KENNEDY'S WAY

Alan Kennedy's career in football began in 1972. He played for a number of teams, including Newcastle United, Sunderland and, most famously, Liverpool. He retired from the game in 1991 whilst at Wrexham, where he played his 500th game. He now comments on football for local and national radio, and is an after-dinner speaker.

John Williams has written a number of books on football culture and is also the author of three books on Liverpool Football Club: *Into the Red*, *The Liverpool Way* and *The Miracle of Istanbul*.

MAINSTREAM SPORT

KENNEDY'S WAY

INSIDE BOB PAISLEY'S LIVERPOOL

ALAN KENNEDY AND JOHN WILLIAMS

MAINSTREAM
PUBLISHING

EDINBURGH AND LONDON

For Mum and Dad, the people who made me, and for
Jane, Michael and Andrew, my dream team
Alan Kennedy

For Sylvia and Joy, Leicester City and Liverpool
John Williams

This edition, 2005

Copyright © Alan Kennedy and John Williams, 2004
All rights reserved
The moral rights of the authors have been asserted

First published in Great Britain in 2004 by
MAINSTREAM PUBLISHING COMPANY (EDINBURGH) LTD
7 Albany Street
Edinburgh EH1 3UG

ISBN 1 84596 034 3

A catalogue record for this book is available from the British Library

Typeset in Futura and Janson Text
Printed and bound in Great Britain by
Cox & Wyman Ltd

Contents

Chapter 1

ROME, 1984

'Alan Kennedy is a special player: he always scores in finals.'

Kenny Dalglish

EUROPEAN DREAMS

What does 1984 mean to you? A cash-card number perhaps? Think of the *year* 1984, 20 years ago now. Do you imagine tales of state terror mapped out by Orwellian futurists? Think again: think sport. There was probably an Olympic Games going on somewhere in 1984: the year sounds about right. France won the European Football Championships, the beauty and power of Platini, Tigana and Giresse writ large: and no English hooligans to spoil it all. But for football fans from Merseyside, 1984 meant either glory or revival, depending upon your Red or Blue persuasion. Everton finally had a team and their own FA Cup victory to cheer in 1984, Andy Gray dumping both goalkeeper Steve Sherwood and Graham Taylor's Watford at Wembley. Everton fans now had the promise of a bright new Blue era, led by manager Howard Kendall and an ex-Kopite battler, Peter Reid, to challenge their dominant Red neighbours. Even League titles beckoned for Goodison in 1985 and 1987. But for Liverpudlians, 1984 was less about a potential Blues revival than it was about a new manager, Joe Fagan, and a unique Reds' football trophy Treble: the League Championship won (again), the League Cup retained and, best of all, for the fourth time in eight years, the recapture of the European Champions Cup. Indeed, 1984 was a good year to be alive as a Liverpool football fan – and as a fan of English club football.

And note, very carefully, the precise use of the word 'Champions'. Because before naked cash and the search for global TV audiences became the ultimate drivers of the European game, the original Champions Cup was the all-or-nothing terrain of the European football cream only. We are talking authentic champions here. In 1984, for example, the English champions, Liverpool, were required to beat the champions of Denmark, Spain, Portugal, Romania and finally, in their very own backyards, the champions and best club side in Italy, to claim the European football club title. Everything was at stake on each leg of this historic journey at a time when Liverpool Football Club, already champions three times, was both feared and revered in Europe, a favoured target and a respected foe. All of this meant that there could be no doubt that Liverpool was certainly the best club team in Europe in 1984. They had triumphed the hard way, in routing a talented Benfica side at the Stadium of Light, surviving a horror semi-final night in Bucharest when even the local police were after Merseyside blood, and by holding a galactic Roma team in their own turbulent Olympic Stadium, to eventually claim the silverware in a mind-numbing penalty shoot-out. No one – not even the most blue-blooded Evertonian – could argue that this latest Liverpool triumph in Europe was merely some knockout Euro cakewalk. This was the real McCoy.

It was three years earlier in 1981, in Paris, and after an uncharacteristically chaotic League season, that Liverpool had last won the European Cup, under the guidance of the master, Bob Paisley. The unlikely Reds hero on that occasion was not a Dalglish or a Souness. Instead, it was a feverish and sometimes disorganised converted left-winger, who was now a head-down left-back; a man who had spent most of the season injured and concerned about his long-term future at the club. A man the Liverpool fans already called 'Barney Rubble'. The North-east's Shiney Row old boy, Alan Kennedy, signed by Liverpool in 1978, was recalled from injury by Paisley for the Champions' final against the most famous football club in Europe, Real Madrid, at the Parc des Princes. Before Paris, Kennedy had played just one match after a six-week lay-off with a broken wrist. He was not match fit, not even close. But with the match heading for extra time, the Liverpool left-back broke forward late on to collect a Ray Kennedy throw-in before scoring the winning goal in the final minutes. The Kennedy name was thus already destined for perpetual illumination in the Anfield Hall of Fame. Kennedy had even added to his credit among Liverpool fans by also scoring in winning

League Cup finals in 1981 and 1983. He had no right to hope for more European reward just a few years later. But he was going to get it anyway.

Three years on, following unacceptably early Reds' European Cup exits, first in Sofia (1982) and then at inhospitable Lodz in Poland (1983), Liverpool were on the European Cup trail once more. Bob Paisley had retired in 1983, an unprecedented three European Cup wins to his name, and smiling Joe Fagan was the new man in charge at Anfield. Finally clear of injuries, Alan Kennedy was now a fixture in a Liverpool back five, a unit that, collectively, missed just one League game in 1983–84. Crazy Zimbabwe goalkeeper Bruce Grobbelaar made mind-boggling saves – and occasional howlers – in the Liverpool goal; Phil Neal, at right-back, made sunrise seem inconsistent; and Alan Hansen and Mark Lawrenson offered talent, pace and class – and cryptic one-liners – to burn, at centre-back. Other new men had also staked their first-team place at Liverpool since the 1981 final: teak-hard Irish ball caresser Ronnie Whelan in midfield; the endlessly energetic Sammy Lee and Aussie Craig Johnston alongside him; Steve Nicol, a versatile young Scot; and a certain Ian Rush, to icily plunder goals up front – 32 League goals alone in 1983–84. Liverpool had been remade since Paisley's marvellous 'golden generation' of the late '70s. This new side looked powerful and fluent, but it also seemed much pacier than earlier versions. Why not another serious tilt at Europe?

The Liverpool backroom staff badly wanted to win the big title in Europe once more. Alan Kennedy, it would be fair to say, was slightly less focused than this. He was greedy for more medals, sure, but he also hoped for a few more European nights of football laughs, adventure and celebration – and a welcome break from midweek training at Melwood. Certainly, the last thing he had on his mind, as the club's players boarded a charter flight to Denmark in the autumn of 1983 to begin the new European campaign at little BK Odense, was that nine months later he might be reeling on a foreign field in Rome, trying to feel his legs and control palpitations and sweaty palms, as he faced the perceptibly expanding Roma international goalkeeper Franco Tancredi – and a howling Roman crowd. Kennedy had a penalty kick to win yet another European Cup for Liverpool. It was the stuff of which dreams – or more properly football nightmares – are surely made.

WALK ON

After the trauma of that Rome night, Liverpool and Alan Kennedy were back at the very top of European football once more. It was to prove a short stay. The real Liverpool nightmares lay just ahead at the Heysel Stadium in 1985. After the Brussels débâcle all English clubs were banished from European competition for five seasons. Graeme Souness and Ian Rush, respectively lead enforcer and goalscorer extraordinaire at Fagan's Liverpool, both left Anfield for foreign excursions and big money. These were painful, wilderness years, when the English game – and later Liverpool Football Club – lost their way. Alan Kennedy himself would soon lose his own bearings and fall out of love with Anfield, wrecking the later stages of his career as a result. By the early '90s another football club, just 20-odd miles east down the M62 motorway, would be on the way to dominating the English game almost as completely as Liverpool had done in the '70s and '80s. But Manchester United would not dominate European football. No English club would ever do that again in quite the same way.

In the 20 years that have followed that crucial penalty kick in Rome in May 1984 the question Anfield followers have been asking most often, the puzzle which haunts us all ever since the trembling Alan Kennedy faced Tancredi, is: can Liverpool ever return to the halcyon days of two decades ago? Souness himself, Roy Evans and the cerebral Gérard Houllier have all failed this crippling test as Liverpool managers who came and went following the deeds of a great player turned great manager, Kenny Dalglish. The latest Anfield boss, ex-Valencia coach Raphael Benitez, faces a huge challenge in a new globalised era in which 'Liverpool' is no longer a universal by-word for world footballing excellence, and Anfield is no more the preferred destination of every talented young footballer in Britain, never mind the focal point of ambitions of the new foreign football mercenaries that all top clubs must now chase. Back in the early '80s Liverpool whistled and the stars followed. Today these talents hear other voices and feel their wallets instead. History dims quality in an era of instant gratification. Liverpool must find a way back to the very top in European football, of course, but no one should make the mistake of thinking that this will be easy. It won't be.

Alan Kennedy had no illusions that Liverpool were signing a 'world-class' left-back when Bob Paisley splashed out a record £330,000 fee for the Newcastle United man in August 1978. But he knew, just as Bob did, that the club were signing a real Liverpool player. Kennedy could play, sure, but he also recognised that he was fortunate, indeed, to share a dressing-room for more than seven years with rare talents like Souness, Dalglish, Hansen and the rest. These were the coming stars of the British game and of European football:

the key outfield men at Liverpool under Paisley and Fagan represented pretty much the last of the rich seam of Scottish football talent that had graced the English game for more than a century. Players like Alan Kennedy, Jimmy Case, Sammy Lee, Craig Johnston and others were the vital glue that held the truly great Liverpool teams together. But by May 1984 Kennedy had also worked hard at his game, had scored crucial goals for the club, and could reflect on six injury-interrupted but satisfying years at Anfield, during which time he had already won one European Cup, five League titles and four League Cups. 'Show me another left-back with more medals,' he would say. Who could blame him? Europe now beckoned again for Kennedy and for Liverpool: he was ready for the challenge.

This book charts Alan Kennedy's life in football but it also looks more broadly at the Paisley and Fagan years at Anfield and some of the men who made it. It looks at Alan Kennedy's problems after Liverpool and his life in football today, as well as his views on why Liverpool have since failed to match these glory years of European dominance. But where else to start than with Alan Kennedy's own story of that marvellous last successful Liverpool European Cup campaign of 1983–84? Having disposed of BK Odense, Athletic Bilbao and Benfica in earlier rounds, Liverpool faced Dinamo Bucharest in the European Cup semi-finals. Theirs was a fierce challenge. But a story was unfolding here that would mean that the Liverpool left-back Kennedy would actually score winning goals in two Champions Cup finals for Liverpool, an incredible tale. And who could have foreseen that outcome for the modest and shy boy rejected as a youngster by his native Sunderland FC?

* * *

IT WAS 20 YEARS AGO TODAY . . .

We fancied ourselves now we had reached the 1984 European Cup semis. The four teams left were Roma, Dinamo Bucharest, Dundee United and Liverpool, so no prizes for guessing that we were all hoping to get Dundee. We had hammered Aberdeen a few years before in Europe, so we were comfortable with Scottish teams. We knew Bucharest would be a difficult trip and that Roma would be a handful – they were full of good players. We drew Dinamo, a real challenge, so the Liverpool staff had to work out how to make the trip as painless as possible for us. In their semi, Dundee United won 2–0 at Tannadice and then lost 0–3 in Rome, but the referee of the second leg admitted much later that the game had been got at. What, in Italy? Big shock! After they'd been beaten in Rome, the Dundee lads said that they had been done, that they were conned. It certainly looked dodgy: the Scots lads knew that they'd been slaughtered by the ref. We weren't that surprised: we knew that nobody in Europe wanted an all-British final because we were so dominant at the time in European football.

The first leg for us, against Dinamo Bucharest at Anfield, was a battle. We won it 1–0, little Sammy Lee getting the winner, a header in the first half. They were completely cynical, trying for anything, and we didn't play that well. But Joe Fagan said that at least we got a decent result: that we had something to take with us to their place in a fortnight's time. We knew we'd need this 'something' all right, because their captain and best player, Movila, decided to have a little go with Graeme Souness. I thought at the time: 'He's a bloody brave man, this little Rumanian.' The referee, André Daina from Switzerland, could see it all starting but at this stage he was just saying to everyone, 'Calm it down, take it easy.' There was nothing blatant or really violent in it so far, it was just very niggly, some very cynical tackles. That is until this fellah Movila easily beat Graeme with a real bit of skill and you could see Graeme saying to himself: 'You're not gonna do that to me again, friend.' So as this guy turned away to play a one-two, Graeme turned right into him and caught him with a beautiful right cross, smack on the jaw. It pole-axed the guy, he went down flat, but the play went on. The referee didn't see it: no one really saw it.

Now, as this guy was having treatment, all their players gathered round and got excited and started pointing – as they tend to do – at Souness. And Graeme knew what he had done and he'd done it well, to be fair. This fellah was then carried off with a broken jaw, the full business. Afterwards, when the lads all started talking about it in the dressing-room, Souey just said: 'Listen, whatever he got, he deserved it. End of story.' We won the game, but all the talk afterwards from them was: 'We can't wait to get you lot back to Bucharest.' I don't think they meant it as a welcome! After the match, their players said that this Souness guy had wound everyone up in the newspapers; that he had riled their players and their fans and then knocked their hero right out. So we knew we were in for a pretty hostile reception out there. Tin hat time. But when Graeme's in that type of combative mood all you can say is: 'Bring it all on: we'll take it all.' This was also part of the Liverpool Way, of course: we all stuck together as a team and if we're going to go down fighting it will be all of us, not one of us. We weren't afraid of going over there, not at all. Even though when we got there there were Bucharest policemen all over the place who drew fingers across their throat and said to us: 'You are dead.' It was intimidating, but Souey was just laughing it off, he wasn't taking any notice. His view was that you just had to stand up and be counted at these games.

As we were coming out of the tunnel for the warm-up in Bucharest we could hear all the boos from the 60,000 crowd: it was deafening. Graeme's at the front, he's the captain, but it was aimed at all of us. We were all just eyeing the crowd as if we were saying: 'We'll take you on all right: all of you.' Graeme loved it, of course: Souness would take it all on himself if he could. He had received threats from the police and from the Dinamo players, even from the hotel staff. People were staring and spitting at him, he'd got the lot. Even the police and army guys patrolling the crowd were joining in the booing as we were warming up. Whenever Graeme got the ball in the warm-up, the booing really took off. So when someone passed the ball to him and the crowd was getting ready to boo, he would just dummy it, so the booing would stick in their throats. He was getting them back, making them madder still. You could just feel the tension rising. We were all going: 'Oh, Graeme, please, there are 60,000 lunatics here and the police are all against us. They'll all be on the pitch in a minute!' Souey, of course, couldn't give a shit: he was absolutely loving it, loving it.

Kenny and Rushie kicked off and the ball came straight back to Graeme (boos) and he played a lovely ball out to me on the wing, with the boos still ringing out all around the place. So I'm starting to panic now, because the crowd's on *my* back. But gradually we started doing what we said we were going to do: play it over the top, turn them, and let's start again from there. Graeme was obviously a marked man and a couple of their players had a pop at him, but he's far too clever for that. And he also got a couple of them on the way back as well, because he was very good at doing his little bits and pieces off the ball when he needed to. Graeme was a hard target. Frankly, the game was shit. We had a lot of flair in that Liverpool team, but sometimes you just have to abandon flair to get a result. This was one of those occasions when we said: 'Hey, we're not playing any pretty football here. We're just going to lump it forward and let Rushie dig in.' It was a bad pitch, but Rushie – who was shipping some punishment himself – was brilliant, and he scored the two goals. It was Ronnie Whelan who set him up: Ronnie got the ball from a shortish corner and feinted to cross with his left foot, first time, but he decided to just flick it up with the outside of his right, through the defender's legs, to set up Rushie. One-nil, and we'd only played 12 minutes.

Suddenly, the crowd began to go flat. And now Dinamo are struggling: they are always struggling from here, because they *so* wanted to kick Graeme Souness and no one could get near him because he did everything right. He just moved the ball on whenever they tried to get to him. Orac scored for Dinamo, a top free kick, but with six minutes to go Rushie scored again, from a pass from Souness of all people! We won the game 2–1, and the tie 3–1 on aggregate. We'd shown a lot of character and discipline and we were in the final. After the match, nobody on their side shook Souey's hand; nobody wanted to mix it with him. But we'd won, even if we thought we'd given away a soft goal which got them back in it for a while. There was just no way we were going to lose that game. All the other stuff was just a distraction: we'd done our job, but we were lucky to get out of there so easily. If the scoreline had been closer for longer, and if their fans had started getting onto the pitch, for example, the police were not going to do anything, not a chance. It was an intimidating night all right because they just *hated* us – they hated Graeme the most – but they hated all of us. But we came through.

In the dressing-room afterwards Joe Fagan told everyone to be really quiet and then he started cheering out loud like a madman – he was delighted with the character we had shown. And he was in his first European Cup final as the Liverpool manager. Now we had to get out of the stadium, get our stuff from the hotel and get back home. It's always nice to get home from a difficult place – a hostile place – one where you have to go and get a result. Especially that one: I wasn't always sure we were going to get out of there, definitely the worst place I've ever played for sheer hostility. All we had to do now was to face 60,000 rabid Romans in the 'neutral' Olympic Stadium. Easy!

ROMA, 1984: 'THEY DON'T WANT US TO WIN IT.'

To be honest, we thought it was very unfair that the European Cup final of 1984 was played in Rome. UEFA had only picked the stadium for the final about a month before. And what if Dundee United had got through? A Liverpool v. Dundee United final: and all the way to Rome to play it? I don't think so. We were annoyed, so I'm sure Liverpool's chief executive Peter Robinson said something to UEFA about the fact that we had to go to Rome, Roma's backyard. The Italians said: 'Well, didn't Liverpool play a European Cup final at

Wembley in 1978?' Well, yeah, but Wembley isn't Liverpool: so why not play the 1984 final in Milan, or Turin? We knew we had to just suck on it in the end, because we all felt that UEFA and the lot of them in world football wanted Liverpool out of the way because we were too successful and they didn't like it. They wanted us out of the competition. Joe Fagan used that feeling with us before the match to wind us up: 'They don't want us to win this.' We had a bit of the old 'siege mentality' about us at the time, but there is no doubt that the odds were purposely stacked against us to make sure we didn't get a result. I think we all believed that.

We had them watched, but we had no great dossiers about Roma. We just knew they were a good side: Falcao and Cerezo, Conti and Graziani. Bloody good players. They were definitely the favourites, but we also thought the pressure was on us to win the English Treble because it hadn't been done before. Because there was a gap between the end of the season and the European final we went for a week's break and training in Israel, mainly to chill out and for some drinking and relaxation. We ended up doing a bit of fighting too as it turned out! We took the British press with us, but the Italian press thought we were crazy. Then we got our thinking heads back on when we got back at Anfield. We all knew the likely Liverpool team, which was terrible, really, on the rest of the squad, but easier on Joe. He wouldn't have to disappoint anyone. It was: Bruce in goal; the back four had been the same all season – Neal, Lawrenson, Hansen and me; Craig Johnston, Sammy Lee, Souness and Whelan were in midfield; with Kenny and Rushie up front.

Joe then decided we needed to practise a penalty shoot-out against the reserves – just in case. I think we lost it about 1–5. Tony Parks had saved a penalty in the shoot-out for Tottenham against Anderlecht in the UEFA Cup final a few weeks before and I remember seeing him on TV run off down the pitch. Afterwards, I was thinking: what a hero he is. He was a national hero, and we all wanted to be that man. Scoring a penalty in Rome for Liverpool meant you could be a hero, but everyone at the club was more worried about the possibility of being a failure. I think that's how Hansen and Lawro, and a few of the others, thought about it. Some of the Liverpool players you think should score were missing penalties in the practice. So Joe made everybody have a go. I know I was just as bad as anybody else. I kept on putting mine to the keeper's left – and missing. And this was only up against a young Liverpool kid in goal, who was not the tallest or strongest of keepers. After a while, it became a bit of a fun thing: 'Aye, you have a go next – put it in that corner.' We all started messing about. It wasn't taken that seriously because, to be honest, we weren't any good at it and we didn't think it would get that far in Rome. We thought 120 minutes of football should produce a winner.

Joe had probably worked out in his own mind who could take two or three of the penalties, if we needed them: Phil Neal, Ian Rush and Souness. Maybe, Kenny. But I knew I was in with a shout, because I know Joe Fagan, Ronnie Moran and Roy Evans would have asked our youth man and European scout Tom Saunders who he would trust to take a penalty. They respected Tom's views, thought he was a good judge of character. Tom once said about me that if there was a fight going on somewhere, I'd be one of the first to go over the top: that I'd want to be involved. And someone else said to me: 'Aye, that's because he wants you to be the first to get shot!' Tom thought I was pretty reliable, good in a crisis, a fighter. The staff all probably compared their five choices for penalty takers. They must have gone into it in a bit of detail, but who was going to be the fifth penalty taker? I was probably about number eight or number nine in line at that time. I'd taken one pre-season in Holland in a penalty shoot-out – and missed it. Alan Hansen had also missed one: his was worse than mine. I had taken a couple of penalties, way back in youth team football. I reckon I'd probably taken a handful of penalties in my whole life in competitive games, and none that mattered as a professional. It is quite unusual, actually, to ask someone to beat the keeper from 12 yards in that kind of situation, from a cold start. It looks easy, but everyone can get the wobbles.

'WE'VE GOT TO PUSH THEM BACK'

Joe named the team and the subs about an hour before the game in Rome. There was very little atmosphere in the Liverpool dressing-room: actually, it all seemed quite nervous. Ronnie Moran was scurrying around, busying himself and trying to calm people, but was mislaying things and getting in the way, making things worse. People just wanted to get out, get it over with. At the time, most of the Liverpool lads liked the singer Chris Rea and a few of us had even gone to see him perform. We had a Chris Rea tape in the dressing-room and Dave Hodgson, one of the subs said, as we were about to come out, that he thought the Italians looked a bit nervous. So why don't we sing them a Chris Rea song, 'I don't know what it is but I love it', just to wind them up? Everyone said not to be so stupid – that this was the European Cup final. But when we got in the tunnel, Hodgy and Craig Johnson both started singing it and the rest of us just joined in. It was a way of breaking our nerves, and putting the wind up them. The Roma players were gobsmacked: they must have thought we were lunatics. As we got on the pitch we were still singing and we were even getting louder. All these cool, international footballers, now they all just looked scared shitless: first blood to Liverpool.

Joe had told us to concentrate on keeping the ball at the start and we had some good possession, got the crowd quietened. There were loads of clouds from the flares from the Italian end, and the match took a while to settle. There had been no real chances when Phil Neal went forward from right-back and passed the ball wide to Craig Johnston. Craig crossed it to the far post and Ronnie Whelan went up with Tancredi, the Roma keeper. It looked like a foul: continental referees normally give them when you even touch a keeper and Ronnie had jumped into Tancredi. But, there was no whistle, and when Tancredi fell and dropped the ball, Roma just panicked. A defender whacked the ball against the keeper's head: it was quite funny. Typical Liverpool, Phil Neal had kept his run going right into the box and the ball fell directly to him: he put it in with the outside of his right foot.

We thought it might be a little easier now, because the onus was on them to come forward and we thought we might be able to nick another on the break. They came right back at us, but we were comfortable. But just before half-time Conti got the ball in from the left byline and his cross cut out both Nealy and Lawro, who had gone across to cover. Pruzzo got in a great little cushioned header at the near post. I still remember thinking: 'Brucie will get that,' but somehow it looped over him and inside the far post. When you lose a goal so close to half-time, away from home in Europe, you end up sitting in the dressing-room wondering about the sort of lift it will give them. You could hear the crowd outside: the place seemed to be buzzing. But Joe was good. He said at half-time: 'Look, don't worry about that goal. We've got to push them back a little more. They've had the last ten minutes of the first half, but we've got to get back to what we were doing at the start – and start creating some chances.' He was right: we hadn't been able to get our front players going at all.

In the second half there seemed to be a lot of play stuck in the middle of the field. I got into a really terrible phase of play and after about 60 minutes I was having a really bad time. I remember getting the ball and just giving it away all the time. Conti was switching wings and giving me bad problems. I was in real trouble. Ronnie Whelan was looking at me as if to say: 'Fucking hell, what are you doing? Help me out. I'm just a young lad.' I had a word with him, I said: 'Listen, Ronnie, I'm having a nightmare, but bear with me, and I'll try to play my way out of it.' So Ronnie sat in with me for a while, and he helped me get over the worst of it. Then Brucie seemed to make a couple of really important saves, because by that stage we had started to hang on a bit. I felt *I* was hanging on, especially. I'm sure the boss must have been thinking about bringing me off before the end, but it was Kenny and Craig Johnston who got substituted. We made it to 90 minutes, still no more goals. At full time Joe said: 'Penalties are a cruel way to decide any game. So let's get out there and make sure we don't need them.' But by this stage both teams were tired, and frightened of making a mistake. It was still about 75 degrees. To be honest, at this stage you end up pretty much playing percentage football – get it up the touchline, away from our goal. I told Ronnie just to dig in, and no one really looked like scoring. When the match was over, I suppose we thought that we had done well enough, holding Roma on their own ground for 120 minutes. We, maybe, hadn't done quite enough to win, but we deserved something. Penalties.

* * *

THE PENALTY TAKER'S FEAR OF THE PENALTY

Alan Kennedy and the Liverpool players now faced a new test. Penalty kicks have always been a controversial feature of football, a strange and foreign intrusion in the beautiful game. Right back in the early days of football in England in the late nineteenth century, gentlemen amateurs refused to score from penalty kicks or to defend them, arguing that their award assumed that some players were willing to behave like 'cads' and deliberately foul opponents. How little they knew. Initially, goalkeepers were allowed to run at penalty takers, to challenge them for the ball, but by 1905 this was outlawed and in 1930 another law change demanded that the goalkeeper stand on the goal line and 'not move his feet until the penalty kick has been taken'. Most goalkeepers agreed that this gave too much advantage to the penalty taker: no goalkeeper who actually wanted to try to save a penalty kick could afford to wait until the kick was taken. So goalkeepers always moved, even if good penalty takers later waited for their movement – and picked another place. And goalkeepers have always been advantaged psychologically in their battle with the taker by the key fact that, although fans have their hopes, nobody ever expects a goalkeeper to save a penalty. His is a wager against nothing. Even though three out of ten penalty kicks are missed – saved by the keeper, blasted wide, hit high over the bar, twanged off posts, launched by David Beckham into outer space – goalkeepers are still treated as conquering heroes, magicians, when the ball is somehow kept out from the spot. The odds on scoring from a penalty are only about 1–2 on. And how many odds-on wagers fail to deliver? But it is still the penalty taker who is vilified, disowned for missing his kick, rather than the goalkeeper for allowing his precious goal to be breached. Which means that in real life we would almost all prefer to be goalkeepers rather than penalty takers. It is low-risk, high-reward work.

If you stand on a penalty spot, roughly 36 feet from an open goal in a local playing field, then missing a penalty kick seems almost impossible. The goal looks gaping. Add a goalkeeper and things look different – but not that much different. Andrew Anthony in his book *On Penalties* calculates that a penalty taker has roughly 180 square feet to aim at, allowing for about 12 square feet of a mobile goalkeeper. This is a lot of space. He estimates that a firmly struck kick, at say 60 miles per hour, allows a goalkeeper roughly half a second to respond. In reality, keepers concentrate on defending the area close to the centre of the goal. If a player hits his kick reasonably well and within a yard of either post it is almost impossible to save. Anything high up and on target or well hit along the ground also has a good chance, because in the time available to react it is almost impossible for a keeper to get in position to make the save. Everything seems to be in favour of the penalty taker. Remember three things only: make your mind up; don't change your mind; make a clean contact. Easy. Except that not everyone has the sort of personality needed to take hold of this in-built advantage and actually make it work. And everything becomes much harder once you add a stadium to your open field, a hostile crowd, millions of television viewers, a long and lonely walk to the spot, some deep psychological warfare with the opposing goalkeeper – who has nothing to lose – and the realisation that the man in the bubble is actually you. The recognition that whatever you do over the next ten seconds actually matters and will do so for the rest of your life – for yourself, and for the people whom you most love and respect – will make most of us retch. Nothing can now be postponed.

Penalty shoot-outs were introduced in football in 1970 to deal with the choking international fixture list and the growing problem of defensive football in major international tournaments. The shoot-out, it was thought by the game's masters, could also act as an antidote to boring matches for armchair viewers who actually preferred theatre or human drama to the deep complexity of sport. It was aimed at the sort of people who liked the idea of watching grown men get publicly humiliated: at all of us, in fact. But for the football professionals the shoot-out was first seen as a lottery, an unsatisfactory way to end any contest: not really a victory at all. Why not count corners or shots at goal? Not that those measures told you anything useful about the pattern of a football match. But players and coaches soon got over this principled objection to shoot-outs, and even playing for penalties would eventually no longer be seen as a negation of the sport. After all, penalty kicks could also test nerve, skill and invention, the staple diet of any football contest. In 1976 the Czech player Antonin Panenka tried to change the entire way in which the penalty shoot-out was conceived in football. In the European Championship final against West Germany in Belgrade, Panenka took the deciding kick, a huge moment for the Czechs. He neither tried to place the ball in the corner, nor ram it at the centre of the goal: instead, he nervelessly and gently chipped the ball into the middle of the net, as the German keeper Maier flung himself aside to try to make a save. You had to see this thing again and again to truly comprehend it. What an act of incredible chutzpah and poise by Panenka – and one of utter humiliation for the Germans. The Czech's skill and audacity seemed to say that even the crude banality of the penalty shoot-out could be converted, instead, into a thing of worth and beauty – and one of deception.

In 1984, and way before the England World Cup and Euro Championship penalty traumas that were to come, Liverpool Football Club were not serious at all about preparing for penalty kicks. The club's coaches disliked practising any dead ball situations and Liverpool had never been involved in a penalty shoot-out that really mattered. The Liverpool staff preferred to trust such matters to the intuitive decision-makers among the players the club had so meticulously assembled. What's more, most Liverpool players were, frankly, hopeless at penalties. Rubbish. We might look inside the dressing-room for the reasons why. The team ethic at Anfield and the ruthless dressing-room exposure of individuals who stepped out of line in any way, made any odd remark, or even wore different clothes, was hardly aimed at supporting the kind of individualism demanded by this kind of test. Okay, the club's regular penalty taker, Phil Neal, and also striker Ian Rush were pretty reliable, and the captain Souness would step up, if required. After that, it was take your pick. Dalglish hated the exposure of the penalty spot, and those smooth and silky centre-backs, Lawrenson and Hansen, simply cowered and hid when the matter was even raised. The new Scot at Anfield, Stevie Nicol, might have a go: he was certainly young and recklessly brave enough. A fifth taker, the suicide spot? Whelan? Sammy Lee? Who? Alan Kennedy was willing, but he couldn't score from the spot in training to save his life: banjos and elephants. 'Let's just hope it doesn't come to this' seemed to be the feeling from Joe Fagan. Christ, it is Roma in Rome, after all. If UEFA have their way, Liverpool will probably get hammered anyway. But Liverpool had survived: now they – in particular a trembling left-back – would need to keep their nerve.

* * *

'I DECIDED TO OPEN UP MY BODY'

Everybody in the stadium seemed to be excited now – apart from the players. Every player, I can tell you, was nervous, petrified. Who goes first? Which side do we go to now? Had we tossed up to see where the kicks would be taken? We wouldn't have won the toss anyway, because we knew everything was planned to stop Liverpool winning. So the penalties were taken up at the Italian end. Joe and the staff felt there was no point arguing. Joe came round and said to the Liverpool players: 'No matter what happens now, you have all done Liverpool Football Club proud. And I think you'll win this shoot-out thing and we'll take that beautiful cup home, too.' Joe then said to me: 'How are you feeling?' I said: 'I feel all right.' He said: 'Good, because you're taking a penalty.' I said: 'No problem.' And he then just wandered off. Then I thought: *Why* did I say that? Why did I use those words? I probably thought it might not get that far down, that I wouldn't have to take my penalty. Remember, I knew what we were like at penalties. But from then on my nerves really kicked in. I'd never been nervous before, until Joe said those words. Joe now had to go and work out exactly who was taking which penalty. Everybody seemed to be organised on this except me: I had no idea what was going on. All I could think about was: he's picked me. Why has he picked me to take a penalty? But I was also focusing on the lads who were taking penalties before me. I knew Phil Neal was taking the first one, so I started encouraging Phil. But he was fine, he was super confident: he wasn't worried about it at all.

The penalty takers were in the centre circle now and we knew that we were taking the first kick. Joe said: 'Right, I've got the five players here.' Stevie Nicol was now in for Craig Johnston, because Craig had been substituted. Before any more could be said, Stevie had just grabbed the ball from Phil Neal and was striding towards the goal. He had had a word with Phil and said: 'Look, I'm confident: I'm all right, don't worry about me. But I want to take the first penalty, get it over with.' He was young, but he *was* confident. Joe said: 'Aw, just let him get on with it.' It was obviously a mistake, because Stevie blasted it miles over the top and we all sucked in our breath. When he walked back to join us, of course, we all told him: 'Not a problem, mate, they're bound to miss one.' He was only a young kid. But we're really thinking that these Italians are usually pretty good at penalties, they don't normally miss them. Their fellah scored, of course, and the Italians in the stadium were really giving it some now. It was completely nerve-racking. I'm standing there with my arms folded, away from the rest of the lads by this stage, wondering: who's next? Then I saw Phil Neal pick up the ball. Relief! But I'm starting to think that, now Stevie has missed, it *might* just come down to me. My nerves are terrible now: my hands had gone cold. My stomach was tightening. All I could think was: 'Don't let it come down to me.' I would honestly rather that they had won the fucking cup as long as I didn't have to take one. Phil scored for us and then Conti missed. Graeme scored and then they scored another. So we're still level. Then Rushie scored for us. I'm really shitting myself now. All the players who have taken one, they're all relaxed, no problem. You could tell, just by looking at the players' faces, who was still to take a penalty and who might have to volunteer. It was like a walk to the football gallows.

Bruce Grobbelaar had had a few words from Joe, who said: 'Listen, in some way, put one of their players off. I don't care what you do.' No problem for Bruce, who's as mad as a goat anyway. Bruce had a little bag in the back of his net and he went to the bag and started faffing around with it. And the ref says, 'Come on, come on!' Then Bruce started to mess with the cameramen behind the goal: he started biting the back of the net. They all started to have a go at him now. Then he did his famous wobbly knees at Graziani. And somehow Graziani, this fantastic Italian player, proven international, hits the top of the crossbar with his kick and over. Grobbelaar then goes completely berserk, obviously thinking: 'Yeeeeees, yes, we've done it. We've won the European Cup!' We just needed to score the last penalty: that's all. No one else could work it out: we were all in shock. And so I start stripping off my tracksuit top: I'd put it on because it was starting to get cold and I was freezing now. My nerves had been shivering me all over and I was on my own in the middle of the pitch. I was the only player left, though Mark and Alan Hansen and the others were edging closer again because they knew they might have to take the next penalty if I missed. They all thought I *would* miss.

I've got a ball with me. I started talking to myself and thinking: where else would I rather be now? I could be a hero or the biggest villain that ever walked the earth. I didn't feel confident. I was trying to focus and it was difficult because my legs were like jelly. I thought about my family as I was walking up there, because I was really looking for help, some guidance, just over this next 30 seconds. I kept on trying to remember where the other penalties had gone and which way Tancredi had dived. It was exciting watching the other penalties, but I had no idea now where those kicks had gone, or where the referee had stood, anything. I knew that no goalkeeper had yet made a save. I passed Bruce, who had a little bit of a grin on his face. He said: 'Oh no, I didn't realise it would be fucking you to take this!' I said: 'Thanks a lot, Brucie.' At the edge of the 'D' I looked at the keeper and at all the cameramen behind, and I convinced myself that they all wanted me to miss. I put the ball on the spot. I remembered that Joe had said something to me about 'not being afraid to change my mind' because I'd been pinging all my penalties the same way at Melwood to my right – and I'd been missing them all. Joe said: 'Why don't you try to *place* it the other way?' There was loads of whistling and booing and camera flashes. I turned quickly to get my stride right, because I'd never practised this. I was also worried that if I went too slowly my legs might not even get me to the ball. So I ran quickly and at the last second I decided to open my body up and side-foot it with a bit of pace to my left, his right. It wasn't right in the corner, but it certainly wasn't in the middle of the goal. Thank God, he went the wrong way. Everything seemed to happen very slowly now, but only one thing mattered to me: HE WENT THE WRONG WAY AND IT WENT IN!

The whole thing was incredible now: I wheeled away to my right, back towards the lads. My arms and legs were going all ways, and I didn't know what to do with myself, because I didn't really know how to celebrate, or what to do. And as all the lads got to me, I just did a stupid little jump in the air, that's all I could do. They were all on top of me and the shock on the lads' faces said it all. They all thought I'd miss it: 'Did you mean to put it there?' I felt great now: I was a hero after all! At the presentation, just to touch the European Cup again after three years missing out on it was fantastic. Afterwards, we went up to a villa we had booked in the hills and stayed up dancing and drinking until 5.30 in the morning. Two hours' sleep and then a press call, and we were on the plane back home to Liverpool at 11 o'clock the following day. Knackered. Half the Liverpool supporters who went to that game were still in Rome when we were back on the streets of Liverpool, together with what seemed like one million Scousers and the European Cup! Full-backs don't get much credit in football, so this seemed like a dream: scoring winning goals in two European Cup finals. We'd all had a lot of ale, but the second we got off that bus we all soon woke up. Ronnie Moran made his little speech: 'Right: that counts for nothing now. Put them medals away, put them in the wardrobe, and bring them out when you're 65 and then you can appreciate them. See you in 26 days, pre-season training.' The highs and lows in football: a year later, Heysel happened. It is hard to believe that Rome 1984 happened to me: a snotty young kid growing up all those years ago in Shiney Row, Co. Durham.

Chapter 2

A MACKEM BECOMES A MAGPIE

GROWING UP GOOD

Gordon Kennedy from Fatfield in Northumberland and Sarah-Anne Donnelly from Hetton-le-Hole, Bob Paisley's home village in County Durham, were two young people who, like many in their generation, met at a celebration post-war dance. This one was held in Sunderland as the nation and the world were recovering, still giddy, from years of shortages and war. Gordon was a sportsman, a wiry footballer and a keen gardener. He was also a motorcycle enthusiast, his interest in bikes and machines a reminder of his recent war service. Sarah-Anne, four years older than Gordon, worked in a fish and chip shop in her home village and she also loved sport. She was athletic and fit, a pretty young school netball enthusiast. When casually kicking a football around with the boys in her neighbourhood she also noticed – as many of them had – that she had a wicked left foot. Gordon played football for the Royal Ordnance (RO) team at the local factory in Birtley, where he now worked. He was a tricky right winger, only 5 ft 7 in. tall but with some real pace: he was nothing special, but was an honest wide man and clever on the ball. Gordon Kennedy enjoyed his weekly football and his weekend pint in the local, but his job as a draughtsman for the RO, an educated escape from the heavy mining work which dominated the communities from which they were both drawn, was his real passion. He lived for his job and, although the pay wasn't great, it was clean work with some status and it offered stable employment for life, if you wanted it. Gordon was conscious of not ending up as his father had, chained to the mines; he had ambitions to better himself and his family. His work was important, occasionally even exotic for these parts. He was reputed to have taken on some 'top secret' assignments, about which he seldom talked to friends or family. Rumours had it that he once worked on something to do with tank design for the Shah of Iran. This was a long way from the slog and grim dangers of coalmining. It was a way out.

When the couple finally married they moved into a small two-bedroom terrace house in Shiney Row, County Durham. Number 36 Eden Terrace was five miles from the Royal Ordnance factory where Gordon worked and the house backed onto the main street that ran through to nearby Philadelphia. Like all similar houses in the area, number 36 had an open range and also a cool larder for food store, where Sarah-Anne kept her jams and chutneys and Gordon his allotment vegetables. Twice a week – less often in winter – a tin bath was produced in front of the fire for bathing, which Sarah-Anne filled with water heated to boiling over the open range. Sarah-Anne worked hard in the home, cooking and cleaning, while Gordon was hot on DIY and making things for self-improvement. They made a good team: Gordon was serious, occasionally moody, good with his hands and gently ambitious and Sarah-Anne was a sweet-natured, kindly and enthusiastic young woman who was in charge of home and baking and conducting happy and neighbourly exchanges over the back fence. In her spare time – when was that? – she also liked to read. Gordon was reserved and had few close friends, but the couple enjoyed quiet socialising with their many relatives – Sarah-Anne had six sisters, who lived nearby – and at the local CIU social club.

Gordon kept his beloved Royal Enfield motorcycle in the outhouse near the outside toilet, where the coal was also kept, and he tinkered and cleaned it most weekends while painstakingly saving for the car and house he wanted for his expected young family. They both wanted kids and the Kennedys' first born in 1952 was a boy, Keith, a sturdy lad, strong and powerful. His brother, Alan, arrived 30 months later, a more wiry and agile child, and the four lived happily in Eden Terrace, the boys sharing a bed and frequently scragging and gnawing at each other as energetic and athletic boys tend to do in cramped urban spaces which have difficulty in containing them. Like nearly all the young boys in the area, where support for nearby Sunderland FC was taken as a given, these two lads soon spilled outside onto the streets of Shiney Row and played football while dodging the growing number of cars in the neighbourhood. But unlike most of their friends they were both unusually talented and, following the traits of mother Sarah-Anne, crucially both were also left-footed. Initially, Keith's size and physical strength meant that the local street football teams had to be set up in order to compensate for his attributes: ten kids would play five, plus Keith. Eden Terrace also backed onto an area of prefab housing, which was soon demolished into the sort of building site that is made ready for post-war regeneration and is immediately appealing for young boys with adventurous spirits. Here and the local rec were the favourite play spaces for boys for sport and for laddish games of war. Local parents liked their young kids – especially the risk-taking boys – to use the rec, a space safer from local traffic and from the dangers of demolition sites. Some parents would even bring sandwiches and drinks over to check on their lads and so as not to disturb the rhythms of the three- or four-hour football matches which typically stretched out over long summer afternoons and evenings.

Gordon Kennedy had ambitions for his sons beyond what was on offer locally. He wanted them, above all, to grow up respectable and responsible and he ruled them with an almost military precision. Although he didn't himself go to church – Sarah-Anne took Alan – he stressed key Christian values, especially honesty, and also a belief in God. He rarely got into trouble with the law and when he was later prosecuted and fined for drinking and driving it was a cruelly shaming experience for both him and his startled family. The boys both knew their father could be pushed only so far, and no more, because he had the sort of temper that meant a disciplining whack was never too far away if he felt they had deserved it and gone beyond what was acceptable. The boys needed discipline, he thought, to be kept unerringly on the straight and narrow.

The Kennedy boys had weekly pocket money and, as part of a strategy of opening up their horizons, they were also encouraged to save and each was given a savings book for the purpose. Gordon was also something of a stickler for timekeeping. If the boys were just one minute later than they should be when coming in at night, the following evening they would certainly be grounded, no matter their frantic appeals for clemency. Alan was always late. They needed to sharpen up. Young Alan once got caught short racing for the outside toilet and an exasperated Gordon copped him one on the backside, spraying shit across the backyard. He was not best amused. The boys loved their father but they were also slightly afraid of him and of his 'sergeant-major' approach to their regulation. Their early grounding was a loving but disciplined one, a stable and caring environment in which the importance of respect and family loyalty and support was routinely emphasised and clearly understood.

The Kennedy boys were also intrigued – sometimes mystified – by their father's job, in an area where the acceptable 'glamorous' alternatives to working 'down pit' were to become a professional footballer or perhaps a train driver. The boys in the area spent hours either playing or talking about the game and collecting and swapping football cards. Otherwise, they whiled away their time standing on railway bridges dreamily watching locomotives steam to and from distant places about which they could only wonder. Above all else, Gordon Kennedy and his wife were people of routines. He had a set schedule for his work at the RO, and little Alan would often wait at the end of the street shortly after five for a brief ride on the Enfield back home to number 36. Sarah-Anne set punishing standards at home. Saturdays, invariably, meant a short trip to Gordon's parents for tea – always for ham and pease-pudding sandwiches with sauce. Here, at eight or nine years of age, the boys also got their first taste for ale, with a little dark and sweet Mackeson from their grandfather mixed up with lemonade in order to 'build them up'.

Saturday was also football day. As the boys started to go to school Gordon would go to watch first Keith, and then both of his sons, play for the Shiney Row school football team. But Sarah-Anne, too, was a staunch football follower and an active supporter of her young boys in sport. Later, in the early '60s, when either Newcastle United or Sunderland were playing at home in the afternoon, Gordon would take his scrapping young sons to stand and holler for the home team at the match. This kind of dual support for local clubs – even bitter rivals such as these – was still common at this time, and Gordon felt support for local sport should bridge excessive partisanship for either club. Keith liked Newcastle but Alan favoured more their local club Sunderland. At home, after the match, Gordon and his two sons would practise moves they had seen or 'keepy-up' together, their father shaking his head, mystified at their obviously left-footed dexterity.

As is often the way for brothers close in age, the first born and dominant brother, in this case Keith, was more strongly attached to his father, while little Alan drew more sympathy and support from his doting mother, who could also be relied upon to mediate between the boys and their occasionally angry father. 'She took the temper away from him,' according to Alan. 'She was always the sympathetic one. I remember getting whacked from me dad and thinking: "Did I deserve that?" I probably did at the time, but he was one of those who thought:

a clout first and ask questions later. Me mam was always the sympathetic one.' These parents were actually a little like complementary coaches at a professional football club: Gordon harder and disciplinarian, Sarah-Anne softer, repairing. Alan remained very close to Sarah-Anne until she died of a heart attack at just 57 in 1978. But his strong ties to his mother would also soon be challenged by a 'rival' because unexpectedly a daughter, Beverly, arrived surprisingly late in the Kennedy marriage, when Sarah-Anne was already touching 40 years of age.

Bev's arrival, in 1960, meant not only an obvious change in the internal chemistry of the Kennedy household, but also a necessary move to a new, larger council house up the hill in nearby Penshaw. Gordon had actually been saving to *buy* a new place but, when push came to shove, he couldn't afford it. The new house was full of draughts but was a dramatic improvement on the old. It had both a living room and a dining room, an inside toilet and a real bath. And Gordon could also tend his very own garden for the first time. It was bliss. In the early '60s, he also traded in his beloved motorcycle for an old Ford – registration 4890 UP – complete with running boards. The car offered a new family freedom and for the next few years the Kennedys travelled the length and breadth of Britain on 'improving' summer camping holidays. Gordon, especially, loved to seek out unusual places to visit, outposts and places of historical significance. In North Wales, for example, he favoured spots where the locals spoke only Welsh – he liked the extra out-of-the-ordinary 'authenticity' of these 'hidden away' holiday places, destinations far off the beaten holiday track.

Although the car meant a new kind of lower-middle-class expansiveness of the sort enjoyed by increasing numbers of aspiring respectable young English families in the early '60s, money was still very tight in the Kennedy household. Most things were still hard to come by and major household purchases were pretty much always made on the 'chucky' – on hire purchase. They included Alan's first pair of football boots, which, like Keith's, were bought from the local Co-op. The battering Alan was giving his school shoes and the blisters he was getting from kicking around in cast-offs convinced Sarah-Anne that this investment was now both necessary and unavoidable. The boots were bought at least one size too big, of course, and they came with old nailed-on cork studs and embarrassingly thick and bright white laces. But they also meant Alan could now take on, with more confidence and better balance, the bigger, heavier lads with whom he was battling nightly on the rec. He could already easily skip around most of them, his pace and strength getting him out of tight spots. Like many professional football players – Liverpool's Ian Rush among them – Alan Kennedy benefited from having an older brother and from playing mainly with older, stronger boys in rough-house street football games as a youngster. It was good preparation for the trials of the football professional.

FOOTBALL CRAZY, FOOTBALL MAD

At Shiney Row school Alan enjoyed most of his lessons – especially any involving history and geography – and he kept on the right side of his teachers. But he was also a dreamer, mainly about football, and even at this early stage he fantasised about the prospects of becoming a professional player. But he knew that his father was a realist about the importance of education – and that there were no professional footballers at all in Shiney Row. Could he really make it as a player? Alan liked PE of course and he enjoyed the much greater organisation in play that was offered by school sport. After all, on the rec you could go minutes without getting a touch of the ball as a mighty scrum of older lads battled viciously for its possession. But here players were assigned their own domains on a massive school field with real goalposts. Now he could revel in the space and use his skills and his pace to do real damage on the left-wing. And all brutal fouls were actually *called* against crude defenders.

There was no coaching or sports drills at Shiney Row and the teachers who took the school team probably knew little about the game – they were typically more concerned that their pupils were well behaved on the pitch than they were about winning matches. But under the strict eye of Mr Lister (English) and Mr McGuinness (Maths), Alan played as a proud eight year old in the green and white of Shiney Row in the all-conquering Under-11s school team. The team was captained, almost inevitably, by his older brother Keith and it dominated the Lambton and Hetton District League and also won the fêted local Morton Cup. The boys in the squad even put a football chart up on the school wall to show how many games had been played, who had played and how many goals had been scored, etc. No one in the school defaced it – no one dared. It was the first taste for Alan of being a minor local football hero. He already knew that he wanted more of it.

To his father's delight, 'brainy' Keith Kennedy passed the 11-plus and went to Washington Grammar, while Alan eventually went to the optimistically named new Success Comprehensive School. He filled in a questionnaire on arrival at his new school with predictable determination and focus: Q: What do you want to be when you grow up? A: Professional footballer. The new school also recruited some of the familiar old Shiney Row staff, including a disciplinarian maths teacher called Jack Woodley and a Mr Davies, both of whom championed Alan's sporting prowess in his new surroundings. It wouldn't wash with Gordon Kennedy, who was furious at this tack, stressing instead the importance of study and raging, on parents' evenings, at Alan's declining academic performance. He gave the school an ultimatum: until my son does better in his studies I don't want him to play football. According to Alan, the school staff were 'devastated' at this ban, which lasted for three months. The sports teachers at Success appealed repeatedly to Gordon to relent and, missing his football, Alan showed no objective signs of improving in his studies. But, remarkably, his end of term report concluded otherwise. Gordon was delighted. It looked as if the teachers at Success had decided that the school's sporting needs were more important than one father's despairing learning aspirations for his sport-obsessed son. Alan was in the school team once again, even if it was only on the back of a little academic 'creative accounting'.

By this time, Keith Kennedy was already playing for Newcastle United juniors and this new family affiliation with the Magpies was now tugging at Alan's own preference for Sunderland FC. He still went to watch Len Ashurst's and Charlie Hurley's Sunderland – his mother's favourite club – but, under Keith's influence, he had also begun to study more closely the Newcastle team of McGrath, Iley, Marshall, Frank Clark and David Craig. He had also started to keep football scrapbooks, envious of Keith's new prospects in the game. Alan liked the strange ritual at Newcastle United home games of the peanut sellers who threw bags into the crowd in return for a tanner thrown back, and that of kids being passed over heads down to the cinder track at the front of the crowd for a better view of the match. Keith's football successes also spurred Alan on: he still believed that he had the necessary drive and dedication to succeed as a professional player. What else could he do? But a case of Osgood Slatters disease, a bone growth problem in his knees, would mean he would need two remedial operations and experience nine months not playing football at all. Keith's game, meanwhile, was improving under the Newcastle coaches, but at the age of 15 his physical development had also visibly slowed. From the young powerhouse he had been as a boy, Keith was settling down as a stocky 5 ft 7 in., 11 stone young man, and lacking his early physical advantages, his game and his prospects suffered as other lads in the United squad began to overtake him. But Keith also had grit and real leadership qualities, so when he was moved to left-back by the coaches at United he worked harder still at his game. He was determined to make his own living in football, if not at Newcastle then somewhere else in the Football League.

Newcastle United spotted Alan Kennedy at Success School as a spindly outside-left. It wasn't rocket science: the coaches at United had simply asked Keith whether he had any younger brothers or knew of any decent young players. Temple Lisle, a Newcastle United scout, told Keith to bring Alan down to train with boys two or three years his senior on Tuesday and Thursday nights. This kind of arrangement is a useful guide to coaches: how well do young players compete above their age range? It was hardly new for Alan, who was now back working and competing with Keith, this time under floodlights at United's Hunter's Moor training ground. It was hard graft for his two shillings and sixpence expenses: a paper round after school, followed by running to the training area from the bus stop, and then plenty of hill climbs and sprints under the watchful eye of United coaches and a 9 p.m. finish. Alan was knackered by the end, and sometimes at the *start* of training. But he enjoyed the new context for his football and the feeling that he was now *inside* the game. Experienced first-team United coaching staff Geoff Allen and Keith Birkinshaw taught the boys about a new playing formation, something the coaches called 4–4–2. It was a rare revelation, the modern football way. But, worryingly, it also seemed to have no place at all for the conventional left-winger. Where, exactly, was jinky Alan Kennedy going to fit in this brave new world?

Joe Harvey, the Newcastle club manager, during one of his visits to look at the new young crop at the United training ground, had some surprising advice for 14-year-old Alan: he should regard Keith – then a reserve-team player – as a target if he wanted to become a professional footballer: 'You need to push him: he's left-sided, try to get into the side instead of him.' He obviously wanted to spur on both brothers in some healthy domestic competition. But it seemed a strange sort of encouragement to Alan: he had no ambitions to play in defence, or to usurp his own brother at Newcastle. And he had other concerns to deal with. At 15 he went to Usworth Comprehensive in Washington to try to get some O levels – he left with history and geography – just in case his playing prospects bottomed out. It was his father's influence again, though Alan was more determined than ever that his future lay only in football. A little later, he was invited to play for the Newcastle 'Ns', then the United youth team. But the United coaching staff now had a problem. Keith Birkinshaw asked Alan what he thought was his best position, adding: 'Forget left-wing, no one plays there.' They offered him inside-right or left-back. He chose left-back, though he had never played there in his life and had no idea about working in defence. He must have done okay because Joe Harvey told Gordon Kennedy soon after that Alan would definitely be signed by the club, even though Gordon insisted his son must complete his education, at least up to 17 years of age. Gordon Kennedy was still torn about his two sons' obsession with football. He was proud of them, sure, and he enjoyed watching them play, as did Sarah-Anne. But he was still unsure about all of this sport business: football was a precarious job where injuries and loss of form could easily end a career. Keith at least had some qualifications he could fall back on. But how stable were his youngest son's prospects? Joe Harvey had to be cute here. Alan Kennedy was his star recruit, a definite prospect. He insisted to Gordon that young Alan would be well looked after at Newcastle and that he was the club's very best youth player, who was sure to succeed as a professional. But the manager was also wary of saying too much to Gordon. What if this doubting father demanded a signing-on fee for his son as some sort of insurance?

Eventually all parties were satisfied. Harvey had reassured Gordon, who had also done his very best by his reluctant son in his education. Alan had got his chance to be a football professional with a one-year apprenticeship to prove his worth at one of his local clubs. He even began playing at *right*-back now for the Newcastle United reserve team, with his brother Keith filling in on the left. Things looked bright. United at this time were also promising great things in the first team, with a loud-mouth centre-forward called Malcolm Macdonald arriving from 'down South' to add some much needed publicity and attacking gloss to the old northern club. Maybe the young Kennedy brothers, from Penshaw out of Shiney Row, two fit and talented local lads, were actually going to be professional footballers after all.

DAYS OF HOPE AT NEWCASTLE UNITED: THE FA CUP CLUB

In many ways Newcastle United is the antithesis of the sort of club built upon at Anfield by Bill Shankly and Bob Paisley in the '60s and '70s. Historically, for Liverpool and its supporters, the long haul of the League championship has always been the measure of a great club, and also the calibrator of a truly celebrated Anfield team. Liverpool waited 73 years from its formation to claim the FA Cup for the first time in 1965, but this delay was of relatively little frustration to most of the club's core followers. After all, it had taken less than a decade for Liverpool to claim the first of 18 League titles, back in 1901, and this was the true measure of any club's mettle, at least according to local football historians and fanatics on the Red side of Merseyside. The FA Cup, a knock-out morsel by comparison, could wait – though ideally not quite 73 years! But in this part of the North-east at least, Newcastle United's traditions seemed to stress much more the quick fix, the emotional buzz of FA Cup success, rather than it did the honest toil and season-long application of the gritty title challenge. After all, for hard evidence of FA Cup successes the club's fans had only to go back to just after the war for Wembley glory and Jackie Milburn in the 1950s. John Gibson, in *The Newcastle United Story* (1985), makes the point:

> To [Newcastle] United fans the FA Cup had always held the most cherished place in their hearts. Not for them the 42-game slog to the Football League championship, nice and welcome though it would be. The more instant glamour of a cup run – the drama, excitement and finally the big Wembley stage upon which to perform – has held vastly more appeal.

Newcastle United might even have won the domestic Double in the early 1950s but for the players' – and the fans' – obsession with the FA Cup to the exclusion of almost everything else. Jackie Milburn was certainly convinced that the 1950–51 United team was good enough to win the Double, but that it had sacrificed the League title on the altar of the demands from fans for FA Cup glory. Typically, too, for a club so focused on the short run of the FA Cup, injury and transfers meant that the 1951 United team was never built upon for longer-term success: it stayed together only for 12 months after the final. But ten-man Arsenal were still beaten 0–1 by United in the FA Cup final in 1952 and with Milburn at number 9 (28 League goals), 'the bronze bull from Chile' George Robledo (39 goals) alongside him and with the tricky Scots left-winger Bobby Mitchell to dazzle full-backs and supply the crosses, United promised even more glory to come. It arrived, in 1955, with Manchester City the latest FA Cup-final victims and Milburn scoring in the first minute with what was then the fastest-ever FA Cup-final goal. These cup successes further pushed League title aspirations back where they seemed, strangely, to belong in this football hotbed: into the game's Dark Ages.

JOE HARVEY, NEWCASTLE UNITED AND 'YOUNG' ALAN KENNEDY

By the time Alan Kennedy joined the Newcastle club as a professional in the early '70s under Joe Harvey, now the club's manager, there was no realistic ambition expressed at St. James' Park at the start of a campaign to challenge for the League title. The manager began each season by stressing new targets: to improve defensively or to score more goals. But it was never to make an assault on the title. The team under Harvey tried to go forward if it could, egged on by local supporters. Above all else, the locals wanted attacking football and skilful ball players. This usually meant individual skill or a quick release of the ball forward and United struggled to assert themselves in matches, especially away from home, by keeping good possession or starting from a solid defensive base. United midfielders tended to be clever attack-minded passers rather than pacy, more defensive, tackling types. All of this intensified pressures on United's defenders, of course, who argued that the attacking end of the team took too little responsibility when opponents had the ball. It also meant that when he eventually got into the United team the young Alan Kennedy soon learned the importance of 'getting rid' of the ball as soon as possible and especially of the magic solution of 'looking for Malcolm' from full-back.

Joe Harvey, a Newcastle player in the 1950s, had begun learning his managerial trade in Football League poverty at Barrow and Workington before returning to what was then Second Division Newcastle United in June 1962. He did not like what he saw: 'Everything was lax. Too many players were uninterested in what was going on and I knew I had to get a grip of things quickly.' He did: United won promotion under Harvey in 1965 with a side containing a promising young left-back, Frank Clark, a player later to become something of a role model for a raw Alan Kennedy and a European Cup winner at Nottingham Forest in his twilight years as a pro. Back in the First Division, and under the driving on-field leadership of Bobby Moncur, United defended adequately but struggled to score goals – only 50 in 42 games. Harvey bought Welsh beanpole Wyn Davies from Bolton in October 1966 to act as a focal point for the Newcastle attack and to restore the pivotal centre-forward to the football dreams of United's followers.

Newcastle finished a distant tenth in the League in 1968, but amazingly they still made it into, and then won, the 1969 European Fairs Cup competition. This success was not repeated, but Newcastle United spent the next two seasons playing in Europe and also paid their first £100,000 transfer, for Aberdeen's Jimmy 'Jinky' Smith. Smith was a typical United signing, a brilliant but flickering talent, a man who would light up a football match with a dummy or a nutmeg, but who could seldom dominate big games or offer consistent performances across the League campaign. But perhaps United would soon now be threatening, after all, to challenge for the very biggest football honours? A major new football force was about to hit town in the football-daft North-east. It was almost 20 years since the Gallowgate had seen his like.

SUPERMAC

Bandy legged and missing his front teeth after too many fearsome clashes with gorilla types at centre-back, Malcolm Macdonald was no glamorous TV sporting icon. But he arrived at Newcastle United as a record signing from Luton Town stylishly enough in 1971 in a Rolls-Royce, and spouting on about the goals he was sure to score and the trophies his new club would undoubtedly secure with him leading from the front. He was manna from heaven in these parts, both for the wannabe United players like Alan Kennedy, who were bursting for a try at the club, and for the local unwashed who were raised on dominant centre-forwards with lots of chutzpah. Supermac's work rate and first touch were often poor, he had no right foot and he was certainly no team player. He smoked and drank too much and he also had a gob like the Mersey tunnel. But he offered value for money copy, and was likely to provide more than a few thrills and spills on the park. Some of his playing colleagues soon learned to hate Macdonald, precisely because the Geordie crowd loved him so unconditionally and because he could go missing away from the comforts of St. James' Park. But Supermac also delivered if he really felt in the mood: his first home match for Newcastle was against Liverpool – he scored a hat trick in a 3–2 win, and was instantly a new Geordie hero. He also added some welcome glitz to the Newcastle football scene: the Newcastle players were soon buying their clothes from a shop he opened in the city. He drove a Jag while others in the squad stuck to Fords. In his first two seasons in the North-east Macdonald scored 40 goals in 77 League matches, so he was hardly a flash in the pan. Some locals even called him the new Jackie Milburn.

To supply the new powerhouse up-front Harvey signed the difficult but talented left-footed Terry Hibbitt from Leeds United and for a couple of seasons these two big personalities shaped the Newcastle club and the team, into which Alan Kennedy was eventually introduced. Hibbitt didn't lack for confidence or something to say, on or off the park, and his searching over-the-top left-sided delivery to the rampaging Macdonald became the signifier of the Newcastle attacking approach in the early '70s. It brought United an Anglo-Italian Cup triumph in 1973 – another European success – but Harvey's side was still dogged by inconsistency, losing infamously to non-League Hereford United in the FA Cup in 1972 before defeating Manchester United 2–0 at Old Trafford just a week later. Even with Supermac in the team, Newcastle United seemed forever destined for mid-table struggle and the occasional cup thrills.

FOOTBALL APPRENTICE

After just one first-team game for United, Keith Kennedy had, by now, decided that his football prospects lay elsewhere. Now in his early 20s, Keith went on loan at Third Division Bury in 1972 before signing for the Lancashire club for a fee of £5,000. He liked the smaller scale of Bury and the togetherness at the club. He also valued the regular first-team action. His move was actually a relief to both Kennedy brothers who, by this time, were effectively competing for the same left-back role in the Newcastle reserve team. It was also clear to Keith that Alan would soon make this position – and probably the first-team spot – his own. Alan Kennedy was now coming to the attention of local scribes and pundits. In November 1972 ex-United defender Ollie Burton instructed his readers of the *Evening Chronicle* in headline terms to 'Look for Kennedy'. He went on: 'I believe that young Alan will play a vital part in the future of Newcastle United. He has class, poise, aggression and ambition. This boy is already one of our best prospects at reserve-team level.' Praise indeed. The *Chronicle* had already featured the 17-year-old Kennedy in a piece on football apprentices, contrasting the £6–10 per week 'modern' apprentice regime of cleaning, laying out the kit, training and one day at technical college, with the £100 a week lifestyle of the top stars at the club, and also covering earlier experiences of preparations for playing.

Alan Kennedy was now a reserves regular at 18 and Keith Birkinshaw, especially, was pressing for an early chance for him to show what he could do at League level. Alan still had problems adapting his game defensively. He had played pretty much his whole life as a forward and now he was being told his prime responsibility was defending. In fact this ambivalence gave him his unique playing style: he certainly had no fears about running with the ball at his feet and attacking the opposition. He could also score goals. But he still ran mainly with his head firmly down and the coaches focused on getting him to do all of his ball carrying in the right areas of the pitch, while making sure he concentrated on closing down opponents effectively. He studied other attacking full-backs, especially England's Terry Cooper, but he also respected the defensive qualities of Newcastle's own Frank Clark. He liked and admired Clark, an honest older professional in the game and one of the local stalwarts of the Newcastle club. After training, the United players usually went for lunch at the Milkmaid in Newcastle, and while Jimmy Smith and Tommy Gibb and other first-team stars were at the bookies or in the pub, Kennedy and Clark talked for hours about the mysteries of the art of defending. In some reserve games now Alan was instructed by the United coaches not to go walkabout but *only* to defend, in order to improve his discipline at the back. It was frustrating and a steep learning curve.

Kennedy was routinely mixing with first teamers in training now and, although he was shy and more than a little naive given his caring and disciplined upbringing, he also loved the banter and the brutal mickey-taking in training. He was often the subject of it. He was also learning a little about physiotherapy and its priorities from Benny Craig, the white-coated club physio's assistant. On one occasion the medical staff brought in a greyhound for treatment before a crucial Saturday race, moving all United players off the treatment areas in order to get the valuable dog back up to speed! Alan had started noticing other little things inside the club: like the fact that the vaunted United kit was actually rather shabby, poor quality; and that the club lacked basic equipment for training; and that the general training facilities at Newcastle were hardly fantastic for a big First Division club. The training pitches were poor, rutted. Full-back play the Newcastle way was also basic at best. It was made very clear that Kennedy's 'job' – this was hammered into him in training – was to win the ball and give it immediately to Hibbitt or else try to find Malcolm Macdonald with an early punt forward. A lot of the club's play around this time was centred on a raking long ball aimed ahead of the marauding Supermac or else a hopeful punt to the honest, but limited, John Tudor. There was no fancy work required at the back: defenders defended and attackers, well, they did their best.

MOVING ON UP

Alan's first-team opportunity at Newcastle finally came later in the 1972–73 season, at home against Stoke City on 10 March 1973, when United captain and all-round local hero Bobby Moncur was ruled out with injury. Kennedy learned of his debut in the *Evening Chronicle*, where journalist John Gibson picked up most of the news about the Newcastle team and even their opponents. Kennedy used Gibson's copy for information on right-wingers for years to come. There was no major preparation for his League debut, at least not in terms of useful advice from coaches about what to do or the qualities of the opposition. He did get some help from some of the experienced old pros, who offered often quite frightening insights about the 'talents' of opposing right-wingers. He was warned, for example, that Southampton's Terry Paine was a tricky flyer who liked to go 'over the top'; that Manchester City's Mike Summerbee was a real 'hard man' and was more than an abrasive handful, especially if you tried to whack him first. These warnings frightened the young full-back, but the United coaches knew that what Kennedy lacked in native football know-how – which was still plenty – he would more than make up for in sheer, dogged determination, despite his apprehensions. By August 1973 Alan was reported by the *Chronicle* to be 'favourite to open the season at left-back', at United, especially since established left full-back Frank Clark was now moving inside to centre-back. In fact, Alan missed out at the start of the Newcastle season, coming on once as substitute, but making his main impact much later in the season as United's League form predictably collapsed. The reason? As history might tell us, distracting FA Cup business was in the offing, once more.

1974 – AND ALL THAT

By 24 November 1973, with Macdonald in his pomp and a young Liverpudlian, Terry McDermott, signed from Bury contributing clockwork energy from midfield, Harvey's new Newcastle United were a heady second in the First Division following a 1–1 away draw at Everton. McDermott, a real live wire and a Scouse joker, had lived with Alan Kennedy's family in Penshaw for 18 months after first meeting up with Keith Kennedy at Bury. Alan told the new United arrival that he would have a hard job breaking into the United side, especially given Tommy Gibb's honest running in midfield. But McDermott had the scoring touch and Gibb offered an ill-advised 'V' sign to the East Stand at St. James' after a frustrating afternoon and was soon gone. So the club was poised: was this to be the elusive Newcastle title challenge after all? Alas, United won only 4 of their next 24 League games, with Alan starting 15 matches, including a shock 1–0 Newcastle away win at Arsenal.

Although things were going well from a personal point of view at Newcastle, even a young player like Kennedy could see that 'player power' was already a serious problem inside the Harvey camp. This made mounting any serious title challenge – or getting any real consistency in the League – almost impossible. Training was uneven and sometimes shambolic with shop stewards Hibbitt and Macdonald usually close at hand when the fights broke out – as they often did when tackles started flying. In United team meetings the same two were usually loudly to the fore, trying to influence player selection. Training was even cut short on a number of occasions because senior players simply refused to comply. Hibbitt, schooled under Don Revie at Leeds of course, once asked Joe Harvey rhetorically in front of the whole first-team squad: 'What the fucking hell do you know about management anyway?' Joe, a notorious conflict avoider, simply upped and left, leaving behind his loyal senior players – Moncur, Craig and Clark – all eyeing the ground.

Harvey's authority in the club was never complete and, as a consequence, neither was the Newcastle team. In fact, this new Newcastle side was essentially a team of individuals. On the terraces, even in defeat, Newcastle fans could always take home a warming memory of a Hibbitt pass, a Macdonald run or a Smith trick. When Smith returned from injury once in the United reserves he drew a staggering crowd of 21,000. When inexperienced Alan Kennedy began to play regularly at left-back he was often exposed away from home by Hibbitt or others in front of him who were unwilling or unable to defend or cover effectively. He could barely get forward either, because Hibbitt simply wouldn't work back and he would get bawled out by the senior pros for deserting his defensive post. It was a tough baptism in a potentially exciting team.

After games, win or lose, most of the Newcastle squad would go to Roy's Two Rooms or La Dolce Vita in Newcastle for some late-night cabaret and to wind down. There were the usual autograph hunters there, but players could safely stay out in the city until three or four o'clock in the morning, boozing without interference from the press or too much abuse from their loyal fans, even in defeat. After a playing trip to London the squad would usually decamp in Newcastle around midnight for the post-match club drinking sessions, which often went on until five or six in the morning. The informal 'rule' here among the players and staff was not to drink shorts because it 'killed your system'. It seemed to a young Alan Kennedy – still a shandy man – that pretty much everyone at the club liked a drink, from the doorman and the chairman to the youngest players and the tea ladies. Perhaps the 'social side' was just too strong at Newcastle, deflecting from the serious business on the field? But little of the excess ever made it into local newspapers. Players' cars were occasionally written off in drunken returns, but the worst stories of abuse were usually melted away by United club officials. From time to time even senior players missed training because of a mysterious '24-hour bug', aka an overly heavy night on the bevy. Most English football clubs had similar stories to tell, but indiscipline seemed especially rife at Newcastle.

In early 1974 another United FA Cup run was beginning to capture the imagination of the Newcastle players and that of the Gallowgate irregulars. Mind you, it was not an especially auspicious FA Cup start, with non-League Hendon and then modest Scunthorpe United both managing to draw ties at St. James' Park – Alan gave away the Scunthorpe goal as a result of a terrible back pass. He was subsequently dropped. Both these lowly pretenders were despatched in early FA Cup replays, with Supermac among the goals on both occasions. It was a typically nervy Newcastle start to a cup run. But, with Kennedy out of the side once more, a fifth round 3–0 win away to dangerous Second Division Cup floaters West Brom showed this United team somewhere near to their very peak. The performance is still talked about on Tyneside today, with Macdonald at his imperious best and Jimmy Smith dazzling and incorrigible. This was starting to look serious – and Alan Kennedy was beginning to wonder just how he could break back into this Newcastle side.

Another home draw in the sixth round, this time to Second Division Nottingham Forest, stirred the city of Newcastle into FA Cup overdrive. With defender Paddy Howard already dismissed, however, Newcastle went a seemingly conclusive 1–3 down in the tie to a Duncan McKenzie-inspired Forest soon after half-time, at which point the Geordie hordes decided 'no more' and invaded the pitch. Sitting on the bench, Alan Kennedy could sense something was going to happen, that the crowd was itching to get the game abandoned. The teams were off for an eight-minute cooling-off period, during which time John Tudor bawled out to his side in the home dressing-room that, even with ten men, Newcastle could still win this game. After the pitch was cleared, and with the home crowd still simmering,

Newcastle were now reduced to three at the back and a callow Forest lost their way. McDermott, Moncur and Tudor all scored in an increasingly febrile atmosphere. The winner was blatantly offside but no linesman was likely to intervene in this crazy climate. It was, without doubt, a dramatic and glorious Newcastle recovery, but the FA, rightly, decided that the 4–3 result could not reasonably be left to stand and ordered a replay. In fact, it took two more matches to separate the teams, Macdonald, who else, eventually providing the winner at Goodison Park after missing a hatful in the first replay. Alan, now recalled to midfield, was voted United's man of the match in the first replay for his marking job on the elusive McKenzie, an early sign of his positive first-team form. Strangely, he wore his girlfriend's dad's pyjamas the night before the match for luck – and then carried on the superstition right up until Wembley. Maybe 1974 was going to be Newcastle's – and Alan Kennedy's – FA Cup year after all?

By this time Alan was routinely in the United 12 – earning a steady if unspectacular £19 a week – but not always getting the final first-team nod. In fact, Forest revealed they wanted to sign Kennedy following his top Cup replay performance, but Joe Harvey, predictably, would have none of it. Alan came on as a late sub in the semi-final at Hillsborough, which pitted United against a talented young and high-riding Burnley side, and United's only First Division opposition in the entire 1974 FA Cup run. While Liverpool eventually overcame game Leicester City in the other semi-final, for an hour in Sheffield, Burnley positively pummelled Newcastle United. Any sensible referee would have stopped the fight, with United's Northern Ireland keeper Iam McFaul alone seeming to keep the Lancastrians at bay. Then the inevitable happened: with Burnley unable to score, Supermac struck. A long punt downfield from Hibbitt and Macdonald was powering away right through young centre-back Waldron before thrashing the ball past keeper Stevenson. It was classic Newcastle. Then Hibbitt again found Macdonald with a looping left-wing pass and it was done, over: Newcastle United were back in the FA Cup final, while Burnley were simply bemused, 0–2 losers. Supermac had already scored seven FA Cup goals in 1974, at least one in every round. He was now sure that this was going to be his FA Cup year: bring on Bill Shankly's Liverpool.

WEMBLEY, WEMBLEY

The 1974 FA Cup final was Bobby Moncur's last match for Newcastle United and, although we didn't know it at the time, it was also to be Bill Shankly's final bow for Liverpool. For the final, Joe Harvey brought back the experienced Frank Clark to play right-back, bringing in the teenage Alan Kennedy to replace the injured David Craig on the left. Kennedy seemed supremely confident before the match, telling the press that he was 'not bothered at all' by the prospects of a Wembley final and even rashly telling the *Daily Express*: 'We will win. Newcastle can match Liverpool for work rate and overcome them with the tremendous flair we have in the side.' Was he dreaming? Under the unfortunate headline, 'Liverpool Don't Scare Me' the youthful Alan reportedly went on:

> I love to tackle more than anything else. I don't care if the situation is as much as 70–80 against me, I will still go in and have a go. More often than not I come out with the ball as well. Tommy Smith is reputed to be one of the hardest players in the game. I am ready for him. He doesn't worry me in the slightest. I will be doing my best to make him uncomfortable at Wembley. I believe the years may be finally catching up on him. I have always had the greatest respect for Smith, but now I believe I can exploit him. He seems a bit slow on the turn and once you are past him he lacks recovery speed.

It was understandable youthful excess, this sort of copy, and the kind of story that should really have been curbed by the Newcastle management. Was nobody in charge here? No doubt, too, these challenging words went down a storm among the hard men in the Liverpool dressing-room, though they probably did little for the morale of the Newcastle forwards who had to face the still forbidding Smith at Wembley. Not that Supermac was worried: Malcolm Macdonald had his own very public say before the final, warning Liverpool in the press to expect a goal storm. It was crass provocation and, worse, it was almost certain to be rewarded with a beating. In fact, Bill Shankly later claimed that it was actually a routine 0–0 Liverpool League draw at St. James' Park earlier in the season that had really paved the way for the Merseyside club's Wembley success. Liverpool had used the entire width of the Newcastle pitch on that day and had kept the ball for long spells, making – and missing – lots of chances. 'We had played the way continental teams had played,' proudly claimed the wily Scot afterwards to a largely doubting press. Shankly was sure this same approach would produce dividends against a one-dimensional Newcastle United on the wide-open spaces at Wembley. He was, as usual, proved right.

Inexperienced in the ways of preparation for modern cup finals,

Newcastle's League form leading up the game was absolutely dire. Did they expect to just turn it on at Wembley? As well as crowing to the press, the Newcastle players also became distracted and much too involved in a host of increasingly daft FA Cup final media promotions: Alan himself was photographed by the dailies in his full United strip inside a zebras' enclosure at a Durham wildlife park. Joe Harvey took his team to the posh Selsdon Park Hotel in Surrey for a full week before the match, which meant an endless – and boring – round of training, snooker, golf and media calls, when the Newcastle squad could – and probably should – have been preparing in a much more low-key and 'normal' way, and being shielded from the media spotlight. Liverpool, businesslike as usual, kept off the TV and left for London only on the Thursday before the final. It felt like the Geordies were determined to enjoy their big week out rather than concentrate hard on how they might try to defeat their more battle-hardened rivals. It was a crucial error, the United players becoming edgy and uncertain well ahead of the day's events when they should have been relaxed but strongly focused on the task in hand. There were even problems with the United Wembley kit: after a row with sponsors, Newcastle turned out at Wembley in clownish purple tracksuits. It all smacked of the worst kind of crude amateurism, boys against men.

On the morning of the match, in the live BBC TV interviews for the final, Bill Shankly and Joe Harvey had also cut very contrasting figures. Shankly, ever the showman, appeared ebullient and confident, while Harvey looked rigid, a chain-smoking bag of nerves. As the TV broadcast ended Shankly could still be heard off camera saying to the nation: 'Jesus Christ, Joe Harvey is beaten already and the bloody game hasn't even started.' It was hardly a calculated swipe but it was a telling aside, heard by Harvey and summing up well the state of the two camps. For all Malcolm Macdonald's pre-match bravado, McDermott's willing running and Alan Kennedy's youthful confidence, Harvey and his Newcastle side were essentially brittle and out of their depth. Liverpool had finished second in the League that year and were well on the way to building a formidable new team around the emerging England international Phil Thompson, the powerful Emlyn Hughes and the little forward dynamo, the irrepressible Kevin Keegan. 'There wasn't one Liverpool player who didn't feel that on the day we would go out and defeat Newcastle United,' wrote Steve Heighway later. He could see what we could all see: it was a major FA Cup-final mismatch. The 3–0 defeat to Liverpool was actually a blessing for Newcastle: an escape. They had managed not a single shot at goal and, tellingly, at the United post-match dinner there was not too much disappointment, not even at the size of the defeat. Newcastle United's two star players in the final were undoubtedly the youngsters McDermott and Kennedy both, ironically, eventually bound for Liverpool. The FA Cup final, the nation's ritual, the celebratory collective end to the English football season, was never supposed to be quite this easy. Maybe this was even why Bill Shankly decided to step away from the game so dramatically? It was certainly not because he feared for the future of his Liverpool team. At the official Liverpool FA Cup final dinner later that evening the great man pronounced: 'The League is only a formality next season. This team is ready for anything.'

ALL CHANGE AT NEWCASTLE

The 1974 FA Cup-final humiliation also marked the beginning of the end for Joe Harvey, who left Newcastle United at the end of the next season. An up-and-coming 40-year-old Black Country coach from Blackburn Rovers, Gordon Lee, replaced Harvey. Lee was very different to smokin' Joe and he had no time for the big star syndrome. Alan Kennedy was keeping his head down, working at his game, but he was also slowly getting noticed. He was already being eyed up by Liverpool, as a possible replacement for Alec Lindsay, before the Merseysiders finally opted for Wrexham's tough Joey Jones. Alan was even called up by Don Revie for the full England squad in March 1975 to play World Champions West Germany at Wembley. He was thrilled but also gutted: he fancied a go at the Germans but his leg was in plaster, a knee injury sustained during a tasty League game at Chelsea. It proved to be a costly and damaging absence because Arsenal's classy Kenny Sansom had already nailed down the England left-back spot from 1979, the next time Kennedy was seriously in the frame for an international call-up. Alan joked much later in his stand-up routine after retiring as a player that he and Kenny Sansom had one thing in common: they shared between them 88 England caps. But Sansom had 86 caps and Kennedy just 2. It is a good joke, a nice piece of gentle self-deprecation, but it is one that also hurts.

Back at Newcastle, and in his first season in charge, Lee's coaching was more innovative and less demanding than that under Harvey and he did at least care more about defence. But even though United's results had definitely improved under Lee, Kennedy's view was that this rookie manager was still learning the game. Things were now far too slack on the training field and Lee's recruits were mainly his own men, useful and good team players, but they were essentially second-raters. The side still lacked convincing leaders and the inventive Newcastle midfield had long been gutted by a man who was certainly keen to stress the value of hard work over creativity. But, for all this, Gordon Lee's side did manage to reach the League Cup final in 1976, though Manchester City were just too good at Wembley in a closely fought match. It was the loser's trudge up the Wembley steps once more. At 21 years of age Alan Kennedy's record in North London now read: two finals, two defeats.

Malcolm Macdonald finally left Tyneside for Arsenal in August 1976 for £333,333 having scored 95 goals in 187 League games for Newcastle United. In January 1977 Gordon Lee himself left the club, for Everton. Few of the established players at United were really sad to see him leave, but the pro-Lee players at the club lobbied vigorously for his assistant, Richard Dinnis, to be made United manager, some of them even telling the press that they would walk out if the directors failed to satisfy their demands. Many of these guys were probably hoping for a comfortable time under the pliant Dinnis, and for a short spell under him things had even looked promising for Newcastle United. But disaster, as always, lay not too far ahead. As it turned out Dinnis's brief reign actually meant the end of United's short period of relative football success in the late '60s and early '70s. It was also the beginning of the end for Alan Kennedy at Newcastle United.

Chapter 3

RED MIST: MOVING TO ANFIELD

THE LEAVING OF NEWCASTLE

In 1977 Alan Kennedy was still optimistic about his Newcastle United future. He was, after all, a fixture in the side and had England potential and had even scored the Newcastle winner in a feisty derby clash in March 1977 with neighbouring Middlesbrough. Kennedy's speed was the key to his success: he even tried racing professional sprinters at Edinburgh's Powderhall race meeting to hone his pace for football. So when the 1977–78 League season started with a first-up Newcastle 3–2 home win against Leeds United it looked like a promising beginning for Richard Dinnis's first full season in charge, with the adventurous Kennedy again on the score sheet. But it was to prove one of the few decent Geordie football Saturdays in the entire season. At this time Alan was on a basic £230 a week at United with bonuses per point rising from £25 to £60 as the club rose up the League table. Maybe the Newcastle board had a premonition of what was to come, because it was to prove a very low spending season on bonuses for the club's notoriously stingy directors. Despite his popularity with some of the United players, Richard Dinnis was soon shown to be way out of his depth in the very hard business of winning First Division football matches. His squad was ordinary, lacking both class acts and real winners. The whole club seemed to be on the slide. The manager, too, lacked the personality and the leadership skills to turn the sinking ship around. Older Newcastle pros increasingly questioned his credentials, younger players searched for inspiration where there was plainly none.

The dressing-room was collapsing around the manager's ears and everyone could see the signs. Ten League defeats on the bounce followed the Leeds victory, including a 2–0 reverse at Anfield on Kenny Dalglish's scoring home debut. The rangy David Fairclough gave Kennedy a seriously rough ride on the Liverpool right. The full-back thought then that this new Liverpool team might be going places while Newcastle, under Dinnis, seemed utterly directionless. On 10 September 1977, following a gutless 0–3 home surrender to West Bromwich Albion, United slipped into the relegation places: they were never able to climb out again during that season.

A nice man, Dinnis was, mercifully, out of the Newcastle hot seat after only five months in charge, to be replaced by a more familiar and suitably gnarled football veteran, ex-Wolves and Ipswich Town manager Bill McGarry. But it was all too late for Newcastle United – and for an increasingly ambitious young left-back. After just nine League games of this early season torture Alan Kennedy was injured: which proves that injuries in football are not always such terrible news. But this was no laughing matter: it was a knee problem picked up at Norwich, serious ligament damage sustained in tackling Jimmy Neighbour in the first half. Newcastle had already used their single substitute, for a broken leg, and Alan's problem wasn't an obvious break. He could just about stand up, so he would have to stay on, do a job for the side: 'It was really killing me: my knee was wobbling all over the place.' Not only did Kennedy complete the match, he continued to play out the first half exposed at full-back – in excruciating pain.

After the game there was no examination of the injury or a hospital stop – no player wants to be left behind on an away trip and this team coach wasn't waiting for hours outside casualty for anyone. After a crippling trip back to the North-east there was still no hospital visit in Newcastle: instead Kennedy was told to see how it 'settled down' overnight. It didn't; it hurt like hell. The next day, after a sleepless night, Alan finally got some treatment and eventually a diagnosis. It turned out to be a career-threatening injury, medial ligament damage, exacerbated by crude advice inside the club and a reckless attitude towards its most valuable assets, the players. Things were handled no differently at Liverpool or any other English club at the time. Footballers, generally, received poor medical treatment inside clubs; they were constantly at risk.

The injury required ground-breaking surgery, with the surgeon, Dr Stainsby, confiding that this was only the second operation of its type ever performed, involving stitching the ligament back to the bone. Thirty-two stitches later, from mid-October 1977 until early February 1978, Kennedy sat miserably in the stands and watched as his promising football career appeared to be disappearing down the toilet.

There was no established regime then of repairing seriously injured players: basically you set your own recovery programme. Kennedy set out jogging and stretching. 'It was all hit and miss: I was probably doing more damage to it than good.' The new manager at Newcastle barely talked to the recuperating Kennedy: he didn't seem to know who he was. Alan now started to do some hard thinking. Kennedy, an FA Cup finalist and already a 'B' international, with full England ambitions and with a contract coming to its end, was unconvinced by the prospects offered by McGarry or by Newcastle United. Instead of building on the promising years of Smith and Macdonald, United had regressed once more and were now faced with another major rebuild. Kennedy liked the city and the fans, for sure, but he felt he was learning little at Newcastle, and where was the club's ambition to match his own? 'I was arguing with the players, falling out with the manager, who was telling me to do impossible things. I wasn't learning anything any more and we were going in the wrong direction.' He became convinced that he would have to escape the perennially under-achieving FA Cup-fixated football culture of the North-east. He would start looking out for possible offers.

Kennedy returned in midfield ('a month too early, after only one reserve game') and played out the final 17 United League games – with no wins. He began on his return by busting a gut to get results for the club, but by the end he seldom gave his all. As a season disintegrates like this one had into relegation, even professional players begin to look after themselves, are much less willing to lay their bodies on the line. What was the point? Who was going to be here next season? 'We were on a slippery slope. I was just trying to get match fit and hoping for a move to Leeds at the end of the season. I was dreaming about leaving the club.' Then a hammer blow: Kennedy's mother died from illness, at just 57. She had been his driving force, his main supporter in the family. 'I always felt that she had treasured me more than Keith and Bev. While Keith always went to my dad, I was much closer to her. I was also the one who looked after me mam: if I had any money I'd always give it to her.' Alan carried on playing, but it seemed like another signal that things needed to change.

All this uncertainty made pre-season with Newcastle in 1978

potentially very difficult for Kennedy. For one thing, Bill McGarry had offered him decent terms, a doubling of his First Division wages in the Second Division, plus a tax-free lump sum of £6,000. Kennedy asked for £10,000. Alan now needed to get fit and to show his best form in the club's warm-up games – Manchester City as well as Leeds were said to be interested and could be watching any of the July friendlies. But Kennedy also wanted to signal to himself and to McGarry that he was no longer a central player in the United project; that he desperately wanted away. The answer? It was obvious: for the official Newcastle United team photograph he grew a *beard*. This is not quite as daft as it sounds (though it is daft). The whiskered Kennedy soon began to look like a wild outsider inside St. James' Park, a shifty hippy under a manager, McGarry, who was known as a bit of a stickler for discipline and appearance. The new look also offered some personal psychological support for Kennedy: confirmation when he looked in the mirror that he was *definitely* going somewhere – but where, exactly?

SIGNING FOR LIVERPOOL

On his first summer 'B' tour with England to New Zealand, Malaysia and Hong Kong in 1978, Kennedy had done well and had made it very clear to the other touring players that he now wanted a move. 'Do you think your boss might be interested?' The message had definitely gone out through David Fairclough, Paul Mariner, Gordon Hill and others on the trip: 'Technically I was flouting the rules, but everyone does it.' He was desperate to leave. But the City and Leeds interest had now cooled and while big-money moves for strikers and midfielders were commonplace in England at the time, fewer clubs seemed willing to spend major bucks on specialist left-backs. Then it all happened. 'I was hating the pre-season for Newcastle in Scandinavia,' Kennedy recalls. 'I ran and ran and ran in training, and this was all I felt McGarry was good for.' Newcastle United then played Hull City in a pre-season game, a 0–0 draw. By this stage Kennedy was sure he was signing for Leeds, but scout Geoff Twentyman was watching for Liverpool and soon after Kennedy was called in by Newcastle for late transfer talks.

Alan was in for a big surprise. 'When McGarry started to say "L....", I was sure he was going to say Leeds. But he came out with Liverpool!' It was entirely out of the blue; it was Bob Paisley who had actually called. This was typical Liverpool, of course, keeping their business to themselves. If he was interested – *if* he was interested, mind – Alan could fly out to the Liverpool pre-season training camp abroad to discuss a possible move with their officials. *If* he was interested! He wasn't much impressed that Newcastle were asking for more than £300,000 for a local player who had actually cost them nothing and out of whom they had had bloody good service in difficult times (where was his cut?). But he thought he might check out the current European champions, just to see what they had to offer. He thought he might just *swim* out there to meet Bob Paisley and his Liverpool stars if he had to. Liverpool were in the middle of an unprecedented five country pre-season tour, one made necessary by the news that the then European champions had been drawn to play English champions Nottingham Forest in the first round of the European Cup. Bob Paisley was soon nervously referring to this unwelcome early Euro summit meeting as: 'Our cup final in September.' The *Liverpool Echo* was also unnerved, even wondering aloud if the draw had been a 'fix' to scupper one of the dominant English clubs. Above all, Paisley wanted his side strong and up and running by the time of the Forest showdown. Liverpool, European champions or not, seldom really got going in the early weeks of the season: they depended on a gentle introduction to Europe. And, if truth were told, Bob Paisley secretly *feared* Nottingham Forest.

Not that any move to Liverpool would be an easy step up, a guaranteed start for Alan Kennedy. The Llandudno-born Joey Jones, an uncomplicated and uncompromising defender, had been a key figure at left-back in the first Liverpool European Cup win in 1977 and Joey was still a popular, heart-on-the-sleeve fist shaker with both the fans and the players at Liverpool. He broke windows in training at Melwood and Paisley used to send him off on international duty for Wales not with the usual 'Good luck' telegram but one saying: 'Keep out of trouble.' For all his strengths, Joey had some obvious 'quality' problems and had lost his first-team Liverpool place in the 1977–78 season. With Emlyn Hughes approaching the veteran stage and Tommy Smith joining John Toshack at Swansea, Liverpool were beginning to look a little thin defensively. Young Colin Irwin was viewed inside the club as a potential centre-back who could play on the left, but he needed more time to develop.

Joey Jones might not easily be edged out of first-team affairs just yet. He scored for Liverpool pre-season in Dublin and against Basle in a 6–0 Liverpool rout, responding to the news of Kennedy's imminent arrival, according to the *Liverpool Echo*, by giving 'one of his best performances'. Kennedy also knew that his close mate Terry McDermott had spent 18 long months in the Liverpool reserves under

Roy Evans, just waiting for his chance. But at least Terry Mac now had two European Cup winner's medals to ease the pain of all those shitty weekends in the Central League ghetto. It still seemed like a good deal. Alan would be prepared to wait for his chance at Liverpool – if he had to. A local journalist, Bob Cass, then approached Alan in Penshaw claiming that Liverpool had asked him to make contact. 'You had better give them a ring.' There was no telephone in the council house in Penshaw so Kennedy joined the queue at the public telephone box at the bottom of the street and spoke nervously to Peter Robinson. The Liverpool man stressed the signing had to be made very quickly. On 7 August Liverpool drew 1–1 with a strong Bayern Munich side in Germany and were reported to have upped their initial offer of £300,000 for Kennedy to £330,000, a record in England for a full-back. The club was also reported to be making more 'English football history' in the proposed deal by signing a player on a pre-season continental tour for the first time. Happy days: except the player concerned wasn't actually signing.

Kennedy flew to Vienna on 9 August with Peter Robinson to meet with Liverpool officials, Bob Paisley and the players. 'Wee Uncle' Bob was keen to do business before the European Cup signing deadline of 15 August. There was no negotiation about salary: Liverpool offered him £410 per week, plus bonuses, take it or leave it. To get things moving, Paisley even lent Kennedy his own training kit and boots so that Alan could get out of the office and do some early passing work with his prospective colleagues. He needed to settle in, get a feel of his new club and his teammates. Kennedy was agitated, still bearded and playing in a 'foreign' kit on a bobbly pitch. He was also still attuned to the crude Newcastle method of getting the ball in the channels as soon as possible from the back. He was truly terrible in these small-sided games. There was nothing like this in the training in the North-east – and he soon found out he was absolutely crap at it: 'It was a nightmare. I could find anyone over 60 yards, but six yards was difficult. I'm sure Bob and Peter must have wondered have we just thrown away £330,000?' He also felt a few hard looks from some of his prospective new pals – 'A third of a million quid and the fellah can't even fucking pass a ball properly. Joey Jones is better.' It might have been a squad set-up of course but, frankly, he was embarrassed by his performance when he had wanted to do so well. The Liverpool players were in fits. Kennedy would have preferred playing in the Liverpool 'friendly' with FK Vienna the next day: it was his type of contest, a meaty affair, boots – and fists – flying.

Bob Paisley didn't seem to care too much about Kennedy's early passing problems. He told the press: 'He will be a first-class capture. He is fast, likes to move up to attack and should fit into our side very quickly. There would be seven men challenging for the back four positions – Hughes, Thompson, Hansen, Neal, Jones, Kennedy and Irwin. I wanted Kennedy because I wanted more competition for places.'

This is a very smart way of saying: 'We rate this guy, but he's not nailed on for the Liverpool first team.' If Liverpool could just get him *signed*, that is. There was no promise of a first-team place and Alan insisted on returning to the North-east to discuss the move with his dad and sister before touching a pen. This is the real mark of the man, though. Liverpool officials were perplexed. This was the football move of a lifetime, but the death of Kennedy's mother in April meant that his 18-year-old sister was now looking after his ailing, diabetic dad. How would they cope if Alan simply moved on and away from Newcastle? Keith, his brother, told him he had to make the move: when would this kind of chance come along again? His sister, Bev, also urged him to go, but his dad was less encouraging, more confusing: 'Whatever decision you make, son, it'll be the wrong thing.' Cheers, dad. It was not exactly what he wanted to hear. He decided that he could return to the North-east at weekends to check on the family. The *Journal* in Newcastle carried the transfer story, front page, but from another personal angle: Kennedy's fiancée, Shirley Heslop, was being 'left behind' as the £330,000 star headed west. Another life twist in a dramatic week, but a North-east Posh & Becks tale it wasn't. Shirley was soon out of the picture and Alan Kennedy was, of course, signing for Liverpool.

Kennedy drove to the Burtonwood service station on the M62 to complete the deal and to meet again with Paisley and Peter Robinson. But even now the North-west weather almost scuppered the signing – it bucketed down and Kennedy's flash TR7 car gave up the ghost en route to Merseyside, windscreen wipers downing tools. He was close to four hours late, with no mobile phones to convey the news: sunk at Liverpool, or so he thought, before he had even started. But Bob Paisley was a patient and knowledgeable man; he knew that even talented footballers left to their own devices were little more than accidents waiting to happen. He moaned at the delay, but he was still calmly drinking tea and checking the racing form when an apologetic Kennedy finally turned up. The later media event at the Atlantic Tower Hotel in Liverpool was notable for two things: Paisley's public assertion to the press that if Kennedy did not play for England he would throw himself into the Mersey – when the tide was out; and the joke Liverpool 'medical' for their expensive new investment. In a side room the Liverpool doctor told Kennedy to strip off and lie on the bed. He checked his pulse and heart rate and asked about the full-back's scarred and injured knee. He then got himself a drink. This was enough: 'Not a problem, 100 per cent fit, this lad can run all day.' No money could have been more casually – or more carefully – spent. But at least it was all done now, the new man bursting for the challenges that lay ahead. But Alan knew he would still have some Anfield tests to face.

WELCOME ABOARD – AND SAY 'HELLO' TO SOUEY

Alan was thrown in immediately to play for Liverpool in Jock Stein's testimonial match against Celtic in Glasgow on Monday, 14 August. The fixture was part of the deal for Kenny Dalglish's signing for Liverpool in 1977 and the Reds won a tough contest 3–2, Alan scoring on his debut following a half-cleared corner returned into the box by the effortless enforcer of Anfield, Graeme Souness. It was the predictable 'dream debut' according to the *Liverpool Echo*: 'Anfield fans are going to enjoy the new man. He is fast, makes exciting and effective attacking bursts, yet is quick and sure in the tackle. An impressive debut indeed.' Celtic's Jock Stein, no bad judge, was also impressed: 'They have bought a good one,' he said. 'He will give more width to their attack, but will make room for the forwards as they come through. I was impressed with him.' Alan had rather more doubts: seeking to make a run outside Ray Kennedy he had ended up on the cinder track, next to the crowd. The Liverpool Kennedys were certainly not yet on each other's wavelength: it would tend to stay that way.

It was now clear to everyone at Anfield that, unlike the problems faced by McDermott, Alan would start the new season in the first team, ahead of Joey Jones. The rest of the squad inevitably needled Joey about the arrival of the new man. Kennedy thought Jones could offer cover at centre-back and full-back, but the Welshman, deflated by Alan's arrival, left Liverpool in October 1978, first for Wrexham and then Chelsea, his moments of Red glory recorded, but now past. In fact, the 1978–79 season proved to be an important moment of transition for the whole Liverpool club. Many of the key 'Shankly' players had either recently left the club – John Toshack, Tommy Smith and Ian Callaghan were all decamping to Swansea, for example – or were winding down in this season – Emlyn Hughes and Steve

Heighway were more bit players now – signalling the new and distinctive Paisley era had truly arrived. The Paisley team that followed was shaped especially around the three young Scottish players who were now the spine of the newly emerging Liverpool regime: Alan Hansen, Graeme Souness and Kenny Dalglish.

All these guys were young but were already terrific footballers and huge competitors. Moreover, they were also intelligent leaders and thinkers about the game. They had style, a real presence, and they strutted the Liverpool dressing-room, happily talking up the Jocks' cause, while mocking the poor English. They were sharp, brutal to outsiders and other fakers, their Jock dynasty losing some shape only when Steve Nicol arrived later at Anfield. He was a much slower burning influence from north of the border. Dalglish felt most at home on a football field, where he was a brilliant force for Liverpool – he lacked confidence and self-assurance, but not a clever and spiky sense of humour off it. Alan Hansen was a very clever piss-taker and an arch-argument-winner, but it was particularly Souness who was the man who oozed the essential class and menace in almost equal measure, and in pretty much any venue. He was a huge presence and was already, after barely a couple of handfuls of matches in the most successful football club in Europe, a totemic figure on the field and in the Liverpool dressing-room.

Graeme Souness was a real grown-up man and a football perfectionist amidst the jokers and the artless dressing-room banter at Melwood and Anfield. He was also a hard case, an Edinburgh prefab child in wicked search of success and the good life. In this, the strategic use of controlled violence was a crucial weapon. Perhaps only Ray Kennedy at Anfield could occasionally face out Souness, put him off his stride and dispute the Scot's almost territorial dominance inside Liverpool football club: the vital claim to be the biggest lion in the jungle. The troubled 'Razor' could do strange things himself, including picking arguments with his own shadow on occasions, but it was Souness, above all, who defined this Liverpool team and particularly its absolute determination to succeed. They all hated losing, naturally, but Souey positively *refused* to be beaten – or even to be put down. It was simply not in his nature. Souness, in short, was already becoming the relentless winning heartbeat of Bob Paisley's new Liverpool and he liked to test out the club's new arrivals for himself, put them through their paces. See what they were made of. He especially liked to weigh up the new *English* players, check what they had in their tank. He had only been at Anfield himself for five minutes when Alan Kennedy arrived, but Souey was already ruling the roost at Melwood – and he had remembered those many stray Kennedy passes from the Viennese training farce. 'This new fellah couldn't play, but what else did he have?' It was worth a look.

Playing a circle keep-ball exercise in an early Melwood training session, Alan, still unsure of himself and probably too keen to impress, chased the ball from the centre and right into Souness, catching the midfield man a glancing blow on the knee, a nothing: but this was also a something. The Liverpool players now exchanged knowing glances as Souness simply growled: this was bound to kick off sometime soon. A few minutes later, with Souness now in the centre, he chased the ball and followed through on Kennedy, cleaning him right out. Alan could see it was coming and reasoned that this assault demanded a typical shop-floor response, something to at least show Souey that the new arrival was no soft touch: 'You couldn't back down in that situation. I had to prove my worth to the lads, show them I was one of them. I don't care who it was.' Kennedy launched his eleven and a half stone against Souness's thirteen. He threw a punch and the fighting lasted only seconds until Ray Kennedy and the Liverpool coaching staff stepped in, but it was real enough. Jimmy Case warned Alan later that he had been lucky to get off so lightly once Souness had his number. But Kennedy had stood his ground in his first big Liverpool test; the new man had shown he had bottle.

Liverpool coach and ex-Reds' left-back Ronnie Moran expected some occasional fighting among the Liverpool players in training as the week wore on, and especially as match day approached. Ray Kennedy, Jimmy Case, Souness and even Phil Neal had all had training-ground brawls. Terry Mac was one of those who would run rather than fight. But it was no bad thing, this occasional scrapping, because it showed that the players had an edge, honing their competitive sharpness and a readiness for battle. Matches in England were frequently battles. Ronnie also liked the new men at the club to stand up for themselves in training when the club bullies came in – it was a necessary toughness, a sign of character and important lessons for survival. 'Joe Fagan once told me not to go in too early when they're fighting,' Ronnie smiles, 'because you might catch one yerself. Good advice, that.' Fights between players in training at Liverpool were dissolved away by the coaches by simply moving players quickly on into new activities. Nothing else was said: there was no censure, no remorse. These guys, after all, shared dressing-rooms and showers, bedrooms and battlefields. Bars. They travelled together for months on end, knew each other better than their own families, and they would sort this kind of thing out for themselves over a long season. Players didn't always have to like each other to win football titles, just have a modicum of respect – and trust – for their teammates. For Souness, ever the slightly absurd perfectionist, Alan Kennedy – and many others in this current squad – might never be good enough players for *his* Liverpool. All of five years later, during a match at Fulham, Alan sold Souness short with a pig of a pass. The Scot growled once more and spat out: 'You'll never fucking change, will you?' But at least the new recruit had shown himself man enough to go into battle. And, for now, that was probably enough.

PLAYING TO WIN

Bob Paisley identified Souness and Kennedy as the two key new signings for Liverpool who made the club even stronger than in 1977. Souness reasoned that compliments from Paisley came as often as snow to the Sahara, so at least this was something. 'We have as good a squad as anybody, stronger than most,' Bob went on, and then typically: 'You get nothing for what you have achieved in the past. You have to start afresh again.' This was old-style Liverpool talk, distilled from Shankly's days. History is bunk: you get zilch for what you won last year. Paisley also suggested there were at least ten clubs who offered a potential threat to Liverpool's title ambitions on the brink of this new season. He was exaggerating, of course, but he wanted to show respect, to take nothing for granted. Liverpool, after all, were trying to *regain* the League title from Nottingham Forest, and this task would be difficult enough. Alan Kennedy immediately liked the compact size of Anfield compared to the horrible rebuilding and the general air of uncertainty at St. James' Park. His new club also offered players much more guidance on financial matters than he had ever had before. But his stay in the Atlantic Tower Hotel was unsettling and he relied on Bob Paisley to pick him up for training; he still had no idea about the layout of the city. Liverpool felt like a modern, forward-looking club compared to the static, old-fashioned feel of Newcastle United. He also enjoyed the famous Liverpool players' bus ride from Anfield to Melwood for training, taking care not to sit in any established star's seat to avoid abuse. The bus could often carry 50 players and staff – 'Kids at the front, the lads at the back' – while Bob Paisley would follow on in his car after completing his morning office tasks. Years before, Bill Shankly had reasoned that the players should, 'Get all their talking out of the system on the bus before we start training'. Alan thought the ride served another useful purpose: Joe Fagan and Ronnie Moran could stand at the front of the bus to look into the eyes and smell the breath of players for signs of over-indulgence the night before. The main suspects always insisted on getting all the windows open on the bus, hoping to breeze away the killer evidence.

Training was also very different at Melwood from what it had been at inhospitable, windswept Hunter's Moor in the North-east. Kennedy thought that the training in Liverpool was more focused and much more enjoyable. Finishing off with a game at every session was a major change: 'Pre-season at Liverpool was not a doddle: it was competitive. But it was also easier, somehow. I had the ball at my feet every few minutes, which was a big change. It was hard work but you were always working with the ball.' The three versus three Melwood contests improved the players' touches and everything organised by Fagan and his staff seemed directly geared to the first match. Training seemed to have a real purpose here rather than the repetitive and gruelling conditioning that was usually on offer in the North-east. Early on, the *Liverpool Echo* highlighted, especially, the importance of the signing of Alan Kennedy for Liverpool's title ambitions: 'Enjoy the pacy raiding qualities of Alan Kennedy, the left-sided flair he adds to the other left-sided star, Ray Kennedy, in front of him,' it told its readers. 'He will give Liverpool a new attacking dimension, which I expect will pay handsome dividends.' There would be a lot worth watching at this 'new' Liverpool – and it was coming right up.

PLAYING AT HOME

Alan Kennedy maintains, years later, in his after-dinner speaking act, that he immediately got on the right side of the Kop by firing a warm-up ball miles wide of the net before his home League debut against Queens Park Rangers and knocking off a copper's helmet. He also says that Bob Paisley responded at half-time to Alan's missed passes and mistakes by wondering, predictably, if Oswald had 'shot the wrong Kennedy'. It might even be true. He certainly met Bill Shankly in the stand before the game and admitted to being nervous before his Anfield debut. The wily Scot offered his assurances and quietly passed Kennedy a 'pill' that he claimed would 'calm his nerves'. Aghast, Alan quickly pocketed the medication: which actually turned out to be a boiled sweet. But it still had the desired calming effect – after all, it had come from the great Bill Shankly. It couldn't, however, stop him being nervously and uncharacteristically vocal in the dressing-room and on the pitch with his new team. 'It was mostly complete rubbish,' says Alan Hansen. He would need to settle.

Sharpened by their extended pre-season contests, Liverpool stormed into the 1978–79 season with six straight wins. There seemed to be much more harmony and certainty of purpose at Liverpool than at Alan's old club, Newcastle. Expectations to win and to play well every week did not add to the pressure: this winning mentality had a gelling effect on the staff at Liverpool. Defeat here was never contemplated, was simply unacceptable. It was a breathtaking Liverpool start, but it was not all plain sailing in the new left-back department.

Kennedy struggled to adapt at first, still chucking the ball forward, panicking in possession. He cannot remember ever being shouted at as much as he was in his first few games at the club. Ronnie Moran was in top form here, and even if Alan was on the other side of the field: 'Fuckin' play it short, will yer!' could be heard booming across Anfield. For Kennedy, raised as a footballer on the Tyne, this was a strange world indeed: 'In Newcastle, the shorter the ball, the more chance the opposition had to get it. At that time 50 yards was a short ball to me.' He was happiest and a better player when the opposition had the ball, or when he had an obvious marking job to do, or when he was on one of his 'What happens next?' head down forward runs. At first he whacked the ball high and long when his midfielders wanted it short and attackers demanded it to their feet, and he gave the ball away when good possession of the ball was stressed above all else at Anfield. He learned that he needed always to 'be an option' and to be prepared to 'play in triangles' when any Liverpool player had possession. This was a whole new way of thinking about the game. It took him months to adjust and for a while other players in the team simply didn't trust him to deliver: 'Sure, I felt intimidated when I joined Liverpool. They were the European Champions, full of star names. It took me a long, long time to get the respect of the players. I was always the one who had to work harder on his game, stay behind after training. I didn't mind; if anyone wanted to stay back to do more work, so would I. I was a fit player, willing to learn. I knew I wasn't the most gifted footballer and left-back was my true position – I couldn't play in midfield here, not for Liverpool. It only struck home that I really belonged at Anfield years later, in the 1983–84 season.'

He also had problems early on working out exactly when to attack and when to stay at home and where prickly left-sided midfielder Ray Kennedy actually wanted him to play. There was little guidance on this from the Liverpool coaches. He was told not to worry and to 'play your own game', though this was actually the *last* thing that sophisticated Liverpool really needed down their left side. At Newcastle he had thumped the ball forward and bombed on. Something else was needed here, surely? Souness and Razor were soon cursing 'this fuckin' clown from Newcastle', but he was slowly adjusting, gradually learning the Liverpool Way. Joe Fagan and Roy Evans told him to keep his head down and things would work out. It was difficult. He was still based in a hotel and hated it and he was worried about his early form. He was also worried that he would not hold onto his Liverpool place. The *Liverpool Echo*, still keen to milk the story of an expensive new arrival, continued to support him. Kennedy was soon telling the paper that his early experiences as a 'professional' sprinter offered him a more disciplined rhythm, a more athletic running style than many other players. Liverpool had had another left-back just before the Second World War, Jim Harley, who was a Powderhall sprinter. Maybe history was repeating itself? Graeme Souness preferred to keep his own running down to the minimum. In contrast to Kennedy's early season problems Souey was already imperious, dominating Liverpool matches and scoring goals. He looked like he absolutely belonged here. Only a shock League Cup away loss to Sheffield United in August – and a host of Liverpool bookings to go with it – spoiled his, and Bob Paisley's, early mood.

The first signals of what was to become a growing foreign influence in the English game also came to Liverpool early in September 1978, when Spurs drew up at Anfield boasting two of the recent World Cup-winning Argentinian stars, Ricky Villa and Osvaldo Ardiles. The British press had been full of stuff about these exciting South Americans, of course, and the 'glamour' they would bring to the English game. The dressing-room at Liverpool predictably hated all this media attention on Spurs and their new stars. Who the fuck were these guys anyway? And could they do it here, in the English trenches? Phil Neal said that, in training that week, he could *smell* a great performance coming from Liverpool, rooted in the players' pride in the English game: 'There was that Friday sharpness that said we were going to give someone a clouting.' Tottenham would be made to suffer for all this media froth. The visitors, hopelessly disorganised, were shattered, destroyed in the sunshine in front of the *Match of the Day* cameras. It was a crushing 7–0 win to Liverpool, but, hey, who was counting? Terry Mac scored a classic goal, a length of the pitch passing Liverpool special. 'Take *that* back to the Pampas,' was the message.

Already, the Anfield Reds – Bob Paisley's men – looked unstoppable.

This thrashing was widely billed in the papers as a triumph for 'traditional' British teamwork and skill against South American flair. Tommy Smith, now at Swansea, had said of the Argentinians, after confronting Ardiles with one of his special full-on assaults, 'They can't expect to come here and play fancy flickers. That tackle was to say to him this is a man's league – and he didn't like it. I think Spurs ought to buy a good stock of cotton wool for such poseurs. He can't expect not to be tackled just because Argentina won the World Cup.' The message here was clear: you have to earn the right to play in England, sometimes with blood. It was much simpler inside the Anfield Boot Room: Moran, Fagan and Evans reasoned that the Tottenham midfield of the unfamiliar Argentinians and the talented but featherweight Glenn Hoddle was just asking to be burst apart. They had also sensed a big Liverpool performance all week in training. But all of this transcontinental stuff was really just warming up, no more than shadow boxing, for the real contests that lay ahead: the meetings with Forest in the European Cup now loomed. This promised to be a quantum clash of personal football fiefdoms – with all of Europe at stake.

BRIAN CLOUGH AND NOTTINGHAM FOREST

Alan Kennedy may have joined the double European champions in August 1978 but he also joined a Liverpool club holding none of the domestic football honours, a personal and professional affront to Bob Paisley and his staff. In 1977–78 the Anfield club had been exposed by a new force from the provinces, by Brian Clough and Peter Taylor's unconsidered promoted side at Nottingham Forest. Forest audaciously won the 1978 League championship and, lacking a host of first-teamers, including goalkeeper Peter Shilton, replaced by the unknown Chris Woods, had even beaten Liverpool in the 1978 League Cup final, albeit with a hotly disputed John Robertson penalty. But this Forest challenge was not *entirely* out of the blue. Bob Paisley and the Liverpool coaching staff knew all too well Clough's championship pedigree, of course. Clough, after all, had been in charge at Derby County in 1972 when the Rams' 58 points were enough to snatch the League title from Shankly's hungry new Liverpool. The 'terrible two', Clough and Taylor, eventually fell out with Derby chairman Sam Longson and left the Baseball Ground, stimulating revolts from both players and fans.

The Clough and Taylor partnership was, admittedly, not everyone's cup of tea – Clough was bombastic and rude, Taylor a chain-smoking fidget of devastating one-liners and personal insecurities – but together they were a fabulous team. And they were definitely not to be underestimated, not at home or abroad. Peter Taylor, like Bob Paisley, had an unrivalled eye for football talent. He had cajoled Clough and the Derby board to sign Dave Mackay, Roy McFarland, John O'Hare, Alan Hinton, Archie Gemmill and England man Colin Todd in the early '70s. Clough's talent – like Bill Shankly's – was mainly in player recruitment, more than a little self-promotion, and in inspiring and melding a range of footballing talents into an effective and tough unit. Unlike Shankly, Clough sometimes seemed to browbeat, even abuse, his own players into outstanding performances. Players at Liverpool wanted to play for Shanks and Paisley, for themselves and for the Liverpool club. At Derby County, and later at Forest, players seemed more afraid of disappointing or letting down their occasionally volcanic boss. But Clough also worked endlessly on the spirit and loyalty of his squads, often by daringly preparing unconventionally for major matches and in succeeding in making real stars out of otherwise discarded or unpromising material. He rescued lost causes and tied them to top talent. Forest of the late '70s looked like a side made up of rejected football flotsam allied to the presence of real and expensive class players in key positions. They worked ceaselessly and looked – and were – incredibly difficult to beat.

Again like their Liverpool equivalents, the Clough/Taylor teams were typically built on defensive strength, combined with midfield graft and hard-nosed creativity higher up the pitch. While Liverpool relied on the unflappable Ray Clemence, for example, Forest pinched his England goalkeeper rival, Peter Shilton. 'Worth 18 goals a season,' Clough beamed: it was difficult to argue otherwise. And even to reach the mountainous Shilton, the club's opponents at this time had first to get past another formidable defensive range, the immense Forest centre-backs Larry Lloyd and Kenny Burns. In midfield Clough had re-recruited the hyperactive Archie Gemmill from Derby and re-signed the loyal John McGovern from Leeds. Loyalty was a big issue for Clough. He also played 'smart-arse' workaholic Martin O'Neill wide on the right to back up the deadly finesse of Tony Woodcock and the brute force of Peter Withe – and later Garry Birtles – up front. But the real key to Forest's attacking verve in the late '70s actually lay wide on the left, in the shuffling, portly figure of the unlikely Scottish genius John Robertson.

When Clough arrived at Forest, Robertson was out of the side and, with Martin O'Neill, was on the transfer list. 'Robbo' was a shuffling, chain-smoking, grizzly, overweight mess – 'indisputably the slowest player in the entire Football League', according to his new manager. But he had real native football talent: he could see the pitch. Clough backed Robertson up with aggressive and physically powerful full-backs, and instructed him to pick the ball up deeper and hold onto it longer. It worked. When the opposing full-back got tight, Woodcock threateningly filled the space behind and the ball went long: if he stood off, Robertson dragged the ball forward before passing or crossing opponents to death. And this physical freak, a pint-guzzling, fast-food junkie, never missed a game. No one could hold him or cut off his supply. Clough remarked later that Forest fans never truly appreciated Robertson's talents: too many of them thought he was lazy, even inept. Nobody at Anfield thought the same. For Alan Kennedy and especially for Phil Neal, holding O'Neill and Robertson, respectively, was more than just a headache. It was migraine time, and with top European honours already at stake in early September.

IN – AND OUT – OF EUROPE

For Alan Kennedy his first European Cup match for Liverpool was hardly what he had expected or hoped for. He had anticipated a trip to maybe Iceland or Finland or even a gentle work out across the Irish Sea. Instead this meeting with Forest felt like a typically severe English League game played out at a dank and hostile City Ground. Perhaps Liverpool made the same mistake, saw the Forest match as just another League game and so dispensed with their usual ball-retaining tactics in an away leg of what promised to be a tight European contest? Whatever the reason, Liverpool were found wanting, perhaps convinced by their own excellent early season form and Forest's jitters that this tie – a European final in the very first round – could be decisively settled in Anfield's favour even in the first leg. The awkward Garry Birtles gave Forest a first-half lead as the home team poured forward, and Paisley and his coaching staff would have been happy to take a 0–1 defeat back to Anfield. Phil Thompson certainly was: on the field he kept on hissing at Birtles that a one-goal Forest lead would be easily swallowed up at Anfield. After all, Liverpool had turned round plenty of similar first-leg score lines back on Merseyside with the Kop howling. They should shut up shop now.

But the rest of the Liverpool players were not so content with this limited, managed defeat. Liverpool's form was too good and the players felt they had a point to prove to Forest, a few old scores to settle. The Liverpool midfield rashly pushed on to the very end in search of an equaliser, as the visitors continued to dominate. It was crassly stupid, macho stuff. Paisley was furious, telling them all later: 'We were looking for an equaliser as if it were a League match. We could have sorted this out in the second leg.' Instead, Liverpool were caught on the break late on by full-back Barratt, with European debutant Alan Kennedy probably partly at fault for the goal for losing Tony Woodcock, who nodded down Birtles' cross for the Forest defender to volley home. It was already the defining moment in the tie, something much more difficult to mend. As Birtles jogged past Thompson he slyly asked the downcast Liverpool defender: 'Will *two* goals be enough, Phil?'

The return leg was mapped out for a predicted Liverpool siege – an early home goal and it would be tin-hat time. Paisley himself had turned to a war footing, saying: 'To use a Churchillian phrase, we'll have to fight them in the six-yard box, the penalty box and every other part of the pitch.' But a couple of typical Clough flourishes changed the agenda entirely. Forest were staying in town at a Paradise Street hotel, an old haunt of Liverpool's. Clough was well known for his strange tactics for 'relaxing' his players before big games. The night before a League Cup final some years later he even got his star players out of bed for some reluctant late-night drinking. Now he had another brainstorm and ordered afternoon bottles of wine for his players, 'to help them sleep'. He also made sure that the message got out to the Liverpool base via the hotel staff. It had the desired effect on the hosts: either these Forest guys were mad or they were just super-confident. David Johnson said later that the Liverpool players were freaked out by the sheer audacity of it all. Here were inexperienced Forest, who in a couple of hours' time would play the biggest game of their lives in a cauldron at Anfield against the European champions, and that bastard Brian Clough had them all on the bevy! It was staggering – and a little scary. In fact, it was almost a Liverpool-style stunt. And it worked: the match finished 0–0.

The Liverpool dressing-room was gloom itself later, the singing from the Forest camp bouncing off the old stadium's walls. No one at Anfield was used to this. After all, many of these home players had dominated Europe for two years running and now they could not even escape from rookies in their own backyards. The great trips abroad and the European arenas seemed miles out of reach once more. Paisley and Roy Evans tried to pick the players up, of course, with talk of regaining the championship from Forest, of another League title.

Paisley also publicly doubted Forest's shelf-life on the continent, mumbling that: 'When they start playing in Europe against some of the Iron Curtain countries they'll find life very different and very difficult.' Forest, in fact, won the European Cup at the first attempt. But even this prospect of a Liverpool title challenge suddenly seemed less important to some of the experienced players, definitely second best. Emlyn Hughes was especially downbeat, admitting that he had had 'a nightmare' in both legs. It looked like a long haul back and the TV men at Granada also seemed to think so. As coverage of the Anfield highlights faded away, the TV producers cheekily played the song 'The Party's Over' to the background of Liverpool's shattered players sloping off the Anfield green. This just wasn't funny. The more positive news was that the new Liverpool dressing-room leaders, the three young ambitious Jocks – Hansen, Dalglish and Souness – had still to win an English League title and so, of course, had another new recruit, a certain Alan Kennedy.

In fact, unlike most in this club, Alan owned no valued winners' medals of any kind in football and he even felt that his *serious* football career was only just beginning now he had moved to Liverpool. He was as sick as anybody about missing out here, but he hadn't left his home in Newcastle in order to piss it all away because of the genius of Brian sodding Clough and his smart alec antics. Forget Europe for now, he told himself: he had still come here to win things. And, looking around even this down and defeated Liverpool dressing-room, he knew that he still believed in these players. They were winners, he was sure of that. But what he didn't yet know, despite this choking expulsion from Europe and Forest's apparent stranglehold over Liverpool, was that he was actually now part of the best English club defence – and some good judges would claim the best mainly British club *team* – that had ever played in the English game. Even deflated Bob Paisley would eventually come to think the same way. Liverpool were down, sure, but this despondent, talented squad was still growing: it had plenty more to give. By the time the Liverpool players were showered and dressed a new resolution had already taken hold: a determination that they *were* going to regain the English League title. And that they were going to do it in some style.

Chapter 4

SIXTEEN GOALS: THE ART OF DEFENDING

GETTING OVER FOREST

If Europe proved to be a cul-de-sac for Liverpool in the early part of the 1978–79 season, a route barred by Brian Clough and Forest, Alan Kennedy's new club's initial League form was quite outstanding with only one point dropped in their first 11 games, during a 1–1 draw at West Bromwich Albion. By this stage Liverpool had already scored three goals or more seven times in these early fixtures, including the home rout against Tottenham and a 5–0 Anfield thrashing of Derby County. It was party time. The Liverpool goals were also coming from all parts of the team, with Souness and Ray Kennedy regular contributors from midfield and the perpetually downcast Scouser Jimmy Case weighing in with a hat-trick in a 3–0 home stroll against Bolton Wanderers. But defending is the key to any great team, and this message was drilled into Alan and all the Liverpool squad at Melwood: that goals may win matches but it is defences that win titles. In Alan Kennedy's first season at Liverpool the team leaked only 16 goals, a modern Football League record. No team will ever match it.

The careful balance struck by Paisley in 1978 between attack and defence in the middle of the standard Liverpool 4–4–2 was a key feature here. This is football's central coaching riddle, of course: despite all the fancy talk you can reduce football theory pretty much down to how much to risk, how much to conserve in the engine room. In this Liverpool side all four of the regular midfielders – Case, Souness, Ray Kennedy and Terry McDermott – had plenty of running power and abrasive defensive strength: they could all dig in when required. But all four were also very capable goalscorers, thus relieving the pressure for goals on the Liverpool front two early in that season, Dalglish and the veteran Steve Heighway. So despite this team's obvious defensive strength, the 1978–79 side was not one of simple functional efficiency specialising in avoiding defeat. This was not, for example, what the Chilean player Carlos Cazely memorably describes as the sort of team that employs 'the tactics of the bat – all 11 players hanging from the crossbar'. This Liverpool team could also fly and score goals, 85 of them in this season in the League alone.

Steve Heighway was now reaching the end of a playing career that had begun at Anfield in 1970 with Bill Shankly personally visiting the undergraduate's student digs at Warwick University to try to persuade the Skelmersdale amateur – who had actually been 'scouted' by Bob Paisley's sons – to sign for Liverpool. On arriving in Warwick, Shankly had, curiously, eyed up the nude female posters in this typical Midlands' student house – 'Not bad, this studying lark.' But Heighway himself was much more difficult to nail down. He was no starry-eyed kid looking for a red shirt at any cost. In fact, he knew so little about the professional game that he even had to ask a teammate which end was the Kop when eventually making his Anfield debut in a testimonial match. Steve grew into the job, finally signing for Liverpool for £10-a-week more than Shanks really wanted to pay. But it wasn't all plain sailing. After an early Liverpool defeat, the 'intellectual' Heighway was snarled at by Tommy Smith on the train home for not being 'professional' enough on the field and costing his teammates bonus money because of his casually missed chances. Did this 'fucking student' really care enough about his role at Liverpool? Hard man Tommy took some convincing, but Heighway rewarded the club with a decade of often inspired wing service and vital contributions in winning titles and European trophies.

Sixteen Goals: Goal One, 19 August 1978
Liverpool 2, Queens Park Rangers 1
(Paul McGhee, 28 minutes, 1–1)

The press: 'A harmless looking left-wing cross from McGhee was totally misjudged by Clemence, who allowed the ball to drift over his head and into the corner of the net. I don't know who was more surprised, Clemence or McGhee.'

Alan Kennedy: 'Kenny had put us in front two minutes earlier from a cross I had put in, so I was feeling pretty chuffed. Their guy was crossing it from miles out on Nealy's side and Clem got caught out at the near post, didn't move his feet fast enough. He probably thought it was going over. We were bossing the game and it was my first match in front of the Kop. I thought, "Oh-ohhh, we better get this back quick."

'Stevie Heighway got us the winner in the second half. No one said anything to Clem afterwards but he got some stick at Melwood from the lads on Monday.'

Ex-Everton striker David Johnson effectively replaced Heighway towards the end of the 1978–79 season, making up a more conventional forward partnership with the cunning and elusive Dalglish. As a youngster Johnson, a staunch Liverpool fan, had chosen, against type, to join Everton because he thought the Blues had a much more serious youth policy at that time than did the mob across Stanley Park. He was probably right. Johnson played only 50 matches for Everton, before moving to Ipswich Town in November 1972. Bob Paisley later signed him to replace John Toshack, but the awkward-looking Johnson struggled at first with form and injury at Anfield until making a real impact at Liverpool in 1978–79, and then becoming top scorer at the club in the following season. Johnson was universally known in the Liverpool camp as 'Doc' because he used to carry a little flight bag into training, a treasure trove full of treatments and medications for players' colds and muscle tweaks. With no drug-testing regime yet in place in the game – and with little formal medical expertise available inside the Liverpool camp – the Melwood coaches reasoned that if the occasional powder or pills from the Doc kept their pampered stars happy, then why not? Ronnie Moran and Reuben Bennett were crude critics of players' moans here: they were always on at Hansen and Alan Kennedy about the 'soft' players of today. A good test for the Liverpool Boot Room of the mettle of a real player was to push hard for him to play, even if he was carrying a knock: no coach or manager stood in the way of a willing combatant, especially if he was a key player. Reuben Bennett showed the traditional Liverpool way to deal with injury: he used to scrape enthusiastically for stones in knee grazes he'd incurred in training, using a fierce wire brush. Few of the players could watch.

Sixteen Goals: Goal Two, 26 August 1978
Manchester City 1, Liverpool 4
(Brian Kidd, 23 minutes, 1–1)

The press: 'It was Liverpool's offside trap that faltered, a long pass from Donachie allowing Power to stride through unchallenged, with Liverpool expecting the offside decision which never came. Power moved on, crossed the ball to the unmarked Kidd who seemed to take an age, but finally drove the ball home left-footed into the net, with Clemence drawn yards out of position.'

Alan Kennedy: 'I remember Paul Power running through – he had a long-stride, quite deceiving. Nobody was in charge of playing offside at Liverpool. Bob just used to remind me and Nealy to stay level with the centre-backs. Phil Thommo's job was to encourage us to play as high up the field as possible. If we were caught in no man's land we got a volley from Bob – and later on from the rest of the lads. We were well caught out here.'

But the really big story in this new campaign was the effective end of another great Liverpool stalwart's career – and the beginning of a new one. Emlyn Hughes had signed for Liverpool from Blackpool for £65,000 as a 19 year old in March 1967. A left-sided defender or midfielder, Hughes went on to make 665 appearances for the club, captaining the side to European, UEFA and FA Cup triumphs and eventually winning a career total of 62 England caps on the way. Hughes was a powerhouse, a rugged football enthusiast and a lion-hearted competitor who actually broke the leg of an opponent as a 19 year old in a match that Shankly attended to scout him. The youngster never blinked. He was a born captain and leader, and became a Shankly devotee. Hughes had an especially explosive relationship with 'Beans-on-Toast' Kop hero Tommy Smith, from whom he inherited the Liverpool captaincy in mysterious circumstances. Smith reckoned Hughes 'stole' it, and never forgave him, the two seldom talking even when sharing centre-back duties. Hughes revelled, especially, in Liverpool's European Cup triumphs at the end of the decade, when he liked to tell all comers – and with some justification – that 'the continentals are terrified of us'.

Hughes had played a big part in the new approach to defending pioneered in England by Shankly and Paisley in the mid-'70s. Kenny Dalglish first remembers seeing signs of it in a testimonial match at Celtic in the early '70s when he had had the thankless task of chasing the ball along the Liverpool back line as Thompson, Smith, and Alec Lindsay played very un-English possession football while looking for a channel to explore further up the field. The British defensive tradition had been to produce hulking, no-nonsense centre-backs in the Ron Yeats or Bobby Moncur mould that could repel all comers and especially the aerial kamikaze assaults made upon them by British centre-forwards. But in October 1973 Red Star Belgrade had embarrassed Liverpool home and away in the European Cup playing a more cerebral passing game that impressed the Liverpool Boot Room. Ray Clemence remembers precisely the change in approach these defeats produced: 'When I came into the side the set-up was Larry Lloyd in place of Ron Yeats and Alec Lindsay in place of Geoff Strong. There was still the stopper centre-half – Lloyd was dominating in the air and I had to know what to leave to him and what to take myself. Then, about 1974, Liverpool's defensive tactics changed. We no longer had a big powerful centre-back who was great in the air. We had Phil Thompson and Emlyn Hughes, much more mobile than Lloyd, not as dominant, but providing a new style of defensive play. They were more skilful; there was much more football played by the defence then. Now I had to read the game better, to be more part of the team.'

Sixteen Goals: Goal Three, 23 September 1978
West Bromwich Albion 1, Liverpool 1
(Laurie Cunningham, 50 minutes, 1–0)

The press: 'With only five minutes of the second-half gone Cunningham, Albion's best player by a long way, put them ahead with a splendid individual goal. Cantello pushed the ball through as Cunningham raced past Neal, who would have had to concede a penalty if his challenge had gone in. Neal stood off and Cunningham, drawing Clemence out of goal, made no mistake with a great cross-shot.'

Alan Kennedy: 'This was a great goal, a curling shot around Clem from distance. Fair dos to Laurie, really, Phil Neal just couldn't get the challenge in. The thing about Laurie was that he could switch wings and he was a tricky player, quick, but only over a few yards. He also dropped a good shoulder. It was going to take a special goal like this to get them in front. Albion were a good team then and often played 4–4–2, but with Tony Brown and Cunningham pressing on, which was unusual in those days.'

In European play the Liverpool coaching staff had noted that a more mobile, faster central pairing, made up of players who were comfortable on the ball, worked best, especially since few continental teams played a typical English pressing game high up the pitch and few had the sort of suicidally physical centre-forwards that were more common in England. This also meant that Liverpool could cope better with clever continental forwards, keep good possession at the back and also try to kill games abroad in high-pressure situations – a major advantage. Both Thompson and Hughes had been groomed to play in midfield but despite his competitive style the former probably lacked the pace and the eye for a pass needed higher up the pitch. His strengths were good anticipation, heading, winning the ball and the sideways possession pass. He was also a good reader of the game and a big talker – 'a major complainer', according to Alan Kennedy – and a fist-clenching motivator from the hard school of local Kirkby housing estates. Phil had also watched the club from the Kop, so winning football matches for Liverpool was no simple professional obligation, as it was for, say, a fully committed Souness or a more detached Steve Heighway. Phil Thompson really *cared* about Liverpool football club. Kenny Dalglish said: 'Thommo was like a stick of rock – if you broke him in two you would see "Liverpool" written right through him.' Thompson certainly looked nothing like the traditional British idea of a central defender: he was so thin and wiry that Bill Shankly reasoned that he must have tossed-up with a sparrow for his legs and lost. But he was surprisingly good in the air and brave in the tackle. Ronnie Moran saw Thompson's defensive potential and his huge desire when in Liverpool's reserves, but it was Bob Paisley, and Phil's fellow players, who made him into a great Liverpool central defender.

In some ways, this conversion of players who had the skill and flexibility to play higher up the field to more defensive positions also became the powerful guiding theme of this emerging Liverpool side. Maybe it was part of Bob's astute forward planning? Both Phil Neal and, of course, Alan Kennedy had started their careers in more forward positions and, as a consequence, were now reliable, but also attacking, full-backs with an eye for goal. Ray Kennedy, on the left of midfield, had been famously converted by Bob Paisley from the striker he had been at Arsenal to a gliding and powerful goal-scoring midfielder. Adaptability and flexibility were the key traits here. This new football philosophy, which was aimed at both domestic and European success, meant that all players in the Liverpool team were now expected to be able to play and to want the ball, a big change for the new recruits. The Uruguayan football writer Eduardo Galeano once said that even Brazilian full-backs back in the 1950s used to 'stick like stamps to strikers and peel off the ball as quickly as possible, wafting it to high heaven before it burned their feet'. They might have earned their corn doing the same thing in the North-east of England two decades later, because Alan Kennedy had learned at Newcastle in the '70s only to defend, run and hoof the ball forward. He would have to change more than most. Meanwhile, a lanky young Scot, a gifted cynic, was adding another dimension to this developing theme of playing at the back – and *really* playing. Defending at Liverpool football club would never be quite the same again.

Sixteen Goals: Goal Four, 7 October 1978
Norwich City 1, Liverpool 4
(John Ryan, 80 minutes, 1–4)

The press: 'With ten minutes to go Norwich pulled one back, with a penalty from Ryan. Robson, looking yards offside, was allowed to move into the Liverpool penalty area where he was brought down by Neal. Liverpool's protests were half-hearted, despite the fact that they had legitimate claims.'

Alan Kennedy: 'Keith Robson had a good left foot – I played with him at Newcastle. But he was one of those players who could go down if you just touched him. Nealy thought he was hard done by. Clem would always try to psyche players out for the penalty kick: he had a little routine to try to upset the penalty taker. It didn't work here. I only gave a few pens away at Liverpool – I remember one at Man United, and one against Everton: Andy Gray out-foxed me, but Bruce Grobbelaar saved it anyway.'

TALL, DARK AND . . .

Like Kenny Dalglish before him, Alan Hansen had attended trials at Liverpool, with four other Scots, as a 15 year old – and had been rejected. Hey, mistakes happen. Partick Thistle manager Dave McParland had been watching Hansen in local football as a 17 year old and was taken with the elegant midfielder: he offered the Scot a £250 signing-on fee. Not that impressed with his job selling insurance or even with the attractions of football as a profession, Hansen grabbed the cash and a contract anyway. But there was a catch: McParland wanted Hansen to play at centre-back, a position Hansen hated and one he felt he lacked the attributes for – he was over six feet tall but weighed only 11 stone and couldn't head the ball or tackle properly. He couldn't defend.

At Thistle, Hansen kept pushing up into midfield, but under the later watchful eye of his new boss, Bertie Auld, a hated disciplinarian, Hansen put on a little weight and began attracting the attention of a string of English clubs, including Leeds, Bolton and Newcastle United. All looked at him and concluded he probably lacked both the pace and the upper body strength to play in England. The truth was that Hansen was a late developer, physically, who only reached his optimum playing weight very late in his professional career. Liverpool's Geoff Twentyman watched too and had better ideas about the way the game in England and abroad was headed, deciding in April 1977 to take a £100,000 gamble, three years after Liverpool had originally sent the gangly young Scot back home. It was more like a sure thing.

Hansen made his League debut for Liverpool against Derby County in September 1977 and he started 18 League games in all in 1977–78, filling in at the back for both Thompson and Joey Jones. He also strolled to a European Cup winner's medal for Liverpool against outclassed Club Brugge KV at Wembley in May 1978. He was still learning his trade, adjusting to the higher pace and the physicality of the English League and to the subtleties of Europe, but he looked a natural on the field, a man with time – and more – to play out from the back and one who could also step up with the ball. He loved breaking the pattern of play from the back. He finally ousted Emlyn Hughes near the start of the 1978–79 season, and once Hansen got a run it was clear that he was in the side for keeps. Whilst not a huge talker or a great organiser on the field, and admitting that he didn't always enjoy playing in his early days, Hansen had the lot. His brilliant anticipation and reading of the game, his close control and his basic intelligence, allied to his capacity to carry the ball forward at pace while still seeing the entire playing area, made him the outstanding Liverpool defender of his generation. In fact, he is very probably among the greatest defensive players ever to play for the club.

Sixteen Goals: Goal Five, 28 October 1978
Everton 1, Liverpool 0
(Andy King, 59 minutes, 1–0)

The press: 'In the 59th minute bedlam took over as King shot Everton into the lead. It all stemmed from a patient, well-constructed build-up by Kenyon and Wright in their own half. Out went the ball to the left touchline and when Pejic centred it arrived at the feet of King. The Everton midfielder had time before despatching a rising shot from 18 yards past Clemence.'

Alan Kennedy: 'My first derby, with my old boss Gordon Lee managing Everton. I don't think he even remembered me! Everton were a hard team, they had good, tough players. Evertonians always said: "Forget the League, just beat Liverpool." We both had chances in this game. I think this goal was a volley over Clem from outside the box. As the ball broke to Andy everyone was shouting, "Close him down!" but no one was in position. I think we knew from then on we were going to lose: they really wanted it. I had to live with gloating Evertonians afterwards, but it wasn't like the North-east derby, where the fans lived apart and really hated each other. Passionate rival fans from the same family was something new for me.'

As a Northamptonshire teenager, Phil Neal had typically 'sensibly' turned down overtures from Tottenham's Bill Nicholson to sign schoolboy forms in order to stay on at school and claim his five O levels in case he failed to make it in the game. He eventually signed for Third Division Northampton Town and in August 1968 he made his debut for the Cobblers on the left-wing. In 200 appearances for the club he covered virtually every outfield position. The talented Neal served a six-year lower division football apprenticeship and was watched by several large clubs before, on 9 October 1974, Bob Paisley signed him for Liverpool for £60,000, solely on the basis of scouting reports from Tom Saunders. Neal was 23 years of age and had thought his time for the higher levels of the game had probably passed. How wrong could any player be?

Neal's book, *Attack from the Back*, sums up the defender perfectly because it is a hard-headed and thorough guide to the arts – and privations – of being a model professional player, including solid warnings about the need, above all else, for self-discipline: 'I cannot over-emphasise,' wrote Neal, over-emphasising, that: 'there is no glamour without graft.' He also points out the important two dictums from the Liverpool Boot Room: 'Never lose the ball' and 'Never waste the ball'. Neal followed this advice slavishly. Famously, he made his first-team Liverpool debut in a derby game against Everton at Goodison Park in November 1974, having been withdrawn from the reserves' derby at Anfield on the morning of the match and then being walked across Stanley Park by Tom Saunders, carrying his boots in a plastic bag. The match ended 0–0, Neal more than holding his own at left-back. He began to replace Alec Lindsay towards the end of that 1974–75 season and then happily switched between right-back and left-back in 1975–76 when Joey Jones arrived at Anfield and Tommy Smith was still competitive on the right flank. The other two tough guys scrambled for a place in the side; Phil Neal played all 42 League games. Could either Paisley or Saunders possibly have foreseen this sort of service in Neal while he was at lowly Northampton?

Neal became the most consistent and the most reliable player in the history of Liverpool football club. He barely missed a match. In ten seasons – 420 games –between August 1975 and May 1985, he missed one League match – he was injured at Manchester United in September 1983 and sat out the following match, at home to Sunderland. Neal once played in a boot a couple of sizes too big in order to protect his secret broken toe – and his appearance record. 'I didn't want to lose my place.' Bob Paisley let it go because he always desperately wanted Neal in the side. For Roy Evans, Neal was simply 'not fantastic at anything but good at everything'. Later captain of Liverpool, Phil Neal is the only Liverpool player to win four European Cups, to play in all five Reds' finals and to win eight League championships with Liverpool. It is a remarkable record and one that, almost certainly, will never be matched in England. Phil Neal was, above all, a responsible and committed professional, a reliable defensive rudder when some of the more volatile and talented members of the Liverpool squad threatened to lose their way or were out through injury or suspension. He was, in short, utterly indispensable, Paisley's – and later Joe Fagan's – defensive rock. Can any football club in the history of the game ever have purchased such value and such quality and service, for a measly 60 grand?

Sixteen Goals: Goal Six, 4 November 1978
Liverpool 1, Leeds United 1
(John Hawley, 18 minutes, 0–1)

The press: 'After 18 minutes, Dalglish had the ball in the Leeds net but it was disallowed for a foul by Souness, on Madeley. Straight from the free kick Leeds took the lead with an incredible goal. Harvey's free kick bounced in the Liverpool half, deceived Thompson as the ball ran between his legs and Hawley went on unchallenged. Clemence came out, dived to his right, but Hawley took the ball past him and his gently struck shot hit the foot of the upright and bounced slowly over the line.'

Alan Kennedy: 'This was in the Kop goal. John Hawley, a big awkward forward, scored it but Clem started blaming me. Indirectly, he was probably mad at himself as well, because maybe he could have done more. In the changing-room at half-time Clem was really having a go, saying I should have done better, either covering Hawley or getting back on the line. I had got caught between. I shouted back at Clem, and Bob said, "Calm it down," but I could see Ronnie Moran was seething at me. I would have snapped if he had had a go, because I got so wound up then by the players.'

FIFTH MAN IN THE BACK FOUR

So now we have the Liverpool back four for the main part of this incredible, record-breaking season: Neal, Thompson, Hansen and the new man, the Liverpool rookie Alan Kennedy. They played together 25 times in League matches during the campaign, with Kennedy, Thompson and Hansen all suffering short injury breaks at different moments. It amazed their opponents that they hardly ever practised defending together in training, but they compressed the play, held the line. This was now the top defensive unit for Bob Paisley and, despite the ambitious signing of Avi Cohen from

Maccabi later in the 1978–79 season, it would remain so until the Irish international Mark Lawrenson joined Liverpool in the summer of 1981, thus challenging for all defensive spots, including Alan Kennedy's own left-back berth.

The 'fifth' man in this celebrated Liverpool back four of 1978–79 was, of course, goalkeeper Ray Clemence. Skegness-born Clemence was bought from Scunthorpe United by Bill Shankly in the summer of 1967 for a paltry £15,000, another touch of Glenbuck managerial genius. Clemence was working in the summer hiring out deck-chairs on Skeggy beach when he received the news. Shankly, full of himself, naturally threw the youngster a line, telling him that Tommy Lawrence was an elderly 30 years old and on his way out of Liverpool (he was 27) and that Clemence would soon be the club's first-team keeper. It actually took the new man two years to make his Liverpool debut, against Nottingham Forest, in January 1970. A Liverpool FA Cup defeat at lowly Watford convinced Shankly that he finally had to reconstruct the '60s side, with Ron Yeats, Ian St John, Roger Hunt and Peter Thompson all being phased out along with Tommy 'The Flying Pig' Lawrence. A great Liverpool era had passed – Bill Shankly was building for another.

Sixteen Goals: Goal Seven, 11 November 1978
Queens Park Rangers 1, Liverpool 3
(Peter Eastoe, 29 minutes, 1–0)

The press: 'Rangers had only attacked twice but they took advantage of over-confidence in the Liverpool defence to permit McGee to break clear down the left and lay on the centre from which Eastoe drove in a fine shot into the top corner.'

Alan Kennedy: 'Good shot this one; Clem had no chance. We usually had good games here, but this was looking like an easy win and maybe we relaxed a little. Later at QPR they had the plastic pitch: it was like playing on concrete. We used to have to go down to a local plastic pitch in Walton Valley to prepare, to get our footwear right. Loftus Road is a swirling ground anyway and the football there was pathetic once the new pitch was in. Bad passes were away, gone.'

For 11 Liverpool seasons, from August 1970 until May 1981, Clemence rivalled even the metronomic Phil Neal for Liverpool appearances, missing only six League matches and ending up with 656 major domestic and European games for the club. The Liverpool right-back and his keeper might as well have been joined at the hip. Clemence had few real weaknesses, though early on his kicking from the ground was wobbly – the Kop quickly told him so – and he effectively took over from Lawrence the 'sweeper' role at Liverpool, which was meant to compensate for the lack of pace from big Ron Yeats and later Larry Lloyd. Clemence added things to Liverpool too: the quick throw out from the back, for example, made for an effective counter-attack when under pressure in Europe, especially with two willing, pacy full-backs and Steve Heighway's speed to call upon. Clemence was also a very strong character, a bubbly dressing-room presence, who demanded excellence from all the club's staff and especially his defenders. He wasn't big for a keeper, under six feet and under 13 stone, so his presence in the penalty area had to be registered vocally and through his organisational skills rather than any overt physical dominance. His concentration was his major asset for Roy Evans, especially when Liverpool began to dominate games as they frequently would under Paisley. Here, the art of modern goalkeeping was being converted into a test of mental resourcefulness as much as it was a demonstration of agility and bravery: 'On a Saturday I'd be very vociferous throughout the game and there were many times when I'd come off the pitch without having had any saves to make, but I'd still have a sore throat and a severe headache from the shouting and the sheer concentration of watching the defence. All the information I was giving to defenders was meant to stop the ball getting to me.'

On the very few occasions he lost goals and sensed he might have been at fault himself, it was almost a reflex for Clemence to try to displace the blame elsewhere, so deep was his own personal disappointment at conceding. Like plenty of keepers in an era of a lack of specialist focus in training on the goalkeeping arts, he also fancied himself as a player. Alan Kennedy recalls his special strengths and ambitions as follows: 'Clem demanded the best from everybody and he was a great talker. He looked after us at the back: "Get out there, push out, do this, do that," it never stopped. He was talking all the time: he was our third centre-back. He was also a decent footballer. As a youngster he did play out of goal and in our five-a-sides at Melwood he played as a centre-forward. And Clem could play a bit – all left foot, mind. He liked to score and the players respected him more because of his ability outfield. If he ever got an injury during a game, say a broken bone in his hand or something, he always reckoned he could play outfield. He was athletic, good in the air and in great physical condition. He was very quick over a short distance and very brave.'

Nicknamed 'Nozzle' by the rest of the Liverpool dressing-room, Clem found it hard to get motivated in training. Reuben Bennett had been a goalkeeper and he did some skills work with Clemence, with Bob Paisley working on boxing routines in the gym to strengthen the keeper's hands. But Alan remembers that Clem didn't actually do that much work at Melwood between games, save for a little specialist keeping preparation, usually on a Thursday morning. Kevin Keegan thought that because Peter Shilton was more of an obsessive in training this got the Forest man the nod over Clem from the England national coaches and manager. In fact, Clemence could occasionally piss forwards off in training at Liverpool. He would play around and was easily bored. He hated conceding goals with a vengeance, but he also reasoned that the main part of the defensive job for Liverpool was often done higher up the field or even in the minds of the club's opponents: 'The side was so accomplished. It had strength, flair and passing ability,' he said. 'The longer the season went on, you knew the teams were scared to death of us, and we felt we could get any result we wanted, wherever we went.' There were no home League losses for Liverpool in 1978–79: Anfield, under Clemence's guard, was impregnable.

> Sixteen Goals: Goal Eight, 2 December 1978
> Arsenal 1, Liverpool 0
> (Ray Kennedy o.g., 30 minutes, 1–0)

> The press: 'There was a setback for Liverpool after 30 minutes, Stapleton running into the penalty box evading several Liverpool tackles before hitting the ball low across goal. Clemence dived, but could only palm the ball and Ray Kennedy, strongly challenged by Price, turned it into his own net.'

> Alan Kennedy: 'Arsenal were pretenders, we thought – good, but never brilliant. They had decent players like David O'Leary, Chippy Brady and Frank Stapleton, so they should really have done much better in the League. Away from home we always

had players back, challenging in defence, which is why we conceded own goals sometimes. But we never really got going in this one. This loss started a hard spell for us.'

MIDFIELD: IRON FISTS, VELVET GLOVES

It was an old Paisley and Shankly maxim, of course, that effective defence starts from the front. This approach had been especially honed in Europe, where the Liverpool staff instructed the club's forwards and midfielders to hunt in packs and close down continental defenders and midfielders, who were not used to having their possession of the ball challenged so keenly. This Liverpool midfield offered both goals and a fierce competitiveness. On the right-hand side was Jimmy Case, a tough little south Liverpool electrician and son of a boxer and rugby player, whose father worked as a fitter's mate on the railways. Case's was an unselfish and uncomplicated presence, one who would happily put his foot in when things got rough. You wanted Case in your side: his mother, Veronica, had spent all her bingo earnings on football boots for Jimmy when he was a kid, so he had a lot of inner-city emotional investment in becoming a fixture in this Liverpool team. He showed it.

Case signed relatively late for Liverpool, as a 21 year old from the South Liverpool club, and he immediately wanted to impress his new manager, Paisley, in training. After a few hefty challenges in a practice match between the first team and the reserves he caught the manager's eye all right – he ended up brawling with Alec Lindsay. Jimmy Case badly wanted to succeed for Liverpool Football Club – sometimes too badly. Alan Kennedy remembers, with a shudder, the alarming contests he faced defending Newcastle United's left flank against the right-sided combination of the brutal Tommy Smith and Case: 'Jimmy wouldn't try to take the ball around you, he wanted to go through you. He was a very hard player. I looked at those two and thought: "What sort of wall am I going to hit here?"' The answer was always: a very competitive and uncompromising one. Jimmy was aware of his limitations, saying: 'At Anfield I would come in white with my work effort and rely on pressuring oppositions to command the midfield.' But Jimmy and the Liverpool coaches had also noticed that Phil Neal's development as a true international-class defender – and Phil Thompson's pace to cover behind the full-back – had begun to offer the right midfielder much more freedom to go forward in 1978. It also meant he could eliminate some tiring running from his game. All of which meant more goals: he and Neal contributed 12 vital League goals in this 1978–79 title season, a huge bonus given the solid Liverpool defensive strength down the right.

If Jimmy Case was a handful on the field he was a double-barrelled problem off it. His big pal, his personal master of disaster, was the strolling and deceptively easy-going Ray Kennedy. The pair were inseparable – and they were also frequently in trouble. Graeme Souness described them as having 'the closest relationship I have ever seen between two footballers'. Today, their escapades as part of a title-winning, high-profile football club would be screaming front-page headline stuff: they mixed with minor Liverpool gangsters; sold FA Cup final tickets to known touts for tens of thousands of pounds; brawled with hoteliers and punters and sometimes their own teammates; and routinely bad-mouthed and intimidated the British football press pack. As Ray himself admitted: 'We were an explosive mix and when we went out together, something always seemed to get out of control.' This was something of an understatement.

In the early '70s Ray Kennedy was a talented, if complex, young Geordie who struggled to keep his weight down and who had finally sickened of the endless working and running and getting hacked down up front, even for a club such as Double-winning Arsenal. He thought football – and life – had more to offer than this and he got little of what he called 'ball satisfaction' in his final season in North London. He had visibly lost his appetite for the game and for the South when Bill Shankly signed him up for Liverpool, effectively to do much the same job for the Anfield club. Ironically, Shankly was gone before Kennedy's Liverpool career even got off the ground. By this time he was no longer forward fodder – but he still had his demons to deal with. From the start at Liverpool, Ray Kennedy was often a moody and difficult man in training, perhaps displaying early signs of the serious illness that would dog him in later life. He moaned so much that the senior players called him Albert Tatlock, after the grumpy *Coronation Street* TV pensioner. He was also explosive and unpredictable. Phil Thompson describes Kennedy as: 'A bit of a schizo. Sometimes on the training ground he would get a look in his eye that was very threatening. He was sensitive and would hit out if anyone said something against him.' Tommy Smith noticed this unease and Kennedy's innate suspicion of others: 'Off the pitch Ray was erratic. I used to call him "The Susser" because he was always sizing people up and would take a dislike to a particular person. He wouldn't say it to their faces at first, but then might suddenly blow up with aggression.'

Sixteen Goals: Goal Nine, 16 December 1978
Bristol City 1, Liverpool 0
(Joe Royle, 67 minutes, 1–0)

The press: 'Former Everton and Manchester City striker Joe Royle had the pleasure of scoring the decisive goal, although for much of the match he received such poor service that one would hardly have expected him to do so. However, he did not have to do anything spectacular, for when Gillies knocked a cross back to him midway through the second half he found himself all on his own, seven yards out. Scoring was a formality, though, from his jubilation one might have thought that City had won the FA Cup.'

Alan Kennedy: 'Royle wasn't on his own because I was jumping with him! It was a great cross and Joe out-jumped everybody, including me. He came in behind me and got up so early and so high that he put his knee right in my back. All I remember was the pain of his knee. We were always scared of Joe Royle in the air – he was a handful. It was a horrible match, bad pitch. Gerry Gow and Souey were kicking shit out of each other, I remember that. City roughed us up and the crowd were really into it. Their Cup final, but we were poor.'

On the field, in an era when keeping the ball was becoming a central theme for the best sides in Europe, Paisley admired Ray Kennedy because of his sure touch and his expert shielding of the ball: 'He was so strong that an opponent virtually had to knock him over to take possession.' Ray was unsure at first that he could play in midfield at all: that he had the mobility, pace and energy to cover the left side. He had to get much fitter – he slimmed from 14 stones to nearer 12 – and to learn the job and use his intelligence, economy of movement and reading of the game to much greater effect. According to Roy Evans: 'When Bob moved him to midfield he thought at first he had to run up and down the left-hand side like an outside left, but he soon learned that that was not necessary. He was meticulous, very organised.' Kenny Dalglish agreed. He thought Ray 'a clever player' and 'probably the best finisher at Liverpool'. This was praise indeed from a master striker. Souness said: 'He had a great eye and was good at closing people down, so he didn't have to run that much. We were the best midfield ever.' The best ever? Well, would you argue with Souness?

Given his prickly personality and his careful sussing out of supposed 'fakers' and dull time-servers, Ray Kennedy was unlikely to see eye-to-eye with all, or even most, of his Liverpool colleagues and he soon fell out with his new left-sided partner, Alan Kennedy, whom he didn't rate as a Liverpool recruit. This was partly a personality clash, though the new left-flank partnership actually worked well in straightforward footballing terms. Alan's pace and enthusiasm certainly helped to cover both for his own errors and for Ray's limitations and the two North-easterners were seldom embarrassed defensively as a pair. What's more, together they offered a real goal threat to match that posed by Neal and Case on the right: in 1978–79 the Kennedys together contributed 13 League goals, making 25 goals in all from the Liverpool flanks for the season, more than one-quarter of the entire club League tally. They may not have thought much of each other, but the unlikely Kennedy 'brothers' were actually building the sort of formidable partnership down the Liverpool left flank that could both defend and score goals.

Sixteen Goals: Goal Ten, 3 February 1979
Liverpool 2, West Bromwich Albion 1
(Alistair Brown, 67 minutes, 2–1)

The press: 'Albion confirmed their new-found threat by getting a goal back after 67 minutes through Alistair Brown, only the third goal Liverpool have conceded at Anfield this season. Hansen, sadly off form and obviously feeling his leg injury, sliced a wild clearance to give Albion a corner. Taken by Tony Brown, his namesake was left unchallenged as he rocketed a header past Clemence.'

Alan Kennedy: 'Alan Hansen was struggling and I got an injury in the first half: a clash of heads between me and Brendon Batson. Brendon didn't feel a thing and Ronnie Moran came on to treat me and said: "Aww, you'll be all right," but there was a big egg coming up on the top of my head. Brendon had a big Afro at the time and John Wile came up to me and said:

"What's it like to hit your head on a coconut?" We weren't the bravest or the best in the air and Ron Atkinson would have said to them: "Get some crosses in, they won't fancy it." He was right.'

In the centre of the Liverpool midfield the brilliant, hard-nosed young Scot, Graeme Souness, ruled uncontested. He missed one League game in 1978–79 and scored eight League goals, mainly at the start of the season when his form was quite unimpeachable, even by his own formidable standards. Souness was Liverpool's midfield co-ordinator, its pass master and its quality controller, but he was also its defensive guard: he snapped into tackles and frightened attackers from running at the Liverpool rearguard. He wanted no goals against, seeing such concessions as a personal stain. Souness was also the chief Liverpool dressing-room bully and occasional prankster, once, pointedly, coming into training with fake stick-on cold sores for the whole squad when poor Terry McDermott had already arrived with the real thing. It brought the Melwood house down.

When he first joined Liverpool the headstrong and occasionally violent Souness looked as if he might suffer from endless suspensions due to his excessively physical approach to playing. He liked to undermine the opposition, stake his claim, but this approach frequently went too far. He needed to cool his wings. This clash with the rule makers was no good to Paisley: he liked Souness's desire but he wanted his enforcers on the field, not neutered in the stands. Joe Fagan gave the young Scot some useful advice: let your reputation work for you. Stay on your feet and don't go lunging in so often. It worked, though Souness still never ducked a direct physical challenge and he remained susceptible to seeking out revenge on or off the pitch, especially on those rare occasions that games had started to drift away from Liverpool. Graeme Souness, above all, hated losing, even seeing it as a slur to his edgy manliness. His very first derby game, against Everton in October 1978, was also the first defeat of Liverpool's record-breaking season. Afterwards, Souness stalked the Goodison goalscorer Andy King in the players' bar, where the Everton man was quietly drinking with his girlfriend and suggested that the two men return to the darkened Goodison pitch to settle their differences 'man to man'. King simply laughed and told the furious young Scot to 'fuck off'.

Souness impressed Ray Kennedy both at Melwood and on the field, no mean feat: 'I had great respect for Graeme. He was a good professional, and very, very tough, but he had to be.' He had to be, because Souness liked to mock the so-called 'hard men' in the ranks of opponents. He derided them because they might be able to kick, but could they play? Souness, himself, despite lacking a little in pace and being an ordinary header of the ball, could do most things brilliantly on a football field and was utterly ruthless in pursuit of success. Perhaps his leadership qualities and his fearlessness were the things that made him stand out above other midfield players of the time who possessed some of his obvious technical ability. 'Among midfielders,' says Alan Hansen simply, 'Graeme was the king.' Souness, above all, expected to win and didn't much care what route to take as long as it had some style and, ideally, it offered ample opportunity to humiliate lesser opponents. He also expected the very highest standards from his playing colleagues. Usually, he got it.

Sixteen Goals: Goal Eleven, 13 March 1979
Liverpool 1, Everton 1
(Andy King, 75 minutes, 1–1)

The press: 'King, scorer of the first Everton winner against Liverpool for seven years last October had never been seen before this. But he became their points saver and here again he snapped up Latchford's pass and drove the ball high into the net – only the fourth goal Clemence has conceded at Anfield this season.'

Alan Kennedy: 'I missed this game; Bob left me out. I had been playing number four because Emlyn Hughes was playing and he wanted to keep the number three. Emlyn was putting pressure on Bob to play at left-back. So I went to see Bob. McDermott, Thompson and Hansen, the single lads like me, all said that I was the record signing – I ought to have it out with him. Bob just said: "Be patient: I'm trying a few things." I felt lonely and insecure: I always thought I had to play at my best to hold my place at Liverpool. You want the team to lose when you're not playing, because you're that desperate to get back in. Bad times – you go in the dressing-room but you just feel out of it.'

Winning – and also fighting – were not quite so important to Souness's other main midfield partner at Liverpool in 1978–79, the mischievous and easy-going Terry McDermott. Terry Mac once confided to Alan Hansen in the Liverpool dressing-room before a major Liverpool match that he wished he was now sitting in the same spot two hours later with a cool pint of lager. He was no fan of training and sometimes worried about playing. Terry preferred leisure to 'work' and liked to 'build up' to home matches stuck in front of the TV set at Anfield for as long as possible watching his beloved racehorses, even as kick-off approached. Bob Paisley sometimes watched with him. According to Jimmy Case, 'Terry Mac would watch the racing until 2.30 p.m., loosen his tie at 2.40 p.m. and then go straight onto the pitch, without a warm-up.' It could have been Sunday League football. McDermott was one of the few bought players in the 1978–79 Liverpool squad that had served a major apprenticeship in the club's reserves, where he sometimes struggled to match the taxing standards of Ronnie Moran and Roy Evans. He would need some time to become an established Liverpool footballer.

When he was playing badly in the reserves the slender Scouser with a perm called himself 'Terry Gone Off' after the crack German midfielder Reiner Bonhoff. When McDermott eventually made it into the first-team squad at Liverpool he was substituted so often at first that he called the little wooden box containing the numbers of the player to be subbed 'the toaster' because his number ten used to pop out of it so frequently. Sometimes, when his number inevitably came up he would run off the pitch backwards, as if being reeled in like a fish. 'We both hated the Kemlyn Road flank,' he once said of his partner in crime Ray Kennedy. 'If I played there in the first half and they were moaning I used to warn Ray at half-time and we would have a laugh.' It was his humour, in fact, that kept McDermott going against early adversity at Anfield and he was always upbeat in the dressing-room, a welcome contrast to the tub-thumping of Thompson, the manic focus of Souness, the formal willingness of Phil Neal or the edgy calm of Ray Kennedy. It was good to have Terry Mac around because of all his daft tricks and sayings. On the field, McDermott was a superb runner, a player who could keep up over distance with any member of the Liverpool squad. His perm meant he steered away from heading but his finishing – seven League goals in 1978–79 – and his unselfish work in front of the Liverpool back four were priceless to the team. McDermott was a roadrunner midfielder who could get ahead of the ball and still get back to mop up in midfield while the Souness and Case partnership made opposing midfielders think twice about fast breaks. It usually worked.

Sixteen Goals: Goals Twelve to Fourteen, 16 April 1979
Aston Villa 3, Liverpool 1
(Allan Evans, 32 minutes, 1–0)

The press: 'The first goal came when poor covering and tackling allowed Cowans to stroll through for a shot which Ray Clemence seemed to have held comfortably. He had the shot in his hands, lost it, and it fell to Evans, who was given the easiest of scoring chances.'

(Phil Thompson o.g., 40 minutes, 2–0)

The press: 'It was gift time again eight minutes later. Evans made a poor header from a right-wing centre, the ball bouncing towards Clemence's waiting hands, but Phil Thompson, trying to clear, sliced the ball away from the goalkeeper. It hit a post and rolled slowly over the line as Clemence scrambled back in an attempt to retrieve it.'

(John Deehan, 84 minutes, 3–1)

The press: 'With Liverpool totally committed to attack they left themselves open to a breakaway goal. Deehan went through unchallenged from what seemed like an offside position. Clemence raced out of the penalty area trying to block the Villa striker, but Deehan stroked the ball through his legs from 20 yards out.'

Alan Kennedy: 'Easter Monday was a big test because Aston Villa were building towards a good team. We were a bit tired, but Clem couldn't hold the Cowans shot, it was that well hit, and Evans just forced it in. It was a scrappy goal for us to give away: we thought we'd get back into it. But Villa took the game to us. The second was a lack of communication – even in a defence like ours. Then Dave Johnson scored for us and we really went

at them in the second half. But Deehan got away on my side –
we thought he was offside – and he hit one well from the edge
of the box. You could see Bob was mad later, seething. He
wanted to have a go at somebody. Thankfully, Phil Thompson
got most of it.

DEFENDING FROM THE FRONT

Up front in 1978–79, David Johnson and Steve Heighway shared
strikers' duties in the Liverpool team alongside the incomparable,
ever-present, Kenny Dalglish. The Scot scored 21 League goals to
Johnson's 16 during the season and he would dominate Liverpool
forward play in the late '70s and early '80s in partnerships mainly with
Johnson and then with a young predator called Ian Rush. Though
lacking the provocative swagger and confidence, perhaps, of a Souness
or the easy assurance of an Alan Hansen, Dalglish was a brave and
technically brilliantly gifted striker who was also, unusually for players
at the top end of a football team, refreshingly unselfish and a real team
player. Defensively this was especially important to Liverpool because
it meant that the midfielders and forwards, led by Dalglish, left few
easy options for opposing defenders in possession. Winning the ball
high up the pitch – turnover ball – could also produce vital goals: it was
a lesson rammed home often enough by Joe Fagan. Bob Paisley was
hugely impressed with Dalglish and saw immediately that he had
typical 'Liverpool' qualities: 'I'd seen Kenny playing for Scotland,
watched him on television, and the more I saw of him the more I
became convinced that he was what I called a Liverpool-type player. It
was his attitude to the game. He wasn't flashy. He did the simple
things and he was consistent too. He was rarely out through injury
either. His timing was immaculate and his head ruled his feet.'

Dalglish's ego-free willingness to chase apparently lost causes also
meant that early clearances from the Liverpool rearguard were often
converted into valuable Liverpool possession in the opposing third,
especially when the striker got his backside stuck into opposing
defenders: the Scot had amazingly powerful thighs and hips and a low
centre of gravity, which invariably allowed him to wrap his body
around the ball and away from defenders until help arrived. He always
wanted the ball, viewing it as a personal affront if he was refused
possession: Alan Hansen said that Liverpool defenders learned to give
the ball to Kenny, simply to avoid an argument. The defensive
strength at Liverpool during this season also meant that even a solitary

strike by one of their main target men – by Johnson or the peerless Dalglish – was often enough to settle a contest. It happened six times in the 1978–79 League season alone, 12 vital points. Much more frequently, though, this Liverpool team was scoring goals as well as preventing them: 14 3-goal or more hauls in the 1978–79 League season, including a 5–0, a 6–0 and a 7–0 win. For the new Liverpool man, Alan Kennedy, winning football matches – and winning them well – was slowly becoming part of a new way of life. Despite the Forest European disappointment, the early League Cup exit, his fall-out with Ray Kennedy, and the general problems of fitting in at a new club containing some very big characters, football at Liverpool was actually beginning to feel very, very good.

NAILING DOWN THE TITLE

Off the field, the fan cultures in the English game were overheating in the late '70s. Liverpool's record-breaking season coincided, for example, with the growth of the hooliganism problem at Anfield and elsewhere in England. The Anny Road boys had recently installed themselves at Liverpool home matches to frighten visiting fans and turn them over, if required. A visit to Birmingham City in September 1978 produced a routine 3–0 Liverpool win, a first goal for Alan Kennedy and reports of the 'Battle of St Andrews', with fans from both sides removed from the ground after rivals had pelted each other with bricks and even darts. The *Liverpool Echo* was later full of letters from despairing fans complaining about the antics of hooligans. The horror of Heysel was still seven long years away, but the early signs were all around.

It was certainly no country lane stroll for Liverpool at Goodison Park on 28 October, a short trip that produced the club's first League defeat in 12 matches with only one other point dropped so far, at challenging West Bromwich Albion. After this local setback a Liverpool home draw followed against a rough-house Leeds United before wins against Queens Park Rangers and Manchester City put the Reds' title challenge back on track. There then followed the only slightly uncertain phase of the whole Liverpool League season: an uninspiring 0–0 away draw at Tottenham followed by home wins against Middlesbrough and finally against bogey side Nottingham Forest – two goals from McDermott ending Forest's incredible record run of 42 League games unbeaten. But there were also 0–1 away defeats, at both Arsenal and at lowly Bristol City, where Joe Royle scored the winner against a decidedly off-colour Liverpool. This sequence of only two wins in five games and four away games with three defeats meant that, at the end of the year, Liverpool and Everton, now managed by Alan Kennedy's old boss Gordon Lee, were tied at the top on thirty-three points, with West Bromwich Albion lying just behind. It looked like a title chase to the finish.

What then followed was probably decisive: five straight Liverpool wins, including 3–0 at Manchester United, a vital 2–1 win against then second placed West Bromwich Albion and a 6–0 home blitz against Norwich City, while Everton faltered. Most of these Reds' wins came in February 1979 – pretty much the whole of January was wiped out for English football because of bad weather and during this enforced stoppage Albion briefly went to the top of the table. This unscheduled winter break brought two things for Alan Kennedy personally: first the return of some good form and second a new rival for his full-back berth. Earlier in the season Kennedy had had a tough time against West Brom's tricky Laurie Cunningham, but back at Anfield in the return in February 1979 the new man thought that he had finally won over the Kop, with one crunching tackle on the dangerous winger seemingly turning things around for him. He powered on for the rest of the game, the Reds deposing Albion, once more, at the top of the table. The *Liverpool Echo* thought Alan's performance against the championship rivals was 'his best game in a Liverpool jersey. His attacking gifts have never been in doubt; his tackling has not been at the same level – until this. An outstanding display, which he relished as much as the fans.' After the drubbing of Norwich City – with Alan Kennedy on the score sheet again in another rousing show – 'I should have had three' – an old Bob Paisley critic, John Bond, admitted: 'Liverpool are the best club side in the world, the best British post-war team. Their game has reached a new level. They are in a different class and the title has to be theirs.' Maybe Bond knew the game after all.

Sixteen Goals: Goal Fifteen, 24 April 1979
Southampton 1, Liverpool 1
(Nick Holmes, 75 minutes, 1–1)

The press: 'It was against the run of play when Southampton snatched the equaliser as Steve Williams, their best player and the only man in midfield who competed with Liverpool, made a great run down the right and his fine centre was headed home firmly by Holmes.'

Alan Kennedy: 'Holmes was a good left-sided midfield player, a dangerous runner: they caught us in the air again. Southampton were a good attacking team, especially at home, and The Dell was a hard place to play. The crowd were on top of you, a poor stadium; there were always people climbing all over the place. They usually worked very hard against us. I put in a cross for Dave Johnson to score early on. Bob always said that 1–0 is never enough, especially away, though, sometimes, weak teams gave up the ghost against Liverpool once we got ahead. But Southampton weren't discouraged. This was a great result for them, but Bob thought a draw was okay for us.'

Israeli international Avi Cohen arrived at Anfield for a trial in January 1979, advertised extravagantly as the 'Beckenbauer of the Middle East'. In fact, he had come ostensibly to replace the 'Beast of North Wales', the departed Joey Jones. Cohen's arrival was an early sign of the new global reach of Liverpool – the club's first overseas recruit since 1954. It was a disconcerting moment for Alan Kennedy, but he told himself to continue to make his mark and he would hold his place. It wasn't that easy. After a good personal run, Alan played a poor 45 minutes in a 0–0 draw at Chelsea and found himself out of the Liverpool team. Typically, neither Bob nor any other of the Liverpool coaching staff explained why he had been dropped, sowing more seeds of doubt that he might not be able to make it in this exalted company after all. League draws followed for Liverpool, at Coventry City and at home to falling Everton in March – Andy King scoring again, the only player to score two League goals against the Reds in that record season. Alan also missed a hard-fought sixth-round Liverpool FA Cup win at Ipswich Town, a victory clinched by a 'wonder' goal by Kenny Dalglish. The League and Cup Double seemed a distinct prospect now for Liverpool, with Manchester United waiting in the FA Cup semi-final. Another run of five straight League wins between 20 March and 14 April – with Alan finally regaining his place – was interrupted only by these heavyweight semi-final clashes.

This was not an outstanding United side under the dull Dave Sexton: it lacked the flair of the Docherty team that had beaten Liverpool in the 1977 FA Cup final, for example, and was heading for a sorry mid-table League finish. Joe Jordan and Lou Macari were supposed to offer goals along with Jimmy Greenhoff, while Steve Coppell and Micky Thomas worked hard on the flanks and Sammy

McIlroy offered support from midfield. McQueen and the tetchy Buchan, with Gary Bailey behind, were hardly impregnable at the back. On paper this looked like a win for Liverpool. In the first meeting, at Maine Road, Hughes replaced Alan Kennedy in a 2–2 draw, Alan Hansen scoring a late equaliser for Liverpool. Surely Paisley's team would now complete the job at Goodison Park? Instead, Bob Paisley switched from the familiar Liverpool 4–4–2 in order to accommodate Steve Heighway for Jimmy Case up front and Liverpool lost the crucial battle for midfield – and the match – to a Jimmy Greenhoff goal. Paisley admitted later: 'I blamed myself because, having drawn 2–2 in the first game, I made a tactical switch for the replay which, later, I recognised had been a mistake. It wasn't individual players who were to blame – it was my own failure to stick with the style that suited us best; that was the game we had perfected. Yet on the night of the replay, and at Goodison Park of all places, I switched to 4–3–3 and we failed to translate pressure into goals. We paid the penalty.'

This defeat was Emlyn Hughes's last match for Liverpool, a game too far. Hughes, the only Englishman to lift two European Cups as captain, remarked later that he had played in five outstanding Liverpool championship teams, but with only two truly great players – the Scots, Dalglish and Souness. Paisley now told the veteran England defender that the club would have to let him go. The United FA Cup defeat was a severe setback and 12 days later, on the 16 April 1979, there was another shock for Liverpool. After those five League wins without conceding so much as a goal – including a 3–0 drubbing of FA Cup finalists Arsenal – Ray Clemence was beaten three times at Aston Villa on Easter Monday. Villa were certainly no mugs: they were slowly building a title team themselves under Ron Saunders and led 2–0 at the break. This was unfamiliar half-time territory for the Reds. David Johnson replied for Liverpool in the second half but John Deehan slammed the door shut for a famous home win. A furious Bob Paisley confronted Phil Thompson in the Villa Park baths after the match, enquiring in his quivering North-east twang whether the Liverpool man thought that the captaincy was now just 'too much' for him? Thompson's jaw dropped as Paisley stalked away. The other players, who were all listening in, toyed mercilessly with the defender on the bus journey back; Liverpool had still only conceded 14 goals all season and now the boss wanted to bawl out his new captain, his defensive brick.

It seemed a harsh judgement, but typical Bob, who had warned:

'When things go wrong at a club it can usually be traced back to an attack of ego somewhere within that club at one level or other. It is our job to stop that happening at Anfield.' Was this an attack of ego or an off-night in an otherwise exemplary defensive League season? History could prove a difficult judge.

> Sixteen Goals: Goal Sixteen, 1 May 1979
> Bolton Wanderers 1, Liverpool 4
> (Graeme Souness o.g., 62 minutes, 1–2)

> The press: 'Liverpool scored all five goals, because Graeme Souness, so desperately keen to win his first Championship medal that he was back helping in defence on one of the very few occasions Bolton attackers got the ball up, put through his own net in a last-ditch attempt to send it wide.'

> Alan Kennedy: 'Always a poor pitch at Bolton, and one massive open terraced end. Bolton were workmanlike, but lacked quality. We were already 2–0 up when Graeme netted for them: we always seemed to get somebody in the way! We conceded 16 goals, but three or four of them we scored! It was never going to matter here, and Souey was working hard to clear – another sign of the togetherness of the team. Kenny and Ray Kennedy got goals for us later on against big Sam Allardyce at the back for them. I wasn't surprised we won well here. None of us were.'

The defeat by Villa had left Liverpool still a little shaky in the League, with Paisley eyeing up both WBA and the approaching Nottingham Forest below and blasting: 'We were absolute rubbish at Villa and the championship's still wide open.' But an uncertain 1–0 Liverpool home win against Bristol City and away draws at Southampton and then at Forest were followed by a crushing 4–1 victory at Bolton Wanderers, Ray Kennedy netting twice, putting Liverpool just two victories from wrapping up the title, with four games left. A 2–0 home win against Southampton, with Phil Neal scoring twice from open play, confirmed the all-round scoring strengths of this Liverpool team as well as their championship credentials. Fittingly, their recent conquerors from Aston Villa were the crucial opponents at Anfield on 8 May, on the

40th anniversary of Bob Paisley's arrival at Liverpool as a player. He was now in sight of his third League title as a manager.

This title countdown was also a huge thrill for a man with less than a year's Anfield service: in front of a packed Kop, Alan Kennedy scored the first Liverpool goal in the championship decider after just 47 seconds, a scrappy six-yard box affair, a deflection from a shot by Jimmy Case. 'But what,' asked Alan Hansen in mock criticism, 'was the Liverpool left-back doing in the opposing penalty area after less than one minute's play?' The Kop chanted in response to the goal: 'Nottingham Forest – you're not champions any more.' It ended as a Liverpool stroll, 3–0, with further goals from Dalglish and McDermott. There was no presentation on the pitch. Instead, Ronnie Moran came round the dressing-room later, with a huge cardboard box, handing out the truly terrible sponsors' plastic awards – there were no medals. Kennedy reflected on his ugly prize for winning the oldest football championship in the world. It was hardly a memorable moment, and Ronnie was predictably grizzly: 'There's yours, there's yours,' he griped, on his way round. 'And remember: pre-season starts in two months and six days: you might be off tomorrow, but we've also got training on Thursday.' Typical Moran. The Liverpool players celebrated well into the early hours, before being captured live on TV the next day getting 'totally bolloxed' again at Chester races for the whole of the following afternoon.

ALL BETS ARE OFF

Alan Kennedy had played 37 League games in his first season and Liverpool had won the title conceding just 4 goals at home, equalling the home League wins and points total, and scoring 51 home goals, an incredible record. Their 68 points beat the previous record haul of Leeds United and equates to 98 points today, with 4 more matches played. Liverpool had scored 13 more goals than the next highest League scorers in 1978–79 and conceded 10 fewer goals than the next meanest defence, equalling Arsenal's 1935 League goal difference record of plus 69. Kennedy confirms that the Liverpool team had actually talked little about the new defensive record they were threatening to establish – they had no idea about the previous low. But, typically, they did know that the *Sun* had had a wager with Ladbrokes at the start of the season on any team scoring 2 goals a game: which meant that Liverpool's final haul of 85 goals, following a 1–0 win at Middlesbrough and a 3–0 victory at Leeds, promised £50,000 winnings from the newspaper. The players had to resort to the courts to collect their reward, claiming, against Inland Revenue demands, that betting tax had already been paid on this windfall. The Anfield players knew something about betting. Some Liverpool players usually had modest 'saver' bets on other competitor clubs, for example at the semi-final stage of major cup competitions. Why not have a little 'insurance' down in case Liverpool missed the final or lost at Wembley? No Liverpool player ever tried to lose a match, of course – the cash and other rewards of winning were always greater than any bets placed on an opponent. But it made sense to take account of the possibility of failure – and a potential loss of earnings.

There was no point backing any other title chasers this season: Nottingham Forest, in second place, were eight points adrift at the end of the title race, with Everton some 17 points back. This was a crushing Liverpool triumph by any measure and it was achieved with Bob Paisley's own team – only Clemence and Thompson as regulars had survived from Bill Shankly's side. Later, key players such as Thompson, Hansen and Souness would all agree that this was the greatest Liverpool title side of all: it was defensively watertight but had great attacking verve, using a squad of just 15 players, with David Fairclough and the emerging Sammy Lee making only a handful of appearances between them. This title win also meant another Liverpool crack at the European Cup. Maybe Alan Kennedy would actually get to play in the big league in continental Europe this time? Nothing was certain from hereon in – except, of course, that this Liverpool team would now play more great football and win more trophies. Who else, in the rest of Europe, could possibly stop them?

Chapter 5

MEN OF ANFIELD

BOB PAISLEY AND THE KENNEDYS

Bob Paisley knew the footballing Kennedys from Penshaw well – or at least he knew Alan's mother Sarah-Anne; they grew up in the same North-east mining village of Hetton-le-Hole, an extraordinary production line at the time for professional footballers. The youthful Paisley was, by all accounts, a bit of an unlikely jack-the-lad: he used to chat up the girls who worked in the fish and chip shop where a young Sarah-Anne Donnelly served Friday fry-ups. The teenage mining men and aspirant village footballers were determined to have their fun on a Friday and Saturday night, of course, and Sarah-Anne could help them out – they had her six other sisters to consider. It was not always clear that Bob knew exactly which sister he was talking to, so the young footballer had to try to keep his courting stories straight.

Sarah-Anne watched the youthful Bob Paisley play for local football clubs and even tracked his professional football career for a time. She may have had a crush on Bob. It seems bizarre that from this innocent beginning Bob Paisley would later become a famous Liverpool football manager, a world figure in the sport, and would end up more than 40 years later signing one of his early young admirer's sons for Liverpool for a record fee. The men would win League titles and European trophies together and Alan would even score the crucial goal for Bob's third managerial European Cup triumph. Alan's mum would have been tickled for both of them, her two footballing heroes with roots in little Hetton. Sadly, Sarah-Anne died just before Bob Paisley took her ambitious son to Anfield: it would have been quite a Durham reunion.

Bob Paisley's imposing father Samuel worked at the Hetton Lyons colliery and, like the young Gordon and Sarah-Anne Kennedy were to do much later for their own lads, Samuel Paisley did what he could to offer an escape route from a life down the mines for his own four sons. He bought Bob his first football boots at six years of age and instilled in him the importance of physical fitness, encouraging the keen young sportsman in both his football and his cricket. The young Paisley already had an interest in the workings of the body and he studied racehorses and athletes for signs of how he could improve on his own conditioning. Bob played County football for Durham and had an England schoolboy trial in 1933. Like Alan Kennedy, he was an eager student of the game, determined to listen more than to talk and, as he put it, to 'learn something every day' from his teachers and coaches. Also like Alan, Bob dreamed of becoming a Sunderland player, but he was rejected as being too small after a trial as a 15 year old.

Having suffered early rejections by the professional ranks, Bob turned, instead, to local amateur club Bishop Auckland and in 1939, after Bishop had won the Amateur Cup, he was finally spotted and signed by Liverpool manager George Kay. But the impending Second World War meant that Paisley effectively lost seven years of his Liverpool playing career. His League debut finally arrived against Chelsea in September 1946, an emphatic 7–4 Liverpool win. Like Alan Kennedy's first championship season, this first season for Paisley as a Liverpool player also suffered from a delaying January freeze. But Bob played 33 times for his new club as a hard-tackling defensive midfield player in a League campaign in which the North-east's Albert Stubbins and Merseyside's Billy Liddell excelled up front for Liverpool and which was finally decided in the middle of summer, on 14 June 1947. Liverpool, and Bob Paisley, were the first English post-war football champions.

The seasons that followed were disappointing ones at Anfield, but Liverpool did reach the FA Cup final in 1950, to face Arsenal. Bob had scored in the semi-final defeat of Everton but he then got injured and the Liverpool directors – the Liverpool team was chosen by the board at the time – decided to omit Paisley from the final team. Liverpool lost 2–0 and Bob was visibly shattered by his exclusion, later claiming that this crushing disappointment stood him in good stead as a manager when he had to make similar decisions by leaving established players out of big games. League decline swiftly followed at Anfield and, in 1954, Liverpool were relegated to the Second Division. This was enough for Bob Paisley the player, and he hung up his boots after 278 appearances and 13 goals for the club. He thought about a fruit and veg business or maybe – a player's old stand-by this one – opening a newsagent shop. But his native football intelligence and his childhood interest in fitness and training meant that Paisley was invited by the Liverpool chairman, T.V. Williams, to stay on at Anfield as reserve-team trainer and physio. It was an inspired appointment. Assessing and treating the body, a Paisley obsession, and doing some coaching were better than working, and it offered a base in a sport – and a football club – that he loved. Paisley took the job. He never looked back.

Neither manager Don Welsh, nor his replacement, Phil Taylor, could drag Liverpool out of the Second Division and in 1959 Reuben Bennett joined the backroom staff at Anfield to work on players' fitness with Bob and to counsel those Liverpool players who were working their way back to the first team. Soon after, Paisley stepped up to first-team trainer, just in time to welcome a new Liverpool manager, a stylish young Scot called Shankly. Nessie Shankly, Bill's wife, later called these two men, Bob and Bill, the 'terrible twins' because of the way they so obviously complemented each other: Bill was impulsive and forceful, Bob was quiet and thoughtful. Bill would exhort and inspire his teams to greater heights, while Bob could carefully assess players and offer astute, direct advice – and almost magically deal with their injuries and fears. For Shankly, injuries were a personal betrayal; for Paisley, they were a challenge to his understanding, patience and healing skills. In the football public's eyes, the '60s and early '70s at Liverpool belonged to the messianic Shankly but Paisley was there, always close behind, balancing and chivvying. In the background too were Ronnie Moran, Roy Evans and especially Joe Fagan, listening and learning. Ronnie also did some shouting – lots of it. In 1971 Bob was appointed assistant to the manager, which meant that when Bill Shankly impetuously decided to retire after the Liverpool FA Cup final hammering of Alan Kennedy's Newcastle United in 1974, Bob, reluctantly, stepped up to the managerial plate. He didn't do a bad job either, winning League titles in 1976 and 1977 and European trophies in both years, including Liverpool's first European Cup, in 1977. If Shankly had laid down the foundations, Bob the Builder was fast erecting a glorious Liverpool footballing edifice. Whisper it, but Paisley was actually already outperforming the adored Bill.

THE LIVERPOOL BOOT ROOM

By the time Alan Kennedy arrived at Anfield in August 1978, Bob Paisley had already built a new Liverpool team to better any of those constructed by the great Liverpool moderniser, Bill Shankly. But Bob was not alone. The backroom staff assembled by Bill Shankly was integral to Liverpool's later success, of course, and in August 1979 Joe Fagan was promoted to assistant to the manager and Ronnie Moran became chief coach at Liverpool, with Roy Evans in charge of the club's by now utterly dominant reserves. It was a formidable cabal, balanced for increasingly cold-eyed decision-making by the canny Paisley, sympathetic morale-raising from the kindly Fagan and the young Evans, and strategic brute rollicking from the abrasive Moran. Bob Paisley especially knew well the value of the two older men in the Liverpool backroom. In August 1979 he said of the promotions for Ronnie and Joe: 'They are vital parts of our life and have thoroughly earned their higher status. I am blessed by having two men of the calibre of Joe and Ronnie to work with me, men prepared to work 25 hours a day for Liverpool. These two never talk about hours. They just get on with the job.'

Bob was certainly right about the hours these guys worked. Few of the Liverpool players ever visited Anfield or Melwood, day or night on any day in the week, when Joe was not already there, deep in conversation with one of the staff, or Ronnie was not busy mumbling to himself or chivvying on an injured player or a perceived malingerer. Joe Fagan was a very modest man and a good coach. He was hugely respected by the Liverpool players, especially the demanding Graeme Souness, who worried that Joe's only weakness was that he was just 'too nice a man; you always fear someone may take advantage or undermine his authority'. For Alan Hansen, Joe Fagan was a 'common-sense' man who had an intuitive feel for the problems of players – he could identify the smallest drop in performance and come up with simple, but effective, ideas to put things right: 'He was a master of saying the right thing at the right time.' Joe, more than the other senior Liverpool staff, adopted a deeply caring, almost pastoral, role with the players at this time, regularly asking about families and other problems at home. He was the first port of call for any Liverpool player in trouble or needing advice, and he raised his voice only sparingly – which meant that when he did get animated at Melwood players actually sat up and listened. Whilst the Liverpool players routinely let rip in training with oaths and blasphemies, the worst gentle Joe could muster was 'You bloody buggers!' Kenny Dalglish said of Fagan: 'Joe acted as a buffer between Bob and the players, taking the sting out of situations before player–manager incidents erupted. He handled things so well he should have been in the diplomatic service.' But Joe did also have his tough side, a line you could not cross, which came much more into play when he became club manager. He once dropped the saintly Kenny Dalglish and let the Scot discover his own fate in the tabloid press. On another occasion, Alan Kennedy was caught daydreaming in a Melwood coaching session that was focused on defending and rather than resort to general criticism – usually Joe's way, to spread the pain – he launched into Alan, pointing out that the session had actually been put on specifically for him: if he could be bothered to listen, that is. Like scolded schoolboys, the squad was briefly silenced – only to erupt again on the bus back to Anfield, replaying the incident time and again, with Kennedy as the unfortunate fall guy.

Ronnie Moran played 'hard cop' to Joe's more understanding Boot Room role, but Moran's real strength was motivational. Ronnie was reputed never to use the same words twice in his gee-ups with players, so they could hardly claim they were hearing the same tired, old song. Not that this stopped them complaining. Ronnie also searched tirelessly for new ways of getting something extra out of players, even if – especially if – it meant niggling away and getting under the skin of his edgiest charges. No one at Anfield, after all, paid Ronnie Moran to be popular, although he also had a sharp sense of humour, giving as good as he got in the frantic Liverpool dressing-room exchanges amongst players. He was especially affectionately tough on the so-called Liverpool 'big heads': the real stars of the side like Souness, Dalglish and Ray Kennedy, who, according to Ronnie, thought they knew everything. But it was not *all* stick from Moran: Ronnie would also offer words of gentle encouragement to individuals, usually out of earshot of the other players, in order to maintain his grizzly reputation. When he gave individual praise – frequently on the back of a general lecture about how today's players had it far too easy – it really meant something because it was such a rarity. It meant more still to a new player like Alan Kennedy, who was currently keeping warm Ronnie's old number 3 shirt for Liverpool and trying to make his way at Anfield. Moran seldom let Alan forget this history or his current responsibilities on Liverpool's defensive left side. Kennedy was standing, after all, on the shoulders of football giants.

BOB THE BUILDER

Bob Paisley, himself, seemed a very straightforward figure in the eyes of the public: a gentle 'father figure' who stepped very reluctantly into Bill Shankly's shoes only because he thought he would be letting the club down if he refused. Who else could take charge? Chairman John Smith finally persuaded Bob to take over by offering reassurances that, although he would be allowed to select all transfer targets, he wouldn't be involved in any of the financial dealing with players. He could leave that to Smith and Peter Robinson. So Paisley became one of the first real authentic English football coaches in the modern era. Paisley, essentially a shy man, lacked some of the obvious warmth of Bill Shankly: he wasn't the sort of manager who would put his arm round favourite players, for example, and give them a comforting squeeze, the way Shanks sometimes did. He was much too reserved for that. Paisley also said that Shankly had steel tips on his shoes so you could hear him coming down the next corridor. This was not Bob's way. He preferred not to be recognised or to cause a storm. Bob later recalled a piece of advice from his headmaster that had guided him in his management style: 'He told me if you had something to say, then you should speak softly . . . that way they would listen. That's the approach I tried to take.'

Ronnie Moran thought Paisley was an especially good assessor of the different needs of players: 'He knew the game inside out and the biggest thing for me was that he knew the players inside out, individually. He knew the ones who were going to work hard and the ones who didn't want to work hard and who needed the most rollockings.' Ronnie, of course, could easily point out the latter group and was more than happy to oblige. Bob told Roy Evans that a player had to have something that made them stand out: either the way they kicked the ball, or great pace, or a big football brain. If you had two of those things, then you had a chance. Publicly, Paisley was an 'ordinary' working-class man of few airs and graces: he was 'wee uncle Bob', or 'Dougie Doins', who happily shuffled between Anfield, the betting shop and home in a flat cap and carpet slippers – he wore slippers because of an old ankle injury from his playing days – carrying a mug of tea and with a copy of a tabloid newspaper stuffed cheerily in his back pocket. How could this bluff North-easterner, who looked like a regular old stager from any West Derby pub, possibly match the best football brains in Europe? In time, they would all have to look and learn.

But Bob certainly had his early doubters, even inside Liverpool's dressing-room. Ray Kennedy, for example, was hugely unimpressed by his first Liverpool team meeting under Bob: he was bewildered by the vagueness and the organisational chaos he encountered. It felt totally unprofessional. Expecting bravado and insight from the ebullient Bill Shankly and his vaunted backroom men, instead the new Liverpool manager, Paisley, seemed nervous and withdrawn, mumbling endlessly about 'what's its' and 'doings' and using other weird North-east phrases like 'jag down there' that nobody understood. Lots of the Liverpool players affectionately impersonated Bob's clotted Durham accent especially, later on, the chief dressing-room clown, Terry McDermott. Nothing of real use seemed to be said at all at these meetings. So, when Bob finally drifted off on this occasion, the ex-Arsenal man, Ray Kennedy, turned to Tommy Smith, the Liverpool captain, for guidance. Tommy shrugged and the brash Kennedy told him that, compared to Arsenal, Liverpool was, surely, a 'pork pie and pop outfit'. Smith, predictably, was furious. But Ray Kennedy soon learned of Paisley's real strengths, saying: 'He knows the game so well that he has beaten teams with his tactics before the players step out onto the pitch. That's his secret, the way he lines his teams up and the formation he plays.' Bob undoubtedly had something – an inner belief and a knowledge about the game – that was difficult to summarise or reproduce.

The truth was that Paisley and his coaches had little interest in over-complicating the game by turning to the modern football theorists or to the sort of technocratic language that was beginning to creep into the game. For Alan Kennedy, 'Bob was great at not giving players problems.' In other words, he kept it simple. When the Liverpool England players came back from international squad sessions and began using mild coaching jargon in practice matches at Melwood, for example, the Liverpool coaches often stopped the game and the offenders got a royal ribbing from Bob and the rest of the squad. As Graeme Souness points out, for Paisley, 'getting in round the back' was what burglars did, and only electricians talked usefully about 'positives' and 'negatives'. Bob never used 'coaching' terms like these, Alan Kennedy recalls, and he didn't expect the Liverpool players to either: 'Bob said: "If you want all of that with England, fine, but don't bring it back to Liverpool. It might put you off your game." The Boot Room didn't like complication: books being written about football, what you should do in certain situations, "position of maximum opportunity", and all this kind of stuff. How could that help you out in front of goal? They didn't know enough about it, I don't think. They just believed in the players they had and trusted them to read the game.'

It was rumoured, in the late '70s, that England manager Ron Greenwood once came to a hotel where Liverpool were preparing to play Middlesbrough to ask Paisley, Fagan and Moran to act as assistants for the national side. None of the players knew about the approach and it was never followed up, if it happened at all. The Liverpool trio would almost certainly have refused the invitation to join the FA elite. They spoke a very different language to the Men from the Football Ministry: a winning one. It was also true that Bob had a rather jaundiced view about the role of international football in the lives of his players. He was well aware of the potential tensions that divided club and country loyalties – and of the requirement, above all, that Liverpool players should always give their all for Liverpool: 'A player picked for his country is anxious to do well in order to win prestige, and the chance of representing it again. That's where the trouble starts . . . there are players in the game today who are more interested in representing their countries than their clubs . . . some of these protect themselves in League matches if they know an international game is coming up. It is not easy to adopt that attitude if you are a Liverpool player because our game is based on teamwork, with everyone pulling their weight.'

In fact, unlike at the England set-up, where Liverpool players were surprised by the level of input from coaches, there was very little formal coaching at all at Anfield. The Liverpool coaching staff largely trusted the judgement of the players they had recruited, who, in turn, respected the knowledge and experience of the Liverpool backroom staff. Players were expected to improve, by playing together and playing to their strengths: by moving off the ball, and through the occasional nuggets of experience and knowledge offered up by Bob, Joe, Roy Evans and Ronnie Moran. Liverpool players were getting much more than coaching at Melwood, even if Roy Evans thought it might also be useful to get an FA coaching badge: 'You can learn something from anyone.' Ronnie showed a keen interest in Alan Kennedy of course, who agrees that formal coaching was not an Anfield priority: 'We never got coached at Liverpool. How could you coach a Kenny Dalglish or an Alan Hansen? Liverpool just bought players who could attack or defend or who were comfortable on the ball. Every player was good on the ball. It was the job of the Liverpool scouts to make sure you could play. I had a weakness on my right foot but we didn't work much on that. We believed in our strengths rather than our weaknesses. No one at the club told me to improve on my right side.

'Ronnie Moran, as an ex-left-back, would have a quiet word with me, but no way would he offer coaching. He would just say things like: "Get tight" or "Make him go inside". Ronnie had an answer for everything. You could say to Ronnie: "How am I going to do this?" He'd never read a manual, but he had accumulated knowledge over years. You could have all the coaching you like but it was what you did on the pitch that mattered. Bob always used to say in training: "Options, options, options." If you're not on the ball, be an option. You don't give the ball away but if you do give it away you, personally, have got to get it back. Which means more running.'

INJURY TIME?

Bob's early training as a physio ought to have stood the Liverpool squad in good stead, of course, in terms of injuries and their treatment, but the Liverpool staff's general approach to such matters was actually rather ad hoc, haphazard even. Bob likened players to machines: 'I make the comparison with cars,' said Paisley, once. 'Modern players are like cars running up and down the motorway at 70 mph all the time. They get more wear and tear; their engines are under more constant strain. It's the difference between the older days when cars ambled along country lanes at moderate speeds.' There would be no ambling, clearly, at Paisley's new Liverpool.

Recovery from injury often relied upon Bob's native capacities to diagnose, usually by sight, an injury or even the effects of a change in a player's lifestyle. Or else it depended on the sheer desire of Liverpool players at the time to shake off knocks and strains in order to maintain their place in a dominant and winning side. Mark Lawrenson later commented on Paisley's famous ability to 'read' the purchase of a new car by a player or even the use of a different chair at home by the tiny ways this new item might change how a player moved in training or the way he carried himself around Anfield. A tighter clutch on a new car, for example, could mean more strain on a niggling hamstring or a newly sore Achilles. Paisley could reputedly tell, as soon as a player went down injured, exactly what the problem was, and by watching a player walking or running whether they had a cartilage problem, a hamstring problem, a bad back or a groin injury. He also cleverly invoked homely imagery of togetherness and solidarity in accounting for large parts of Liverpool's success under his leadership. On the 40th anniversary of his stay at Anfield he said: 'We are dedicated to two things – the family and winning. We are a family club, everybody helping everybody else in every department. We don't have any secrets about our success. We regard football as a simple game, but perhaps what gives us something extra is the spirit in the club.'

Some of this was flannel, of course, but taken all together it meant that Liverpool players relied, largely, on Bob's intuition and often on his homespun remedies to deal with potentially chronic injury problems. It also meant that the players' dedication to the collective cause – to 'the lads' and to the staff, to the 'spirit' in the club – usually outweighed any individual concerns about the possibility of longer-term physical damage. Kenny Dalglish recalls, for example, how the club dealt with a troubling pelvic injury he suffered by getting Joe Fagan's wife to tighten up his jockstrap with a few well placed stitches. He played on for the rest of the season in his strange new contraption, preferring Mrs Fagan's make-do needlework to an operation and inevitable absence from the first team. Ray Clemence was astonished by the number of times Liverpool players turned out carrying injuries, recalling an occasion when the Liverpool coaches insisted that he travel to an away match at Newcastle wearing a carpet slipper on a swollen ankle he had turned very badly turned in Friday training. He played, much against his better judgement, and Liverpool won comfortably. Alan Kennedy broke his nose in his first season at Liverpool and suffered pain and breathing problems as a result. Joe had said that he should carry on playing and that he could have the necessary operation at the end of the season. No chance: the surgery finally happened three years later during a peculiarly long close-season break.

The staple response to leg injuries at this time at Anfield was intense hot and cold treatments, followed by capsules – 'black and reds' – to reduce inflammation. The hot wax footbath at Anfield was so feared by the players that its mere threat was enough to 'clear' most muscular foot problems. The Liverpool treatment room was widely seen, by the players, as a place of torture and witch-doctors: a site that seriously threatened your health and your vital position in Bob Paisley's affections. A popular story that did the rounds among the Liverpool players illustrates how treatment 'worked' for the medical staff rather than for the players, for whom it meant only dread. Tommy Smith was, reputedly, on the Liverpool treatment table with ugly lacerations on his legs. The attendant doctor said to Jimmy, one of the Anfield Boot Room boys: 'Jimmy, get me two large Scotches, now. I've got some work to do here.' Even the teak-tough Smithy gulped at this development, anticipating that he would need the Scotch to dull the pain of whatever happened next. Jimmy returned with the drinks and the doctor knocked back both of them in an instant. Smith just gaped, and caught the medic's eye. 'Aww, you'll be all right, Tommy,' the doctor growled. 'On yer way.'

Alan Hansen argues that one of the ultrasound machines at Anfield was unfit for humans; it was actually for use on deep-seated injuries in horses. Ian Rush was later convinced that none of the Liverpool 'medical' staff actually knew how to work their ultrasound equipment because players were simply urged to forget knocks and run off strains. Or they were told to heal themselves. In his fourth season at Liverpool, in 1981–82, Alan Kennedy had a lot of niggly injuries, especially a groin problem that never seemed to go away. He pestered the Liverpool coaches and, for his trouble, he got some unusual do-it-yourself treatment advice – and some cod psychology – at the home of the then European Club Champions: 'The coaches knew about the injury but I used to get through it. Today it just wouldn't be tolerated. I really needed a hernia operation, but I didn't get one. You just had to get on with it. We even used to give ourselves treatment. We used to go into Anfield at half-nine in the morning, say, and Roy or Ronnie might be busy and they'd say: "Listen, put yourself on the ultrasound machine and give yourselves a little bit." Some of the machines they had there were from the 1950s. How did we know that we were even treating the right area? We had no idea. We'd give ourselves a little bit of ultrasound and half the time the machine probably wasn't even switched on. But we thought: "Great, this, giving ourselves treatment." It was a way for the coaches to say: "Look, you're fine. It's all in your imagination. Just get out there and do your training or playing." The Liverpool treatment room should really have had a big cross on it with a message saying: "NOBODY'S ALLOWED IN THIS ROOM, UNLESS YOU HAVE A BROKEN LEG."'

The key theme here, of course, was the thinly veiled assumption that *real* Liverpool players simply did not get injured. And could anyone really afford to be unfit in this outfit? 'Here's the team today,' Bob used to say after his Friday morning meeting. 'If anyone doesn't fancy it we've got others waiting to come in.' He meant it.

WHAT'S THE SECRET?

This intuitive approach to dealing with injuries – along, of course, with help from forward David Johnson's own personal medical kit –

was one of the few authentic 'secrets' of the Liverpool success under Paisley. Although few English clubs at the time were much more sophisticated in the injuries department, Liverpool did suffer an incredibly small number of major injury setbacks and hardly any at all in their largely ball-centred work in training sessions. But the general notion that one could somehow discover the 'secret' to Liverpool's achievements became something of a standing joke at Anfield among the players, Paisley and his coaching staff. Its main expression was in the regular arrival at Melwood of the visiting foreign coach or journalist, each one in search of the magic formula, the elixir of champions. All were tolerated with a genial grin – and all were sent home equally bemused. Alan Kennedy recalls: 'Bob would say to us, in his broad Geordie accent: "Allright, I've got this one. He's from Czechoslovakia. He's come to see us, to see what we do." And they'd say: "Right, Mr Paisley, can we see what you do that makes you so successful?" And we'd smile at each other and train and then they'd go away thinking: "That's incredible: they crossed the ball, had shots at goals, played five-a-side – and then they'd finished. And that was it." "There was no secret," Bob used to say. "Just good players."'

In truth, there was little that was exceptional at all about Liverpool's training. A typical week meant that all players had Sunday off, unless they were injured. The walking wounded reported to Anfield for a check-up and morning treatment for an hour or so, but they also had to report in again on Monday morning at nine o'clock rather than the ten o'clock show demanded from the rest of the players. Joe, Ronnie and Bob would have a regular Sunday morning session at Anfield to go through Saturday's game: the team's form, the performances of individual players, goals conceded, and so on. They'd have a cup of tea with their chat in the Boot Room and other coaches and trainers might also join in this regular weekend pow-wow: Reuben Bennett, John Bennison and Tom Saunders, maybe Roy Evans. So it was for a full seven days a week that these guys were committed to Liverpool during the League season. The players joked that Ronnie had a bed in one of the rooms inside Anfield.

For a 10.45 Monday training start at Melwood, the juniors, the Liverpool kids, would put the first-team training kit out at Anfield, where the senior players met for 10 a.m. to discuss Saturday's game, any TV football, the weekend's drinking and, occasionally, the matches ahead. It was here, too, that the dressing-room wide boys – Hansen, McDermott, Dalglish, Souness – began looking out for the inevitable 'ricks' – the tiny mistakes in expressions or speech – that made certain players the butt of the week's jokes. This relentless testing and banter – which was often cruel and pointed – was also about establishing firm dressing-room cohesion. It was also indiscriminate: as Alan Hansen says, no one in the Liverpool dressing-room was allowed to get above his station, to be 'in love with himself'. The in-jokes and the language codes were a formidable barrier to outsiders and they made the Liverpool dressing-room both an exhilarating, and a forbidding, place to be. This made absolute sense to the Liverpool dressing-room leaders: the best football club in England ought to have the most outrageous, the most compelling and hurtful banter. Just as a wide-eyed Steve Nicol made his way in the Liverpool first team in 1984, his idol Kenny Dalglish experienced a noticeable dip in form. Noting Nicol's devotion to Kenny, Alan Hansen told the young Scot just before the 1984 European Cup final that Dalglish had a terminal illness, which Kenny confirmed by asking Nicol: 'Haven't you seen how badly I've been playing?' Nicol was in tears before dressing-room laughter finally broke the spell. The young Ian Rush almost left Liverpool because he hated the early stick he got about his hick clothes and his Welsh roots, especially from the older 'smart-arse' Jocks in the Liverpool first team. He soon learned – as all the Liverpool players did – to love being on the inside of this strange and insular cult. Everyone looked forward to Liverpool training for the ball work, but especially for the shit-stirring, the jokes and the endless dressing-room *craic*. 'The lads at Liverpool,' Mark Lawrenson said later, 'were champion players, champion drinkers, but also champion jokers.'

Most of the Monday morning talk at Anfield was about the Saturday late-night action in the city. Who had pulled; who drank what; what new places had opened up; and how you had managed to get home. The seniors got changed at their own little pegs – at Alan Kennedy's Newcastle the players had old-fashioned football lockers. Reserves and other players used the visitors' dressing-room. Then it was more wicked banter and more weekend stories on the bus ride down to Melwood. Bob Paisley would follow on later in his Rover car, well away from the shop-floor talk. Monday morning training at Liverpool was hardish, but not too hard. If Liverpool had played well and got a result at the weekend, then it would be an easier session than if Joe thought something needed working on. As Alan Kennedy puts it: 'Liverpool wouldn't punish you exactly, but they toughened it up if the game had gone badly. But everything was still geared around running with the ball.' Another little secret.

The Monday sessions would begin, typically, with stretching exercises, warm-ups and half-laps of the main Melwood pitch: everyone would do it, reserves, juniors, maybe 40-odd players in all. Kit was all-sorts, whatever the players preferred. There was little checking or advice given here. For a while, for example, Ray Kennedy took to wearing a bin liner under his training kit to purge himself from sweat in an attempt to get his weight down. He would sometimes feel faint on the trip back from training, but the coaches used to refuse to open the bus windows, fearing other players might catch a cold. After the morning warm-up, the players were split, for more focused ball work, into first team, reserves and junior groups. Coach John Bennison would take the juniors, Roy Evans the reserves and Joe and Ronnie would take the first team. Ronnie would set the practice out under Joe's command. The 'first team' here would consist of no more than 14 or 15 players. First teamers would then do stamina work and little exercises: shooting at goal; crossing. The Liverpool staff aimed to keep training simple: get the ball in, make the cross. Get the shot in. Five-a-sides. To guard against boredom or laziness, the rules of the small-sided games were constantly changed: scoring only with the left foot or only when over the halfway line. In forwards versus defenders contests the defenders always won – the forwards' teams would leak goals. Players got a bit of everything, but Monday was really a reasonably gentle wind down from the weekend match and the beginning of a slow build-up to the midweek fixture, if there was one, or the weekend game.

Once the season was in full swing there was usually a break in training in the week. Training fitted around matches and was less physical than at many clubs. If Liverpool had a match on Tuesday night the players were off all day Wednesday, unless they were injured. They might then fit in a day at the races, with champagne and plenty of ale to match, or an afternoon's drinking at a local bar or snooker club. Afternoons after training, especially for the single players, were often spent in bars, the bookies or snooker halls. If there was no midweek game, Bob might insist on a double training session on Tuesday, morning and afternoon, maybe some running and some three-a-sides, five or six games in that one session. A favourite practice was six or eight midfield/attackers against four defenders, five including the keeper. The back four and the keeper would play keep ball and the attackers would try to get in and behind the defence, the emphasis for the defenders being on the importance of interceptions and reading the game and forcing opponents to shoot from distance.

This session might be finished off with some longish runs – 50 yards there, 50 yards back.

This was intense work – but not gut-wrenching. It was a tough session, in part, because the coaches knew that Tuesday or Wednesday night was also a nightclub in town night for the senior players, and especially for the single lads. The players were expected – or at least assumed – to go out, to have a good time on a Tuesday night and maybe to continue it on Wednesday night. So Wednesday training was usually low key: either it followed a match, was a match day, or else it was parked in the middle of the players' midweek drinking sessions. Missing the bus to Melwood after a heavy midweek night out was always a possibility. As Alan Kennedy points out, it wasn't recommended: 'It happened to me twice, missing the bus. One of those times I slept in, the other I had a problem with the car. Ronnie gave me a stern look first time and I had a genuine excuse the second time. If you did it a third time you would get the biggest rollicking of your life from Joe Fagan. You knew: but I never saw anyone get fined for missing the bus. How could anyone be late for ten o'clock starting work? One of the excuses from the lads who lived over the water was that there was: "Fog in the tunnel". Bob used to think: "Fog in the tunnel?" Sometimes, after a late night, you might miss the bus. You daren't miss it again.'

Bob Paisley's attitude to players' drinking at Liverpool was pretty relaxed – within limits. A few beers together helped with team spirit, he reasoned, and posed no real fitness dangers, though the usual suspects at Liverpool could easily take this line of thinking way too far. Graeme Souness thought that Paisley was sensibly happy to be in the dark about what his players were really up to away from Liverpool FC: 'Bob had the attitude that if he didn't see it or hear about it, it was all right, and quite often he gave us that impression of those three wise monkeys, allowing us our heads as long as it did not affect what was going on during matches.' But the senior Liverpool players also recognised both their freedom and their responsibilities here – and the very different regime at Anfield compared to at some other clubs. 'There was no strict discipline at Anfield,' recalled Kenny Dalglish later. 'Everyone was expected to have self-discipline. Those football clubs that try to become monasteries rarely achieve success. People respond well to being treated like adults.' Liverpool FC was certainly no monastery; that much was clear. Roy Evans recalls Liverpool playing a German team in a match in Marbella, when the Liverpool players were allowed a drink before the game. The German coach came over afterwards and said: 'Your players were in the bar last night and are in the bar tonight and you beat us 3–0. How do you do it?' Joe Fagan replied, evenly: 'Good players.'

Bob Paisley actually had other, much more potent, fears to contend with than those about his players downing buckets of ale, as Alan Kennedy remembers: 'Bob was strange – he had a mentality that if you had a pint of beer, then most of it is water and you can run that out of your system or piss it away. If you had vodka or brandy it's harder to get out of your system. He didn't mind you having a beer. Plenty of times players would come into training smelling of alcohol. We always thought we could have a good session, work hard, and we could get rid of the poison. There was no "Go and do ten laps of the pitch" after a heavy night. When training was done, at one o'clock you could go off and do what you wanted. Worse than the drink, Bob hated anyone to go and play golf. He was rather you were shagging and drinking than playing golf. Golf made players walk miles, and you might pull a muscle swinging the club. Bob wasn't happy if players organised golf days for testimonials. He could cope with the drinking, but not golf!'

Vodka and golf: a modern footballer's nemesis. If there was a Wednesday night Liverpool game, followed by the usual players' beery night out, then the whole squad was required to come in at 10.30 a.m. for a bath or a sauna at Anfield on Thursday morning. This was mainly so the Liverpool coaching staff could check on the condition of their players after a big night out, use the club roll call to help limit the previous evening's excesses. Bob and Joe simply wanted to *see* their valuable assets in the build-up to the weekend's main fixture. Ronnie Moran might give some players a rub down, but this was mainly a relaxing day. There was no light training, nothing. Then, everything had to be right in training on Friday morning. There was *some* Liverpool work done in training for set pieces, but mainly for defensive duties. None of this was tailored in advance for the opposition, no matter their attacking qualities. Liverpool seldom changed their shape or approach to deal with a specific opposing strength, relying, instead, on the quality of their own players and the reliable shape of the basic 4-4-2 or 4-4-1-1 formations that Paisley favoured – though he would never talk in these sorts of 'tactical' terms, of course. Football players changed and moved their positions, it was argued by Bob, but the dangerous spaces on a football field remained the same, whatever the opposition. Every Liverpool player was expected to close the ball down quickly in their own area of the field, so they passed opponents on once they had left your own space. Liverpool always marked space, not specific opponents.

For free kicks against Liverpool Kenny Dalglish was always the first man in the wall, adjusting and shaping it with Ray Clemence, whilst chivvying at the referee about the award and the exact location of the kick. It usually helped to slow things down. Bob, like Shankly before him, disliked too much preparation in training for attacking set pieces, and was happy to rely, largely, on the spur-of-the-moment decision-making of his lieutenants and the element of surprise this offered. 'Nothing fancy,' was his simple steer on this matter. 'You play what you see, if it's on, try it.' In Europe, however, where defenders tended much more to go man-for-man at the back, for free kicks taken by Alan Kennedy from the left there *was* a little Liverpool plan. All the powerful Liverpool headers of a ball at the time – Ray Kennedy, David Johnson, Phil Thompson – would make a move to the near post, leaving a massive space in the home defence behind, that Kennedy would try to hit. It was Phil Neal's job to fill this hole, and he would seldom be picked up because he would make his runs from such a deep starting position and wide defenders were just not picked up by a man-for-man defensive plan. It wasn't rocket science, but more than once it produced results.

If there was no Wednesday fixture for Liverpool, then Thursday was the big Liverpool training day. Ronnie or Joe would start the session with newly fixed faces by saying: 'Right, let's start getting focused on things, we've got a big game at the weekend.' This was the start of it, the serious training work, though there was still little talk of the weekend opposition. It wasn't pressured work, exactly, but everyone could tell that the pace had picked up, that the coaching was a bit more focused; that the tackles were biting, the small-sided games more competitive. The banter and the joking from earlier in the week and all the training chat about women and drinking was now on the back burner. It was: 'Don't have any fun, any laughs, now.' This was much more serious stuff. Now the manager and coaches were looking forward to Saturday's game, building back up to the weekend's action, with the first-team defenders and attackers playing together in units and the coaches examining defensive and midfield deficiencies that might have arisen in the last match.

Thursday was usually the big training day for everybody at the club – this was even the day when Liverpool's goalkeepers did their main, directed practice. For much of the rest of the training week Ray Clemence was scoring in five-a-sides and doing pretty much what the outfield players did. Thursday was also the day's training that Bob Paisley watched most closely. If a new player was coming into the team an 11-a-side practice might be organised with the reserves – who were told not to 'upset' the first teamers, but who often won this showdown, nevertheless. This was a nervous day for those on the margins and for those trying to hold on to first-team places. For Alan Kennedy, this was an important weekly test to be passed. You could hold on to your first-team place or force your way into the manager's plans for the weekend with a good training show, a sharp performance, in the intense Thursday training contests at Melwood: 'You had to do it well – get your touch right – because that's the time you can impress the manager. If things had not gone well in midweek, on Thursday the passing had to be really crisp, it had to be good and you could impress the manager to get into the squad. A lot of players brought in on Thursday training could try to get into the squad by doing well. Bob was looking all the time now: who's moving well; who's trying harder than others? I was either a centre-forward or a goalkeeper in the Thursday games. I was always trying harder than anyone else. I felt as though I had to.'

SOMETHING FOR THE WEEKEND?

Fridays was sharp, morning ball work, short and sweet, competitive small-sided games and a slightly harder session if Thursday had been a day off – but nothing stupidly aggressive. If it got too meaty on a Friday, the Liverpool coaches would step in quickly to call it a day. The Liverpool players would certainly wind each other up here, the Jocks in the first team maybe playing in an intense six-a-side against the English lads, plus English-born but Eire international Steve Heighway. This was short and sharp but pretty serious stuff, a basis for national pride – and high quality. For a short time, the players on the winning teams in training could vote for the worst player in the opposition. If Graeme Souness was voted worst opponent he simply refused to accept the decision: how could this shower be better than him? All the Liverpool training sessions were tight and focused: the Liverpool staff knew they were dealing with intelligent footballers with low boredom thresholds. Terry McDermott had a natural level of fitness and running strength that seemed to be powered by lager. Ray Kennedy struggled at times and Alan Hansen was no big fan, especially of the early season stamina work. But as long as they put it in on match days, the coaching staff were generally happy to let players find their own levels for training: after all, good training was no goal in itself.

Having followed the players' bus down to Melwood, Bob would start his Friday morning team meeting before training at about a quarter to eleven. The senior players always had a cup of tea, provided by the younger lads, and Kenny Dalglish would bring biscuits provided by a friend in the trade, and always two types: chocolate and digestives. The lads used to fight – and it was often very close to a fight – to get the chocolate ones first. This biscuit competition became another silly, but enjoyable, little Friday morning Melwood routine, part of the competitive dressing-room ritual. The players tried to focus on Bob's words of wisdom, but not all were always up to the task. Terry Mac wasn't a great sitter or concentrator, for example. He could easily glaze over when Bob was talking, only half-interested, daydreaming about something much more fascinating from events the night before. As well as some general comments about Liverpool's immediate opponents, Bob might also offer here just a little something to individual players: 'The outside right's a bit chicken: clatter him early on' or 'They won't pick up Terry McDermott's runs, so make them count.' Bob was also ruthless in his desire to win, telling forwards such as Kenny Dalglish: 'Look, if you're going to get kicked, get kicked in the box. It's worth it in there.' The Liverpool staff never used TV video material with their players to look at recent performances or consider the opposition, even though much more of it was now becoming available and some other clubs were starting to use it. The Anfield coaches trusted their own eyes more than TV analysis.

Bob's Friday team meetings barely changed, even after his European Cup triumphs. They remained short, often perfunctory, and were still stuffed with old, impenetrable North-east slang. He sometimes grasped for the names of opposing players – and even for those of his own team. The two rival Liverpool 'Davys', the forwards Fairclough and Johnson, for example, were often left nonplussed after team meetings when Bob announced that 'Davy' would play up front this week. Which one? Alan Kennedy also remembers that this tactical high point of the Liverpool training week, typically, carried little detail about the opposition, beyond relayed comments from Liverpool scouts about the general playing style of opponents and their obvious preferences, strengths and weaknesses: 'they like to go wide'; 'they are weak on the left side'; 'watch them from corners'. Alan Kennedy describes a typical Bob tactics talk: 'We'd only start talking about the opposition on Friday morning. Bob would come in. Joe would sit down as well, Ronnie next to Clem. But the coaches had no real input now: it was all Bob. Bob would have his table, a board with 11 counters with numbers on, on the treatment table. He always used to wear trainers and would pull his shorts right up into his stomach as if he was a little nervous. Sometimes he would have his tracksuit bottoms on. He loved being the coach. He'd come in and say: "Right, lads, we've got Stoke tomorrow. Now we had them watched last week and Reuben (or Tom) says they play this way, 4-4-2", or whatever. And in three or four minutes he'd talk about their players, the team, the manager and what they did last week and where they were in the League, whether they're good away from home, etc. He would rarely pick out individuals. But he would remind players about the opposition. He would remind me about a Steve Coppell, say. Or he would tell Clem about a Bob Latchford, a big, tough centre-forward. Generally speaking, he would show how the opposition would line up with the counters. He might mention particular players and their strengths and weaknesses from last week, depending on the scouts. He didn't want to talk too much about their strengths: imagine the dossier other clubs would have on Liverpool!'

The tactics board was not much more than a prop: it was more than technical enough for Bob. On one occasion, Alan Kennedy remembers, Bob lined up all his counters and had put 12 on the opposition side. He couldn't work out what system Liverpool's opponents were playing because he had too many counters to choose from. They were playing 4-2-4, but, according to Bob's board, they were actually playing 4-3-4. The players were gagging with laughter as Bob scratched his head. He might even have done it deliberately, to take the pressure off his own players, lighten the session. But Paisley and his staff had little interest at all in dwelling on the qualities or tactics of opponents. Why should they? Few teams in England at this time – barring Clough's Forest, perhaps – studied tactics in any sophisticated way, and Liverpool had many of the best British players, natural on-the-field leaders, already at Anfield. Why not just let them play and let the opposition worry? Paisley's real strength was his intuitive feel for the game and his near unerring good judgement of players. According to Kenny Dalglish, 'His knack of making the right decisions made Bob a great manager.' Paisley was no crockery thrower – he seldom lost his cool – but he did let players know when they had made a mistake. And he had a real presence, despite his deceptive old-world charm and rather shambling appearance. In his own way, he was a real football intellectual and a man with a ruthless streak. For Graeme Souness, for example: 'If we looked as though we were becoming a little complacent, or if we were not performing up to standard, Bob would say: "If you have all had enough of winning, come and see me and I will sell the lot of you and buy 11 new players."'

One or two of the senior players might also chip in at this stage with ideas or views of their own – Bob always asked for players' comments. Emlyn Hughes would certainly offer something in Alan Kennedy's early days at Liverpool, and Steve Heighway and Ray Clemence also often had contributions to make. But most of the Liverpool players were generally ready to go by now, and making obvious points to Bob just delayed going-home time. Bob, nevertheless, enjoyed this little feedback session as long, of course, as it was practical and positive. There was no space here for building up the opposition, for example. Why waste time worrying about the opposition when Liverpool had the best players anyway? Paisley would then announce the squad of 13 players for the following day and pin up the list on the Melwood noticeboard. David Fairclough and, increasingly in Bob's time as manager, Sammy Lee might be names thrown into the squad to keep the more vulnerable established midfielders and attackers up to their game. Alan Kennedy watched nervously for Emlyn Hughes's name on the board in his first season at Anfield and then, briefly later, for Mark Lawrenson's. But, most of the time, 10, if not 11, of these players in the squad of 13 already knew, early on Friday afternoon, if they were in the weekend's starting line-up. Bob seldom threw in late surprises and, from 1978, his team virtually picked itself until players such as David Johnson, Ray Kennedy and Jimmy Case all began to struggle in 1981.

For home games, Liverpool players usually stayed on Friday nights in the Lord Daresbury hotel in Warrington, a quiet and private little out-of-town retreat off the M56. They were picked up by bus, together with Ronnie and Joe, at Anfield at 6.30 p.m. and then had an evening meal together at the hotel. The main reason Bob wanted the players together was to give them time and space to focus on the match, especially from Saturday morning onwards. Early Friday evenings at the Lord Daresbury could actually be quite lively, as players received family and friends and sorted out their ticket allocation: four complimentary tickets per home match, with the option to buy six more at £3 a shot. Tickets for home games, especially, were always a scramble.

Alan Kennedy roomed with the deceptively laid-back Alan Hansen, who always wanted to be ready for bed on Fridays at around 9 p.m. – and no distractions. Joe and Ronnie were usually on the prowl at 9.30 p.m., in any case, to make sure everyone was in their rooms, before retiring, themselves, for a whisky and a chat about the following day's fixture or forthcoming European trips. Alan Kennedy simply describes Hansen, with feeling, as: 'One of the laziest people off the pitch I've ever come across.' Kennedy, full of nervous energy, liked to be active and doing things on the morning of matches whereas Hansen preferred long lie-ins and tea in bed – ideally delivered by his room-mate. Many of the Liverpool players watched the one-liner, sharp US sitcom *Cheers* before getting off for the night, something of a home-game ritual.

There was very little dietary advice at all for professional footballers around at this time, so many established Liverpool stars, internationals Emlyn Hughes and Phil Neal among them, often opted for a pre-match steak at Saturday lunchtime. It seemed to do them no harm: both played more than 600 times for Liverpool and Neal hardly missed a match for the club in 11 seasons. Bill Shankly had reasoned that if boxers preparing for fights stocked up on steak, this obviously 'high-energy' food must surely work, too, for footballers. Alan Kennedy generally opted for something lighter before a game, an omelette or fish, but he also tried to load up on baked beans or peas if he could, thinking that this offered the best chance of a relieving 'clean out' on the toilet before the match. He was also hammered by Bob Paisley before a Liverpool FA Cup tie at Southend once for eating a bread roll – instead of toast – at the pre-match meal. He wasn't even in the 12 to play, but Bob still went ballistic. Generally, Liverpool's was a really basic approach to food – whatever suited, plus myths and anecdotal knowledge – and the Liverpool staff mainly let the players get on with it. It was years later before it was realised that red meat actually took hours to digest and that pasta, not baked beans, might really make you go faster, and for longer, during matches. Dr Vaughan Thomas at Liverpool Polytechnic PE Department criticised professional footballers in the early 1980s for their low levels of fitness compared to other athletes. His comments were summarily dismissed by the football coaching gurus, but given the drinking and eating habits of top players at the time and their minimum upper body and strength work, he was almost certainly right.

At one o'clock on match days the bus picked the Liverpool players up for the short trip to Anfield. On arrival, the Liverpool FC horse-racing fraternity – Hansen, Alan Kennedy, McDermott, David Johnson and perhaps Jimmy Case, too – would go straight down to the players' room to watch the horses on TV, while the rest of the squad signed autographs and sorted out their remaining match tickets. Ex-players – Tony Hateley, Roger Hunt, the great Billy Liddell – and the occasional Liverpool club director, were also usually around the lounge from 1.45 p.m. for a pre-match chat. In the players' lounge, current players could lay their bets by phone but more usually Alan Hansen acted as the club bookie. If Liverpool were winning well, Big Al could even find out how he stood in this buyers' betting market during the half-time interval.

At two o'clock Ronnie Moran came down to collect the Liverpool racing crew, for a few words from Paisley, physically dragging them away from the TV screen. Bob's Anfield team talks were always basic and to the point: 'Don't let yerself down' or 'do what you did last week' were regular standbys. After this little ritual was over, McDermott was likely to want to sneak away again, claiming he was 'off to the treatment-room': he wanted a further update on the day's runners and riders. In the dressing-room on match days, players could barely breathe for the fumes from cheap liniment. Ronnie Moran was warming up reluctant muscles with bottles of the toxic liquid, with Reuben Bennett crudely binding up ankles, cracking stories and demanding from his players, one by one, evidence that they were truly 'up for it' today. Bob moved quietly around the players now, reminding each one in turn about his job, while the occasional favoured local celebrity was allowed to put his head around the dressing-room door to wish the team luck.

The Liverpool chairman, John Smith, also made dressing-room visits, to general player amusement. Smith had a patrician sense of duty to be seen to be interested in the lives of his employees, so he liked to ask the players, in a too-posh accent, about the health of their families, moving swiftly on in turn, not wanting to get in the way, and also slightly wary of aspects of the dressing-room culture that he worked so hard to keep out of the local press. It was his little dressing-room ritual: the Liverpool board meets the staff. Ray Kennedy once replied to these rhetorical questions from Smith about his missus and children by revealing, deadpan, that his wife was actually ill, his house had burned down and his children had been removed from school. Smith, by now oblivious and deaf to all replies, simply moved on with a mumbled, 'Good, jolly good, Ray.' The Liverpool squad, needless to say, collapsed. Ronnie Moran just shook his head: these big-time players today had no respect.

If the Liverpool players did get really properly focused for games at home, it was probably only in this last 20 minutes before kick-off. But it seemed to work out all right, this low stress, informal build-up to big football matches, because in the first two seasons Alan Kennedy was at the club, Liverpool's home League record read: W34 D8 L0. The

Liverpool staff was doing something right in its preparations and training because no visitor really enjoyed coming to play at Anfield and few returned home with anything worth building on. Alan Kennedy claims that after just ten minutes' play against most opposition you could usually spot a crucial lack of confidence or the absence of spirit or talent in the opposition that was a tell-tale sign that another home win was already on the cards. Soon, of course, for Liverpool fans simply winning at home would no longer be enough: increasingly, it had to be achieved with style and with goals, lots of goals. Remarkably, although Alan Kennedy joined Liverpool in August 1978, his first home League defeat as a Liverpool player came more than three years later, as a substitute on Boxing Day 1981, against Manchester City. Afterwards, Joe Fagan read the riot act, a useful wake-up call: Liverpool went on to win yet another League title. Playing at home for Liverpool under Bob Paisley simply meant winning football matches.

HARD TIMES – AND PENALTY ALERT

By the start of 1979–80 League season, Alan Kennedy's second at the club, he already knew most of what there was to know about Melwood training, Liverpool preparations and Anfield success. And yet, in many ways, he was none the wiser. He realised that he was at a very special football club, but why, exactly, *was* it so special? It *felt* different, but there were no magic potions or shattering insights to reveal to the world about Liverpool's methods. Bob, Joe and Ronnie seemed to embody a vast stock of football knowledge, sure, but it must be being transferred by osmosis to the players. The manager, after all, was genial, but he was virtually unintelligible to the first-team squad – and yet all absolutely respected him. No one questioned Bob Paisley's judgement. There was no real 'coaching' at Liverpool, and yet Kennedy felt that he was learning much more about the game than he ever could at Newcastle. He knew, from Ronnie Moran, that kicking towards the Kop end, for example, the wind swirls around the Kemlyn Road corner, often preventing even the hardest hit ball from going out from long clearances. This was vital information, especially for hard-pressed full-backs. He also knew that Liverpool football club was hopeless at dealing with players' injuries, and yet no one at the club ever seemed to get injured or stay injured for long. The Liverpool players drank and ate pretty much what they liked, and yet they seemed to run harder and longer than any of their opponents. Their match-day preparations seemed arcane, and yet opposing teams hated to come to Anfield. Somehow the non-interventionist homespun doctrines at the club – epitomised by Joe Fagan – about the 'simple' game and the 'family' club and 'keeping players' feet on the ground' had the effect of moulding great footballers with large egos into the ultimate team unit. Liverpool spotted and signed the best footballers in Britain, mixed in some honest and reliable artisans, and then made all of them care deeply for each other, for the Liverpool staff and for the club. Perhaps this was the *real* secret? As Alan Hansen argues today, 'What they did that was special and different was that they didn't do anything! There wasn't any coaching: for the 14 years I was at Liverpool, I was never coached once.'

On the commercial side of the British game, meanwhile, there *were* some surprising new developments. In July 1979 Liverpool became the first British club to attract shirt sponsorship, a £100,000 deal with Hitachi, the electronics and white goods group and the sixth largest manufacturing company in the world. Everton mystified everybody by signing a much smaller shirt deal soon after, with Hafnia. Who? The new shirt deals were hedged in by restrictions on the size of the sponsor's name and by limits on the TV coverage allowed of sponsors' brands. Club chairmen argued that the clubs needed new revenue sources. Liverpool's turnover in 1978–79 was £2.4 million, but profits were a miserly £71,000, a state of affairs Chairman John Smith described as 'absurd'. Smith had some tough messages about finances in the game – and at Anfield: 'While we are very successful in football terms, in economic terms we are broke. Clubs like Liverpool cannot exist on the money coming through the turnstiles alone. Costs are going up all the time. Wages are very high – and rightly so – and we have to use every avenue to increase our income.'

A local journalist reported at the time that Liverpool FC was 'virtually bankrupt'. The idea that the mighty Liverpool FC was effectively broke, predictably, did not go down too well on Merseyside and Smith was soon 'clarifying' his remarks in the local press. The seven-man Liverpool board serviced three subcommittees inside the club, covering finance, ground issues and development, but Smith, Peter Robinson and Bob Paisley made day-to-day decisions at Anfield and liaised with the players' committee of Heighway, Thompson and Clemence on pressing matters involving the players. Meanwhile, Football League Secretary Alan Hardaker warned that English soccer at the turn of a new decade was 'bleeding to death' and, prophetically, that English football clubs would 'sooner spend £200,000 on an unknown Yugoslav than spend half as much developing their own players'. The League initiated its own inquiry into the game's finances in a season in which, two years after Liverpool had signed the genius Dalglish for £440,000, Manchester City's Malcolm Allison paid more than three times that amount for the journeyman Steve Daley. In 1979, Liverpool football club were certainly increasingly serious about such things as scouting abroad, increasing gate returns and attracting new sponsors and different income streams. The game was modernising. Even the portly Bob Paisley wore the new Liverpool Hitachi kit for official photo-shoots. His predictions, while he was still a Liverpool player, that footballers would one day become advertising hoardings and earn huge salaries looked closer to the mark by the day.

On the field, an apparently minor incident would later prove to have a major impact on the life of the club and of one of its newest and least regarded players. In the pre-season of 1979, Liverpool competed in a four-club tournament at Schalke in Germany and took part in the club's first semi-serious penalty shoot-out, after a 2–2 draw with Dutch side Feyenoord. This was a sudden-death affair, but five penalty takers were pre-nominated by each club. Phil Neal and Terry McDermott, Liverpool's usual penalty takers, scored calmly from the spot and Graeme Souness followed suit. Feyenoord missed their fourth kick, so Liverpool's fourth penalty taker effectively won the match for the Reds. His name? A (very) reluctant Alan Kennedy. Kennedy has trouble today even recalling this debut as a Liverpool penalty kick taker, and he was certainly no volunteer for the job: he had barely taken a penalty in his life. The *Liverpool Echo* reported routinely on this still unfamiliar type of affair that: 'Liverpool have found a couple of extra penalty takers – if the occasion demands.' Maybe the writer knew somehow that, one day for Liverpool, the occasion most definitely *would* demand, because in Rome in 1984, it would actually demand rather a lot.

Chapter 6

ANFIELD AND PARIS

LEFT-SIDE BLUES

Alan Kennedy was finally settling in at Liverpool Football Club. There was the relief and joy, of course, of a first League title and of finally moving out of hotel living into his new Rainford digs near the M6 motorway for a quick escape up to Newcastle or to Bury to see his brother Keith. He also had a new Anfield football chum. His defensive partner Alan Hansen had been in and out of the Liverpool team, so was looking for a regular roommate: he ended up with Kennedy for seven years. It was bliss for the Scot, because rooming with the new full-back was like having your own personal, sunshine skivvy: he made the tea, got the papers, brought the breakfasts and positively beamed with optimism. Hansen claims now that he once may have made Alan Kennedy a cup of tea – on his birthday. More usually Hansen affectionately exploited Alan's better nature, by nicking his duvet on cold nights, playing gags, bossing him around and using him as a willing gopher. But they were a good pairing these two, not least because they shared left-side defensive cover and Hansen needed a bit of Kennedy's breeziness: the Scottish defender could easily get depressed about his own game. Despite his quality and unflappable appearance, Hansen didn't always look forward to playing, frequently fearing the worst. Nothing, but nothing, seemed to get Alan Kennedy down for long.

Hansen liked Alan, hugely, and remembers him especially for his unquenchable enthusiasm and cheerfulness and his infinite capacity for coming out with funny one-liners – even if they were not always meant to be funny. After a few such Kennedy gaffes, the Liverpool dressing-room began to call him, affectionately, Bungalow Billy, or just Billy for short, meaning not much upstairs: or 'Belly', after a derided cod newspaper columnist, Bel Mooney. Roy Evans claims Hansen was behind most of the nicknames: 'Hansen used to cane Alan for any little mistake he made – in a nice way, all for fun.' Kennedy took it in good heart, as a sign of becoming one of 'the lads'. More importantly, on the field Alan Kennedy was proving his worth to the Liverpool side and he was regarded as a good man to have around in the dressing-room, a real 100 per cent team player. He felt just a little more that he actually belonged.

But Alan still had a few of his own personal demons to deal with about his standing in the Liverpool first team: there were one or two doubters still to convince. For one thing, he still felt let down by Bob Paisley over the Emlyn Hughes affair the previous season. Bob had preferred the veteran Hughes for the crucial FA Cup semi-final matches against Manchester United, at a time when Kennedy, a young, big-money Paisley signing, was actually playing well. Alan felt that Bob had, uncharacteristically, made a sentimental team selection that had badly backfired, that the manager had put Emlyn's personal wishes for a big Liverpool swansong ahead of the best interests of Liverpool Football Club. Had Liverpool actually beaten United in the FA Cup, then Alan was convinced that Hughes would have claimed the number 3 shirt in the final in an emotional Liverpool send-off. Let's just say that Alan was not exactly devastated that Hughes played poorly – and that Liverpool lost the battle with United. For all his great strengths, Bob had neither the personality nor the language to explain exactly why he was leaving players out of the Liverpool first team. Why should he have to? This kind of man management is difficult managerial terrain at the best of times, though apparently not for Ronnie Moran, who would prefer to tell dropped stars, bluntly: 'It was because you were crap last week.' Joe Fagan's job was to talk to the disappointed player and pull him round: it was hard to fall out with Joe. Bob was much more detached: he could simply retreat into his office until someone knocked on the door.

Few Liverpool players ever confronted Bob and even when Alan tried, he could get no good answers about why Hughes should have played against United. Alan assumed it was because it *was* Emlyn: a loved Reds' stalwart in his last days at the club. Alan Hansen once urged Kennedy to see Bob on another occasion when the full-back had been left out, and he later asked Kennedy what he had actually *said* to Paisley to try to elicit a response. Alan replied, in the sort of North-east twang that Bob might be expected to understand: 'I'm yer left-back, yer nar?' It was hardly a compulsive argument. Predictably, the dressing-room slaughtered Kennedy for this little tidbit, repeating the phrase for months afterwards. Anyway, at least this problem was unlikely to emerge again soon: Hughes left Liverpool for Wolves, where he would even win another three England caps to add to the 59 he had won in a glittering career at Liverpool. It was also one more potential Anfield rival removed for Alan Kennedy.

There were other concerns about Bob. A number of the Liverpool players, including Alan, felt that they had been unfairly picked on by Paisley, that they were earmarked as soft targets if things were going awry on the field, or if Bob simply fancied giving someone else a run. A small group of players felt that they were 'obvious' men to be substituted or left out whenever a section of the Liverpool side was malfunctioning. Managers almost always have key players whom they see as being the irreplaceable backbone of the side and Liverpool were no different in this respect. The Jocks *were* irreplaceable, by anyone's standards. But football bosses also know well the players in their squads who are the most vulnerable and easy going and are, therefore, the least likely to complain, or to 'lose it', if yanked off in front of 40,000 critics. Why risk upsetting an awkward customer in public if you can change things by removing a compliant one? It is a simple rule of managerial thumb, still widely followed in the game today.

It was certainly true that star Liverpool players were hardly ever substituted by Bob, no matter how badly they were playing. And he seldom rewarded lesser players for good performances by giving them an extended run when his stars had recovered from injury: the big names at Liverpool usually went straight back into the first team, even if they weren't fully fit. Maybe it was just a ruthless assessment by Bob of the abilities in his squad. Although they respected the manager, a few Liverpool players definitely thought that Paisley too often liked to take the easy route when making changes. This approach made Alan feel uncertain of his place at Liverpool: 'I always felt if there was a bad result it was going to be either Davy Johnson, Terry Mac or me who would be coming off. We were always the guys to go, depending on whether it was defence, midfield or attack that needed changing. I always looked for my number coming up on the touchline. I felt I was always looking to the bench. Maybe Ronnie Moran was looking at me, too, because he'd been a left-back and I wasn't what he wanted me to be. I always felt I had to justify my presence in the team.'

With Emlyn Hughes now gone, the Israeli Avi Cohen and local youngster Colin Irwin were quickly emerging as Alan's main rivals for a left defensive slot. More competition, then, and one of these new rivals was a £100,000 international signing. These new players were primarily centre-backs who could also play on the left side, part of Bob's quest to find footballers who could double up on defensive positions. Neither of them had Kennedy's natural left-footed ability, his speed or his attacking flair. Avi was technically sound and a gifted footballer and he was also popular with the Liverpool players, who had predictably tried hard to teach him some 'useful' English football phrases, such as: 'The manager should fuck off.' But some members of the squad also doubted that Cohen could really cope with the physical side of the English game in the longer term and they thought that he looked too much like a lesser version of Alan Hansen. Who would attack the ball if these two played together at the back? Colin Irwin could probably do that, but he was ordinary on the ball and arguably lacked the pace to play wide. He did not lack ambition though: he told Bob Paisley that he would 'wait until Christmas' to see if he could break into the Liverpool side. Exactly *which* Christmas, he wasn't prepared to say.

Alan was also well aware that he had not yet convinced his left-sided midfield partner, Ray Kennedy, that the new left full-back was true Liverpool class. Ray made it clear that he never considered Alan to be qualified to play for Liverpool, despite his superb commitment and fighting spirit. In Ray's opinion, Alan did not have the natural skill and ability to hold down a regular Liverpool place. Ray felt he had had to help Alan by covering back and reinforcing the left defence. This last sentence should not surprise too much: Alan, after all, was a raiding full-back. Part of the flexibility and danger of the 'new' Liverpool was that this attacking role from deep relied on the cover offered by Alan Hansen and by the Liverpool midfield. Matching the 'rigidity' required in defence with the flexibility that now made Liverpool such dangerous opponents was no easy balance to strike. Hansen often joked that it was difficult to find his supposed defensive partner on the left flank: 'That was the beauty of playing with Alan, you never, ever, knew where he was going to be.' Alan Kennedy seemed to like setting off on a 50-yard diagonal forward run as much as he did a good tackle or defensive solidarity. Ray Kennedy failed to see the funny side: he still thought that defenders should only defend, a big mistake in

Paisley's exciting new team. In fact, Ray Kennedy even thought that Alan's alleged limits in being unable to select the 'right' pass at the right time might have shortened the ex-Arsenal's man's career, by adding to his unfamiliar burden on the left side. Ray commented, unfairly, but typically trenchantly, about his new left-back partner that: 'Alan had no nerves and not much brain, which was why he was lethal at penalties. I didn't dislike him, but we didn't gel on the pitch.' These words were not meant to be diplomatic. This new partnership on the Liverpool left was no football marriage made in heaven, as Alan quickly realised: 'Ray was an experienced player. He wasn't underrated by Bob Paisley, but he was by some other people. You looked up to him: he was a well-made player, an old-fashioned-style centre-forward. When I first came to the club he said to me: "Listen, give me the ball whenever you're in trouble, I'll help you out, and I'll be ghosting in at the far post in case a cross comes in from Jimmy Case." The old nerves came out sometimes in me and he wasn't happy about it. But I found it difficult to communicate with him. The easiest pass – short to him – became the hardest pass for me. The easiest ball became hitting a 60-yard pass into the opponent's box. We worked together okay, but Ray was a stubborn man. He was difficult to get on with. He thought he was the best in the team, so his ego was way above mine: his and Graeme's. Ray was a perfectionist.'

Ironically, the troubled Kennedys, Ray and Alan, had often been mistaken for brothers by the press when Alan first broke into the first team at Newcastle United. In fact, they could hardly be more different in personality and approach to their profession. Alan was gauche, overly earnest, hard working and desperate to learn 'the Liverpool Way'. He was determined to overcome the limitations of his narrow football socialisation at Newcastle – which *did* sometimes mean he gave erratic or hasty distribution from the back. Ray, on the other hand, was coolly knowing and sure-footed, but he was looking for the sort of partnership on the left that would help reduce his running and mask his mobility problems. The personal and professional chemistry here was all wrong. There was very little in the way of mutual respect on Liverpool's left side for much of the time these two men played together. Ray resented Alan's erratic short passing and head down forward bursts and felt the full-back took the 'wrong' option too often. Alan thought Ray was too critical too soon and that *he* needed to improve on his defensive cover when Alan followed through an attack as Bob demanded. Maybe this was just creative tension?

By now Ray Kennedy was probably past his Liverpool peak –

though he still played a crucial role in the successful 1981 European Cup run – and, while placid on the field, off it he and his pal Jimmy Case were also getting more and more difficult to control. When Liverpool lost badly in the European Cup in Tbilisi in October 1979, after the game Jimmy went for the British press in the media suite, snarling at them and telling individual journalists exactly what he thought of them. Ray had to chin him to calm him down, while David Johnson surreally warned the rest of the Liverpool players to avoid the black jam that was being served with the post-match champagne because it tasted of fish: it was Johnno's first encounter with Black Sea caviar. Chairman John Smith eventually managed to calm things down and placate the terrified scribes, but it was a marker of what might follow from the Kennedy and Case duo in full flow.

Terry McDermott was not a man actively to look for trouble, at least not like Case and Ray Kennedy sometimes seemed to do. But Terry was often around when the wheels began to fall off. Terry liked a lager himself and once, when Ron Greenwood reported that some England players had been caught on a late-night binge before an international game and the story and names of the offenders had been splashed all over the national papers, the sage Bob Paisley mused that he'd better ring up Greenwood right away and ask him to send Terry Mac home. The Liverpool man must surely be ill: his name was, mysteriously, not on the list of England miscreants.

'Off the pitch Ray could be very niggly, especially after a few drinks. His size was frightening,' said Terry Mac. 'In practice matches he'd sometimes lose his rag and I remember him even having a go at Phil Thompson in an England training session.' Graeme Souness said later of these three hugely talented Liverpool stars that: 'Everyone knows that Jimmy Case, Ray Kennedy and Terry Mac all left the club earlier than their ability warranted, because they occasionally overdid the leisure time.' This might be true, though Paisley and the staff were always willing to give the players plenty of leeway away from Anfield. But this outstanding Liverpool team also depended, probably more than it knew, upon these same fractured personalities and supreme talents. These three were, after all, in the very guts of the impressive Liverpool engine-room.

In March 1980, after beating Everton 2–1 in the League, Liverpool took the squad to North Wales for a few days' deserved R & R. Terry Mac, Ray and Jimmy Case all had too much pop one night and the last two were arrested after a late-night drunken assault on a pub landlord and his son. The ale, and the fact that the landlord made the fatal error of mistaking Ray for *Alan* Kennedy, caused a disorientated Ray to really lose it – he nailed the landlord and his son, and even the hapless Terry McDermott, for good measure. The police were summoned and Ray and Jimmy ended up in jail, with Ronnie Moran and Roy Evans being called out to try to mend things. Ray even claimed later that it was Ronnie's 'stressful' training sessions that were the cause of his behavioural problems! The two players were eventually fined £150 for affray in a blaze of embarrassing publicity for the club. It was one of the few occasions that John Smith was unable to limit the difficult aftermath of a Liverpool 'night out' with Ray and Jimmy at the wheel of things.

At his best, Ray Kennedy was brilliant company but he was a pretty hard man to get close to – especially if he took against you, as he seems to have done with his new teammate and namesake Alan. Alan Hansen argues that Alan Kennedy thought too much about Ray's moaning and that the 'difficult' relationship between the two was a psychological problem that Alan should simply have ignored. Liverpool FC and his teammates had, in time, learned to learn to live with Ray's occasional irascibility and even to deal with his off-field scrapes with Jimmy Case and others. This was because when the ex-Arsenal man was converted to a left midfield position by Bob Paisley late in 1975 he also became a great football player for Liverpool. But the Liverpool board now had Ray's number: off the field he needed to mend his ways. On it, the Liverpool Kennedys would have to make the best of their differences: after all, there was no left side in the English game quite to match them.

DOWN AND OUT IN TBILISI

The new Liverpool season began with Alan at left-back in a disappointing 0–0 Anfield draw with a spoiling and defensive Bolton Wanderers. Worse was to follow, an early 2–3 loss at Southampton, not a favourite Liverpool venue. Alan Hansen also had injury trouble as the first major fixture of the season loomed – perhaps the key match in the whole season – a meeting with the little known Russian champions Dinamo Tbilisi in the European Cup. It was another too-early nightmare European tie as far as Bob was concerned: the prospect of a second-leg visit to distant Georgia against accomplished but underrated opponents who were already well into their season, while Liverpool were still trying to find their feet. Tom Saunders had made the gruelling scouting trip to Georgia and had come back with an account that no one at Melwood wanted to hear: it was a story of difficult travel, crap hotels, and of tough and classy opponents who kept the ball. But there was worse news: unlike many quality Soviet footballing sides, Tbilisi could also hurt the opposition with goals. A clear win at home was essential for Liverpool to guard against potential destruction out in the Georgian wilderness. This was good advice: Bob took note.

On 19 September, before the first leg at Anfield, a 17-year-old Manchester United fan, a left-sided midfielder from the Home Farm club in Ireland, signed for Liverpool in the wake of stiff competition from United themselves, Spurs, Celtic and even the Belgian giants, Anderlecht. These clubs were good judges. Ronnie Whelan got his first football lesson at Anfield that night, but it was not from Liverpool. Tbilisi had impressed the Liverpool players with their technique even in the pre-match warm-up, and with Ray Kennedy and Hansen out injured, the visitors purred into action from the first whistle, making chance after chance, inspired by the brilliant Kipiani in midfield. Liverpool hung on. Bob Paisley was especially impressed by Tbilisi's movement, as well as by the angles the Georgians saw and used, and by their physical presence: Souness and Jimmy Case, usually so talented and ruthless, were intimidating only shadows. Paisley wrote later: 'Our three men in midfield never got to grips with their opponents.' Perhaps playing David Fairclough, an attacker, instead of the injured midfielder Ray Kennedy, had been a mistake?

Alan Kennedy had seen nothing quite like this before: 'I remember how confident they were in playing and that they had no real forwards: they were much more flexible than an English side. We couldn't get to grips with the fact that they had players who kept playing in the space between the midfield and the forwards. They played it around a lot in midfield and we couldn't get hold of the ball. We just didn't know how to treat this. This was my first real European game and I remember thinking: "This football is really crisp and fast – but the game is passing me by." All I could see was white shirts coming towards me. They had loads of chances. Dave Johnno scored for us but we still couldn't settle and they equalised. We were 2–1 up at half-time but we were still chasing the game. Who had even heard of these? We won, but it stays in your mind because you've been humbled by a team you've never heard of – and one you'll probably never hear of again.'

Chivadze, a marvellously adventurous sweeper, scored the Tbilisi equaliser on 33 minutes after linking up with Daraseliya. Despite Shengeliya's best efforts for the visitors after half-time, and Liverpool's near constant pressure, neither side could add to Jimmy Case's 44th minute free kick for Liverpool. Afterwards, the home dressing-room was hushed, respectful and dismayed. The Liverpool staff tried to talk up the home win, but this 2–1 score line was really no better than a home draw against opponents who felt full of goals. Everyone knew it would take a monumental effort now from Liverpool to survive this tie in the 100,000 capacity Lenin Stadium. Deep down, everyone knew that Liverpool were almost certainly out of the European Cup.

At Nottingham Forest, where Steve Ogrizovic played his one Liverpool game of the season – and made a blooper – Alan Kennedy also picked up a groin strain. The injury meant he would be spared his first true flavour of football in Europe with Liverpool and a crushing defeat. The trip included: the exhausting Aeroflot dog-leg flight, via Moscow; the endless Soviet security checks; the foul Georgian food; the 4 a.m. hotel 'wake-up' call organised by Dinamo fans, apparently under police supervision; and the terrible Georgian weather, pouring rain. George Scanlon, from Liverpool Polytechnic, on the trip as a Russian expert and official translator and a member of the same Bootle boys' junior football team as Ronnie Moran, could do little to help here. He just groaned along with the rest of the party. Hansen and Ray Kennedy were back for Liverpool, but it made little difference. Once Kipiani had outwitted Irwin, replacing Alan Kennedy on Liverpool's left, and crossed for Gutsaev to score after 50 minutes, the writing was on the wall. Further goals, from Shengeliya and a late penalty from Chivadze, produced Liverpool's most comprehensive European defeat since Ajax, under Bill Shankly, way back in December 1966. For two seasons running now Liverpool had fallen at the first hurdle in Europe. Alan Kennedy had yet to play on continental soil in anger.

This defeat was especially hard to take because going out of Europe in early October meant that the League fixture list seemed to stretch interminably and boringly on. No worries there: John Smith was soon arranging mid-season revenue-raising fixtures for Liverpool. Kevin Keegan's Hamburg scored six in beating Tbilisi, home and away, in the next round of the European Cup, but by this stage the Georgians were in pre-season, and a very different prospect. Hamburg lost in the European Cup final to Nottingham Forest, so Brian Clough had now won two consecutive European Cups from under Bob Paisley's nose. After ten League matches, Liverpool were struggling in sixth place in the League and were even reported to be interested in signing Forest's Tony Woodcock. But Bristol City suffered most for the Tbilisi defeat: a returning 0–4 hammering for them at Anfield. Manchester City, Wolves, Brighton, Middlesbrough and Crystal Palace all experienced similar canings from Liverpool in the next few weeks. Scoring goals seemed the least of the club's problems, with Johnson and Dalglish regular contributors and McDermott also chipping in. Terry Mac also provided the main Anfield dressing-room comedy at this time: a 'handbags' clash with Everton's Gary Stanley during a 2–2 draw at Goodison Park in October, which meant a suspension for Liverpool's least likely hard man. By 17 November Liverpool were top: they needed no further invitation to stay there.

QUALITY WILL OUT

By now Alan Kennedy was feeling much more into the job at Anfield. He had seen off Hughes and Joey Jones, Colin Irwin was not challenging, except through injury, and the acclimatising Avi Cohen barely made a Liverpool first-team squad. Anfield was also becoming something of a defensive fortress. Kennedy liked the city of Liverpool and its working-class sensibilities and traditions: its basic decency and lack of flannel or pretence reminded him of his native North-east. He was also struck, not always so positively, by the market ingenuity of the city. When he had a coat nicked in Liverpool on one occasion by a couple of scallies who were 'helping' him unload his car, he was even able to buy it back through a local contact a couple of weeks later for a mere £10. Business, after all, is business.

On the field, local boy Sammy Lee, a butcher's son and the Liverpool squad's chief singer, who actually looked and played a little like Bob Paisley the Liverpool footballer, would begin to get his chance in Liverpool's first team as this season wore on. He eventually replaced the troublesome Jimmy Case, who left for Brighton under ex-Red Jimmy Melia. Case would soon be back to haunt Liverpool. Scouting and Liverpool youth development specialist Tom Saunders was soon lamenting the difficulty in finding talented local recruits for the club, a whisper that has become a roar over the years that followed. Maybe this is a cyclical problem, because Liverpool did, after all, later unearth McManaman, Fowler, Owen and Carragher in one purple patch in the '90s, close to £50 million's worth of exciting local football talent. But for ex-head teacher Tom Saunders, Liverpool's youth recruitment back in 1979 already told him that: 'Although the ambition to become a professional footballer is as strong as ever, the quality of intake is inferior to anything we've had over the past ten years. Youngsters today have options for leisure that were undreamed of only a few years ago. They don't play as much football as when I first began teaching. Recently, I saw my first junior match in Moscow, boys of 10 or 11 years of age, whose technique was astonishing, very, very high. Perhaps we should take the pick of our youngsters and place them in schools of excellence where they can concentrate on the game.'

Saunders said, sadly, that probably only Communist societies could contemplate this kind of intervention in the lives of young boys. But what he was actually signalling here, of course, was Liverpool's immediate determination to try to learn from the Tbilisi experience, as well as pointing to the future rise of centres of football excellence in the English game, which came along long after Tom had given up his Anfield duties and Bob and Joe had moved out of the Liverpool hot seat. Alan Kennedy was actually quite *pleased*, thank you very much, that there was no hot-shot young, left-footed Scouser defender coming through Roy Evans's reserves at the moment to upset his own personal applecart. By the turn of 1979, Liverpool led the League table by two points from Manchester United and Arsenal. That has a rather pleasant – if now unfamiliar – ring to it, don't you think?

Grimsby Town were despatched 0–5 in the third round of the FA Cup in January 1980, leaving Graeme Souness to expound on some of the secrets behind Liverpool's success. He hit it right on the head: great players whose egos are made subservient to the demands of the team. Ronnie Moran and Joe Fagan would have been proud of him: 'The Anfield attitude helps to create success. Everything is played down. Nobody goes around shouting the odds. I can only remember twice in my time with the club when we have been praised after a game or, more truthfully, when we have been told we could not improve: when we beat Bruges at Wembley [in 1978] and when we beat Villa to win the title [in 1979]. The staff went round quite pleased after those games! We are constantly being told to keep our feet on the ground.'

Keeping your feet on the ground was soon not going to be that easy now for Alan Kennedy. After wins against lesser fry in earlier rounds, Liverpool came up against the dreaded Forest once more in the League Cup semi-final in January 1980, armed with a record against Clough's team since 1977 of: W1 L3 D5. Liverpool lost again, this time to a late John Robertson penalty at the City Ground, whilst managing only a 1–1 draw at Anfield, with Peter Shilton predictably outstanding. At Forest, the locals had even chanted 'Liverpool are boring' as the visitors tried to choke the game. In between these contests David Fairclough scored three goals in a spectacular 5–3 League win at Norwich City: Bob still left him out of the return leg against Forest, though it was only Fairclough's late goal as a substitute in the match that saved Liverpool's long unbeaten home run. Paisley took his team back to Nottingham, once more, on 26 January for the fourth round of the FA Cup, again without Fairclough. The striker was beginning to hate Bob Paisley. Three things swung this vital match: Jimmy Case successfully cutting out the supply to John Robertson on Forest's left; Kenny Dalglish showing all of his brilliance for Liverpool; and Peter Shilton actually showing his slip for once by dropping Neal's cross, for Dalglish to score. As the teams trooped off after a 2–0 Liverpool win, Brian Clough said to Bob: 'Eh, bloody well played, you did well there.' It was praise enough. On 19 February, Liverpool beat Forest 2–0 at Anfield in the League, with late goals from McDermott and Ray Kennedy. Maybe this curse was actually over – or was familiarity merely breeding contempt at Anfield? Who cares? Liverpool were gunning for an FA Cup and Football League Double.

By the FA Cup fifth round, Liverpool players always began to fancy a possible run all the way to Wembley. But when the footballing Kennedy brothers, Keith at Bury and Alan at Liverpool, listened to the fifth-round FA Cup draw in 1980, dreams of Wembley were second best. Instead, they heard the words they had waited all their football lives to hear: that their respective clubs would meet in the FA Cup at Anfield. Had the meeting been in Greater Manchester, Keith would really have fancied his chances. As it was, his club were finally sunk by that man Fairclough, restored again and scoring two more Liverpool goals, though the 2–0 score line barely did justice to either Third Division Bury or to Keith. 'In the assessment of the Kennedy brothers,' according to the *Liverpool Echo*, 'there was no doubt that Keith had lifted the honours. The Bury left-back had a splendid game – and so had most of his colleagues in defence.' It was almost the perfect outcome for the massed Kennedy clan who beamed down from the Main Stand: a win for Liverpool; glory and cash for Bury; and a man of the match award for Keith Kennedy. Needless to say, the ale flowed.

Back in the League, Emlyn Hughes inspired his new Wolves side to beat title-chasing Liverpool, 1–0. Some thanks, this: his Anfield mates had all agreed to stay behind at Molineux for a *This is Your Life* TV special for Emlyn. How sad is that? No more, certainly, than the story that as Liverpool were beating Everton 2–1 at Goodison Park the following week, so the great Evertonian, Dixie Dean, died of a heart attack at the match. Soon after this real tragedy, a minor but significant one occurred to Alan Kennedy: he stretched his hamstrings riding a horse and being thrown by it during an afternoon's riding at home. At first he didn't cough to Bob or to the lads. Imagine the stick he would get! But a week later he chased Steve Coppell in a crucial match at Old Trafford and the hamstring went. Coppell crossed and Mickey Thomas scored. United won 2–1. Bob Paisley's views on these unique match preparations by his left-back are, perhaps thankfully, unrecorded. He might have thrown Alan Kennedy himself, given the chance. The injury also meant that Alan missed the first two instalments of an epic, four-game, Liverpool FA Cup semi-final marathon with Arsenal, before briefly returning for the second replay at Villa Park, in which Kenny Dalglish grabbed a last-minute Liverpool equaliser. Sadly, Alan had returned too soon and the hamstring went again. It was Ray Kennedy who made the single crucial error in the third replay at Highfield Road, which meant that his old club Arsenal, not Liverpool, would stumble on to play West Ham United in the 1980 FA Cup final. Dazed and confused, the Gunners were beaten by a Trevor Brooking header. Maybe Bob and Alan Kennedy were just destined never to be FA Cup winners?

But the League was something different. Troubled by injury, Alan made only one more League appearance, in a 0–0 draw at Crystal Palace, but Liverpool powered on, thrashing Aston Villa 4–1 at Anfield to clinch the title, eventually, by two points from Manchester United. It had been a huge strain, the final weeks of the season: Phil Neal even found himself crying during the Villa game, tears streaming down his cheeks, as the tension finally lifted. Five championships in eight years for Liverpool, but this had been the hardest. The injured Alan Kennedy and David Fairclough carried the trophy onto the field for the customary lap of honour. As injuries had struck other key Liverpool players in the campaign, the young guard – Sammy Lee, Fairclough, Colin Irwin and Avi Cohen – had all played a key role in the closing League games and in the FA Cup battles against Arsenal. Bob and Joe could reason that not only had they secured another League title for Liverpool, but they had also reinvigorated and possibly extended the Anfield squad. Alan Kennedy eyed the latest player developments rather less positively: he was still not sure he was the club's first choice left-back. But the big disappointment for all the players and staff had been another failure in Europe. Maybe next season it could all be put right.

OUT IN THE COLD

England played in the European Championships in the summer of 1980, with the country's travelling fans running merrily amok in

Turin: it was not a pretty sight. Clemence, Thompson, Neal, Ray Kennedy, McDermott and David Johnson all played a losing part in Italy. Alan Kennedy, meanwhile, was still lagging behind Mick Mills and Kenny Sansom in Ron Greenwood's England pecking order, so he watched his Liverpool mates, and England, unravel at home on TV. He still badly wanted to play for England, though he despaired of ever being picked ahead of Sansom, who was soon to leave Crystal Palace for Arsenal for £1 million, thus displacing Alan as the country's most costly full-back. Salt in an open wound. But Kennedy first needed to get focused on nailing down his Liverpool place. Even this was not going to be that easy. All the close-season football talk in England in 1980 was about hooligans and falling crowds, chatter which got even louder as attendances plummeted in the early weeks of the new season and a teenage Middlesbrough fan died after trouble at a match versus Nottingham Forest. At Anfield, even Liverpool's gates were soon down in the mid-30,000s, while Everton opened up against Leicester City in front of fewer than 24,000 souls at an echoing Goodison Park.

For all the media comment about the effects of hooliganism and of the decline in entertaining football, it seemed more likely that it was national recession that was the main culprit in cutting attendances. Thatcher's new government produced over two million unemployed nationally and over 107,000 on troubled Merseyside alone. The game's financial guardians, meanwhile, talked, more and more in 1980, about cutting costs and 'rationalising' the structure of the sport: just the sort of language, in fact, now increasingly favoured at number 10. Liverpool's accounts revealed a 40 per cent rise in wages and that two players were earning over £40,000 – almost certainly Dalglish and Souness – though most of the squad were on salaries below £30,000. The Liverpool players never exchanged information among themselves about salaries, though a summer tournament with England and chats with players from other clubs often meant Liverpool's international stars were soon set on having a meeting with Bob or Peter Robinson to talk money. A Football League study group drew up a 'survival charter' for the sport, the main outcome of which was an agreement on three points for a win from season 1981–82. Liverpool's Peter Robinson wanted something much more radical: he talked openly about the need for a smaller and more independent First Division and of the importance of having a new arrangement for distributing TV income. In 1979–80, he complained, mighty Liverpool had appeared 30 times on TV and received just £25,000 from TV income – the same amount as little Rochdale. He had a point. It took another 12 years and the rude intrusion of satellite TV for the major break to come, but English football was already feeling the cold early winds of change. As always on business matters, Liverpool FC was at the forefront of a public call for a big push towards a new football tomorrow.

Bob Paisley, meanwhile, seemed oblivious to financial constraints: he splashed out over £300,000 for another defender – 'Another bloody defender!' – Fulham's 24-year-old England B international Richard Money. Alan thought that it was starting to feel uncomfortably crowded again in the scramble for places at the back at Anfield. In the new pre-season programme, Liverpool struggled for a rhythm and it continued into the season proper, with only three wins coming in the first seven League games, plus an embarrassing first-leg League Cup defeat at Bradford City and a scrambled draw at amateur Finnish side, Oulu, in the European Cup. This European clash, with Avi Cohen in for Alan at left-back, happened close to the Arctic Circle on the worst pitch that any of the Liverpool staff had ever seen – the ploughed infield of an athletics stadium. Annoyed, Liverpool scored ten in the home leg. But in the League, at promoted Leicester City, Liverpool had been rancid, with Terry Mac even goading City teenager Andy Peake 30 yards from goal to 'Go on, fucking have a shot', as the Reds' defence half-cleared a City free kick. It whistled past the startled Clemence. Liverpool lost 0–2, with Bob saying of his disgraced men: 'They couldn't have punched a hole in a wet *Echo*. Their attitude was all wrong, strolling around as if it was easy.' You could tell he wasn't happy.

Alan Kennedy had actually started the new League campaign well and was even leading Liverpool scorer after four League games, scoring with, according to the *Echo*, an 'unstoppable shot' against 'team of the eighties' Crystal Palace and a goal line nod-in against Norwich City. He was certainly refreshingly direct: 'I used to shoot a lot from distance. The manager used to say: "Listen, have two thoughts in your mind when you're running with the ball: are you going to play it forward for a one-two, or are you going to shoot at goal?" They always said: "Have a plan in your head." Mine was always to shoot at goal: one plan. Maybe the Dalglish's and Souness's had two or three plans: they could look ahead. Mine was just one track: I'm playing the ball in, getting the return and shooting at goal.'

But soon the two roommates, Kennedy and Hansen, were struggling for form and fitness, as were some other Liverpool players: Jimmy Case, David Johnson and Terry McDermott, to name three.

Alan also had a knee problem and was instructed to have cortisone injections: 'It was never right for months afterwards.' The coaching staff liked to have the walking wounded strolling round Melwood because, they argued, watching the first team train offered its own incentive to get back. There was no room on the bench for a left-back, so when Alan got fitter he also played a few in the reserves, where the quality was excellent: Fairclough, the young Howard Gayle, Whelan, Ian Rush and Heighway were all regulars under Roy Evans. Liverpool reserves would have nailed most first teams and would have fancied themselves against the Liverpool stars at this time. But even playing winning second-team football kills the spirit in front of small, anorak crowds.

Liverpool briefly got back on track in the League with three wins, but five consecutive League draws followed. Alan played in two of these, but by the end of November, and dogged by injury and indifferent form, he had still made only seven League appearances. He was glad to miss a 1–4 thumping at Wolves, where, inevitably, Emlyn Hughes scored for the home club. Liverpool were dominating matches but plainly struggling to score goals, managing only four in a seven-match League sequence from 13 December, which culminated in a 1–2 home defeat by soon-to-be-relegated Leicester City, and the end of Liverpool's incredible 85-match record unbeaten run at home. Liverpool strikers Johnson and Dalglish eventually ended the season with a miserly 16 League goals between them. By Christmas, Liverpool were off the pace; by the season's end they would be nine points and a crazy fifth place, adrift behind surprise champions Aston Villa.

What went wrong in the League in 1980–81? Problems of scoring goals, injuries, natural wastage, a loss of form to key players, and unusually weak replacements explains most of it. David Johnson was clearly coming to the end up front and Ray Kennedy and Jimmy Case had also already done their best work for Liverpool. The regular Liverpool back four was also frequently disrupted, with Alan Kennedy and Phil Thompson playing only 44 League games between them. In defence and midfield, Kenny Dalglish suffered his first injuries and Sammy Lee had shown his worth but, after a promising start, Cohen, Irwin and Money were clearly not top dollar yet. For once, Bob Paisley and his scouts had not quite got this right. Help was on the way, though: in the *Football Echo* on 16 August 1980 a tiny front page clipping reported that Ian Rush, a shy teenage centre-forward signed by Bob in the summer for £300,000 from Chester, had scored his first

Liverpool goal against Coventry City reserves. In these small tales, great football legends are, indeed, foretold. Right now though, in Europe the picture was better for Liverpool, and a rather forgotten left-back, Alan Kennedy, even made the Liverpool team for the October European Cup clash with Scottish champions, Alex Ferguson's Aberdeen.

The normally placid and silent Alan Hansen paced the away dressing-room at Pittodrie before kick-off and bellowed for a tin hat performance from Liverpool. Surprised? Any Scot who had been despatched to play in England always got slaughtered when he returned north of the border. Moreover, Hansen's inferior rivals for the Scottish national side, Miller and McLeish, both played at the back for the Dons. Incredibly, no one north of Newcastle seemed to think that the sublime Hansen could play at all. He had something to prove, all right. Lots of Liverpool oil-riggers nagged the players for tickets and before the game Bob shrewdly offered the Aberdeen muse Gordon Strachan a 'toffee' by publicly praising the little man, inferring the Dons should win at home. Instead, Terry McDermott scored an exquisite team goal for Liverpool after just five minutes to secure the match 1–0 in Scotland. The tie seemed already as good as over, but back at Anfield it got even better for the home team Jocks: a 4–0 drubbing, including a Miller own goal from a Hansen header and even a penalty area tap-in closer from Hansen himself. 'Don't forget,' says Hansen today, 'I got forward more than any other defender in the history of the British game.' On this evidence, you could almost believe him. The news was less good for Alan Kennedy: a hamstring injury saw him substituted by Avi Cohen and set him up for another few weeks out. He was, to say the least, pissed off.

WEMBLEY GLORY – BUT SILVER AT VILLA

Injury seemed to be dominating this Liverpool season: even the indestructible Dalglish finally succumbed in December 1980, breaking his 147 consecutive-game run since joining Liverpool from Celtic. Outsiders marvelled at how few injuries Liverpool players received: club insiders were simply amazed at the knocks Liverpool players were willing to carry into matches. In January, Alan Kennedy injured his knee again, at Norwich City, and missed six more matches. By the time Europe returned in March, Liverpool had pretty much given up the ghost in the League and had also capitulated, 1–2 to Everton, in the FA Cup. Just two defeats in 21 derbies, but it still looked miserable. The good news? A first League Cup final awaited Liverpool. The partial home and away format seemed to suit the Liverpool team: after all, hadn't these erratic Merseysiders already lost away to Bradford City in their first match of their League Cup run? The other good news was that, after all his injury setbacks, Alan Kennedy was back in the side – and looking for goals. Bob would need him to provide some firepower for Liverpool in the final.

The Reds' route to Wembley was pretty straightforward: after Bradford City were dispatched, Swindon Town were demolished 5–0, and both Portsmouth and Birmingham City were also easily seen off at Anfield, with Alan unhelpfully managing to notch Portsmouth's goal in an otherwise 4–1 Liverpool stroll. The two-leg semi-final with Manchester City was much more competitive, a late Ray Kennedy goal at Maine Road being enough to divide the sides before a Kenny Dalglish effort in a tight 1–1 return draw at Anfield effectively put Liverpool through. Second Division West Ham United dumped Coventry City in the other semi-final. The Hammers, current FA Cup holders and with Parkes, Lampard, Devonshire, Bonds and Brooking to the fore, were running away with the Second Division title: this final was no gimme.

Before Wembley, it was Nottingham Forest's European conquerors, CSKA Sofia, at Anfield in the European Cup: they probably wished they'd stayed behind their Iron Curtain. Back in Bob's plans, this was Alan Kennedy's first serious 'European' game since that startling match against Tbilisi back in 1979. Again, the away team from the East was impressive, the Bulgarians drawing much applause for the quality of their football and their neatness in possession. They also made good chances, but without taking them. Every time Liverpool came forward, somebody – usually the immaculate Graeme Souness – seemed to finish the move off emphatically. Souness bagged three unstoppable screamers. This was as evenly contested a 5–1 shallocking as you could wish to witness, the extraordinary quality of the Liverpool shooting dividing the sides – and closing the tie. All of this meant that Alan's first real European match for Liverpool in Sofia two weeks later – where David Johnson's early goal added to Bulgarian gloom – was a cigar affair, and still no true European test away from Anfield. Alan still managed to concede a late penalty to the Bulgarians, a foul on Yonchev, which was saved by Ray Clemence. This was also Alan's introduction to the Aer Lingus Tuesday morning charter flight that Liverpool always favoured for away European games. Alan was not a great flier and he used to spend some time in the pilot's cockpit for take off reassurance. There was little time for sightseeing or even getting out of the hotel when Liverpool played abroad – Bob wanted to get in and out of Europe as fast as possible, as Alan recalls:

'Bill Shankly and Bob Paisley never trusted the foreigners. They always thought the dressing-rooms were being bugged. Bob would never even accept cups of tea at the stadium. The coaching staff used to call trips to Europe 'missions'. For them, it was like dropping bombs on war targets. Bob hated the iron curtain countries, especially. They were grey and dull, which was why we always got home as soon as we could. The staff thought we might get kidnapped! But we didn't really want to see places – we just wanted to play our football and get home.'

Just before the League Cup final at Wembley, West Ham were tanked, 1–4 at Upton Park by Dinamo Tbilisi, in the European Cup-winners' Cup: the English finalists could at least compare notes on the quality of Georgian passing and technique. The final itself was a poor advert for the English game. Liverpool, unusually captained by Ray Kennedy, were missing Thompson and Johnson and played Irwin and also the by-now-waning Heighway behind an isolated Kenny Dalglish. It meant that Paisley's side had plenty of the terrible new Football League ball, but made few real chances. Alan recalls: 'It couldn't have been a great game to watch and we were playing with a stupid ball that had a blue and a red panel in it. It looked out of shape and horrible – just like the match.' Extra time seemed inevitable a long way out. With just two minutes remaining of the full two hours, a controversial goal seemed to have settled it. Step forward one Alan Kennedy – aided by a quirky Welshman.

The oddball referee, Clive Thomas, had already ruled out a first-half Sammy Lee effort because another Liverpool player was deemed offside and interfering with play. The Welsh official now decided that the prostrate Lee was *not* in goalkeeper Parkes's eye line when Alan – 'continuing the move', as Joe and Bob insisted that he should – got forward and virtually chipped the ball over Sammy's prone body from broken play to score in the closing minutes. The truth was that Clive Thomas liked a bit of public attention, the occasional media storm, and this decision would certainly guarantee the weekend's sport headlines. The Liverpool bench couldn't care less: Alan Kennedy, and 100,000 others, were sure it was the winning goal. And yet Liverpool, of all clubs, managed to concede an equaliser in the dying minutes, Terry McDermott fisting out a goal-bound header from Alvin Martin, and Ray Stewart scoring from the spot. Perhaps it was justice, but Paisley fumed afterwards. Deserving to win is not an issue, of no importance. Liverpool had got themselves into a great position to win and then, unforgivably, had thrown the opportunity away. Not good enough.

The replay at Villa Park was a very different affair, a riveting attacking treat, notable for Ian Rush's (largely anonymous) Liverpool first-team debut in place of the injured Heighway, a terrific over-the-shoulder volleyed goal by Dalglish, and a header from Alan Hansen, in off Bonds, to reply to Goddard's early strike for West Ham. Phil Parkes bravely kept the margin to one goal. Later, the Liverpool players seemed to be joined by just about every scally from the city as, led by the returned Phil Thompson, they went up to collect their medals in the Villa main stand. Afterwards the Liverpool Boot Room sat down together for a quiet drink and a closer look at a trophy that would actually become very familiar to them over the next few years. They could reflect that there would at least be some silver in the Anfield bank at the end of this strange, injury-disrupted season. Alan Kennedy also now had scored a goal in a cup final and had a cup winner's medal to his name when, at one stage, his season had looked ruined and his very future at the club had seemed threatened. Anything else good that happened this season, he thought, would be a bonus. Anything.

GERMANY CALLING

Actually, it looked as if nothing else good *was* going to happen: Liverpool stumbled on in the League, through an undistinguished list of draws and defeats, and against Bayern Munich at home in the European Cup semi-final, their familiar scoring failings re-emerged. Souness and Johnson missed out for Liverpool and Rush and Heighway started against the Germans, which was no great case for optimism. The young Welshman had been moping around the club all season, an immature outsider, not seeming to fit in or get on with the lads at all. He just didn't have the strength of personality to join in with the banter and he absolutely hated being the focus of it. He also didn't really look like he could play and he was definitely no goalscorer: a wasted £300k, for sure. What was Bob up to; had he lost his touch?

After a predictable 0–0 Anfield stalemate, Bayern's German international captain and future Maoist Paul Breitner began to get in some useful practice for a touch of the old repentant office worker toiling in the fields, by parading round L4 and telling anyone who would listen that this Liverpool side – like all English teams – was 'unintelligent' and that the tie was now done. The Liverpool players had already heard the celebratory singing from the away dressing-room, but this was unacceptably taking the piss. Who were these fucking Germans anyway? Souness and Hansen, especially, bristled: 'Get a team out, and we can still take these posers over there.' Joe and Bob were actually not that dismayed by a home 0–0, and sensed that the arrogant posturing from the visitors had potentially handed Liverpool a lifeline. Newspaper clippings started going up in the Liverpool dressing-room, an ominous sign for any opposition. Training in West Derby would be very interesting over the next few weeks – if only Liverpool could get a decent 11 fit.

There would be no counting Alan Kennedy in on this revenge mission: he had got injured again in this game, after a clash with Breitner, and it was another chaotic *Emergency Ward 10* Anfield injury story: 'I'd obviously broken my wrist, but Terry Mac had already come off with a dislocated thumb. The doctor just said at half-time: "Can you move your wrist?" I just got sent out for the second half.' Typically, the club decided after the game that Kennedy and McDermott could get their X-rays at the hospital the next morning. Neither wanted to miss the post-match drink, so they both went out boozing with the rest of the squad: Alan was unable to hold a glass or, later, to sleep at all. At Fazackerley hospital the next day the wrist needed to be realigned and set: Kennedy fainted from the excruciating pain involved in the process. The doctors told him it would be eight weeks minimum in plaster, or a pin in the wrist. He took the cast. His season was over.

Alan Hansen stills dines out today on inviting Liverpool supporters to name the Reds' defence that started in Munich in the semi-final return. He'll throw in the champagne if you can also name the bench. Ray Kennedy and Jimmy Case were kept awake the night before the match in Munich as Paisley, Fagan, Moran and a whisky bottle loudly tried, well into the early hours in the hotel room next door, to settle on a Liverpool team. This looks on paper now like a run-of-the-mill result in a European tie: two draws between heavyweights, with away goals just counting in favour of Liverpool. But that detail says nothing. Hansen reckons this was one of Liverpool's greatest ever performances in Europe. He's right, of course: well, he *is* Alan Hansen. Walking into the unique cobwebbed-style Olympic Stadium in Munich that night to get a feel of the atmosphere, the Liverpool players crossed the running track to ask travelling supporters about the pieces of paper flying around the ground. They were flyers for Bayern-organised trips for the final in Paris. They really were cocky bastards, these Bavarians. This, plus Breitner's smugness, was plenty enough motivation: depleted, unfancied, injury-plagued Liverpool were now going to win this tie, whatever it took.

Alan Kennedy had mixed emotions as he listened to this game on the radio, his injured arm in a cast, nursing a drink with friends back in a Liverpool bar. Only professional players can think this way: he feared the worst, win or lose. A loss would cap a poor Liverpool season, but if this makeshift Liverpool team actually pulled off a shock win without him, what real chance did he have of getting fit and making the final? Would Bob even pick him? There are few things worse in football than drifting around injured and ignored while your clubmates are in the spotlight and preparing for the highlight of their careers. Who could want that? Perhaps an honourable defeat for a weakened Liverpool now would be the least painful option all round? He felt guilty even thinking like this, but it was hard to see a Liverpool win. Irwin and Money replaced Thompson and Kennedy at the back for Liverpool, while Souness returned, but was still struggling. For one of the few times in his career, Paisley prepared a specific plan for the opposition, Sammy Lee to shadow Breitner. But plans always meet events, especially in football: Kenny D lasted only seven minutes before sustaining serious ankle ligament damage. What now? Bob decided to throw traditional German organisation into chaos by presenting them with a problem they were unlikely to have covered in their dossiers: he sent for his Toxteth option.

Liverpool-born Howard Gayle came off the Reds bench, having played just a handful of games towards the end of the League season. Frankly, Bob wasn't sure about Gayle, didn't understand him. It was a clear case of culture clash. Here was a traditional, older North-east village football sage meeting a proud young inner city black man: it was like two Britains colliding. Howard did not suffer fools gladly. He had plenty of pure Toxteth fire, allied to talent and pace, but did he have the steel and discipline to do what the seasoned Dalglish could do? Did he? Gayle was brilliant: he ran the Germans ragged. While Howard ruined all those nice German travel plans, it was Ray Kennedy who scored the vital 83rd-minute goal for Liverpool, languidly stroking home right-footed low down to Junghans' right-hand post following a first-time pass from a hobbling David Johnson. Johnson had run his heart out for Paisley, but when the notoriously hypochondriac forward signalled to the bench that he had to come off, that his hamstring had *really* given way, Paisley famously turned to an armed security guard nearby and asked to borrow his gun. 'If his leg *has* gone,' murmured Bob, 'let's complete the job and shoot the bastard.' Naturally, Johnson stayed on. Rummenigge scored for Bayern but it was too little, too late. On the whistle, Hansen hugged Joe Fagan while others looked harder for the skulking Breitner. Back in Liverpool, Alan Kennedy was reluctantly jigging with celebrating supporters while gingerly cradling his suspect arm. Shit! But maybe he still had a chance of making this final? It looked hopeless, but he had to give it a real go: after all, how many European Cup finals come any player's way, even at a club like Liverpool? And who knows what might happen now if he could just get fit and back into Bob's team?

PARIS, FRANCE

It was a desperate race to get key Liverpool players right for the European Cup final against Real Madrid in Paris on 27 May. Alan Kennedy – six weeks out – and Phil Thompson managed to get back only for the very last League game of the season, a narrow home win against Manchester City. Kennedy played with his arm in a lightweight cast that he had removed just before the final. Dalglish didn't even make the City match and Sammy Lee also missed out, to Jimmy Case. Bob had given no assurances to Alan that he would actually play in the final, even if he got fit, but in the game against City Alan thought he had shown some of his old erratic attacking potential. He was optimistic. A week's intensive treatment later, and Bob's innate conservatism meant that, on the day of the final, he had reverted to his most trusted side – though he had not always trusted it this season. The established Liverpool back four were reunited; a fit-again Lee just edged out Jimmy Case in midfield; and, crucially, a patched-up Dalglish was partnered with Johnson, once again, up front. A distraught Ian Rush was squeezed out of the final 16 by the Bayern semi-final hero Howard Gayle: the Welshman decided he would have to leave the Liverpool club.

This looked as solid and as talented a side as Bob Paisley could possibly muster but, because of injury, it was one that had played together only four times in the League that season. It was short of form as well as fitness, so Bob expected no standout performance from his selection. But he felt an overwhelmingly strong will to win in the Anfield camp. Liverpool faced a far from classic Real Madrid, led by the German hard man Stielike and relying largely on the pace and guile of forwards Santillana and Juanito and the Englishman Laurie Cunningham who, himself, was returning from long-term injury. Real coach Boskov leaked some of his pre-match anxiety by teasing Bob that his Liverpool team was too old. He was half right: Paisley was already planning major changes, but reasoned that there was probably one more big night out left in this Liverpool generation. No special travel plans were made by Peter Robinson and Bob for the final: the club would do things as they always did. Liverpool travelled to Paris on the Tuesday evening for a brief training session in the stadium and stayed in the Trianon Palace hotel in Versailles. There was some early disruption in the camp though: a UEFA wrangle over the TV coverage of sponsors' logos on the Liverpool kit. Peter Robinson was soon toiling to try to sort it all out, and it added to the inevitable edginess among the players as kick-off approached. The official itinerary says that the Liverpool party were to leave their Versailles base for the stadium on Wednesday evening at 6.30 p.m. for an 8.15 p.m. kick-off. This seems impossibly tight today, but it was the way Bob and Joe kept nerves among the players to a minimum: get them to the ground as late as possible, do the job, get out. Why should a major final be any different? They certainly needed something to keep Alan Hansen calm: as soon as he saw the massive Real Madrid flag that cloaked the entire Spanish end of the ground as he came out with the Liverpool team, he feared the worst. But then the elegant young Scot *always* feared the worst.

The 1981 European Cup final was certainly no sporting eye candy, played out, as it was, by two very under-prepared teams in the oppressive Parc des Princes on a pitch that had its problems. This was primarily a rugby stadium and signs of battle could still be clearly seen on the field. The Liverpool players were dismayed and beforehand Joe Fagan had warned them about high bounces coming off the markings of the pitch, which seemed to be set like concrete. After a few minutes' play a long ball did just that, ballooning off the Liverpool 18-yard line and up into Phil Thompson's considerable nose. Hansen, of course, was creased. The state of the pitch, Dalglish's rustiness and an injury picked up early on by Graeme Souness meant that Liverpool failed to function at all in the first half, though a nervous Real had been no great shakes themselves. Cunningham had a couple of early shows against Alan Kennedy on the Liverpool left, but nothing too serious. In fact, the match was meandering apologetically towards extra time and possibly even to penalties, when one unscripted moment of the unexpected won the European Cup for Liverpool.

Goals do not come at this level directly from throw-ins: defensive organisation snuffs out risk. Full-backs do not win games like these, especially when these matches come towards their arse-clenching climax. Full-backs stay at home, shut up shop. But not this unpredictable, unquenchable full-back, and not this Liverpool. Alan Kennedy was about to become the unlikeliest of Liverpool heroes: 'I'd had a couple of shots at goal in the first half, so I'd gone close a couple of times already. Bob had told me to keep on my feet against Laurie Cunningham because he was a decent winger, but to try and get forward when I could. Cunningham went past me after about 15 minutes, left me on my backside, so I thought I was going to get a right rollicking at half-time. But Bob said we were not pushing up enough and there was too much of a gap between the back four and the midfield. We struggled to cope as they picked up the ball and ran at us . . . It was Sammy Lee who won the throw-in, but Ray Kennedy took it and Real had not picked anyone up. I didn't think I'd get the ball: I thought I'd be picked up, that I was clearing a path for someone else. But Ray threw it towards the edge of the box and it hit me on the chest and bounced down, and their centre-half, Cortes, took a wild swipe and, for some reason, missed it. Maybe it was a low bounce on that dodgy pitch. Now I was coming in at an angle on the six-yard box. Dave Johnno and Kenny were in better positions, but the keeper made my mind up for me. He made a movement to his left, expecting the cross, and the ball went into the near post. If the goalkeeper had stayed where he was it would have been an easy save.'

Augustin *had* leaned a little to his left, but he also looked content to have dived under Alan's ferocious shot, which actually hit the goal line high up close to the centre of the Real goal. Standing up, it would have taken a brave and athletic keeper to parry this haymaker away: so cross out 'brave' on the Augustin assessment form. Defender Cortes had clearly been deceived by something, or had simply misjudged his tackle as Kennedy powered on. When you watch it from behind again on TV, you just expect to see the ball squirt out to the right from Cortes's boot. It is almost as if the ball really does disappear once it is masked from the camera by Alan's body. But Alan had also been brave and single-minded enough not to turn away, not to flinch, as the giant defender hacked aimlessly at his run. Once in clear sight of the keeper, Alan had only one thing on his mind: the word 'goal' actually formed soundlessly in his head as he saw the Spanish keeper sway out to his left. As his left foot swung through the ball, Alan Kennedy's life would never be quite the same again.

Almost asphyxiating with excitement, but still checking for possible linesmen's objections that might yet ruin this dream, Kennedy ran wildly towards the Liverpool fans behind the goal. But where were his fucking teammates? Had his effort actually been disallowed? Was he, right now, making a complete arse of himself in front of this crowd and millions of TV viewers, as the match continued behind him? His doubts suddenly lifted. 'You lucky fucking sod!' – the first welcome words he heard from McDermott, as the lads finally caught him. Relief: he had scored, after all. Not surprisingly, the goal also energised Kennedy for the final few minutes, adrenaline racing, even though he was still far from match fit. He even got in another shot on target before the final whistle. Real had simply faded away and Alan Kennedy, tongue firmly in cheek now, was disappointed later that there was no man-of-the-match award, which usually offered a car or a big money prize to the winner. In a pig of a match such as this, the scorer of the winning goal usually had a big claim. He was actually a good bet to win, he kept telling anybody who would listen. No one would.

The trophy presentation had its own element of farce, because the UEFA official concerned seemed so overcome by events that he was determined to hold the European Cup aloft himself! Not likely. Phil Thompson finally dragged it off the suit: a Liverpool lad captaining his home town club to the greatest club honour in the game was not having some smarmy Italian bigwig stealing his moment of glory. In fact, within 48 hours the European Cup would end up behind the bar at Thommo's local, the Falcon pub in Kirkby. Typical Liverpool. In the Liverpool dressing-room later the Reds' stars continued to insist that Kennedy's was no 'proper' goal to win a match of this importance. It was a jammy cross, a sliced clearance. Alan was too tired and too happy to argue. Bob Paisley, now three-times European Cup winner, insisted that it was a shot, of course it was, and he scolded those critics who had wanted or expected a better match saying: 'Sometimes you have to win these games the best way you can.'

Of Alan Kennedy's winning goal, Bob said: 'It was Alan at his unpredictable best, for I swear that half the time he doesn't know himself what he's going to do next. Without any disrespect I'm sure he'd know what I mean if I say he's not a typical Liverpool player. While he has enthusiasm and heart in abundance, and is totally committed to the team's cause, he's not the type to see a move three or four passes in advance. Alan's the instinctive rather than the calculating type. He reacts to situations rather than creates them.'

This was a fair assessment by the manager and was, arguably, as articulate and perceptive a comment about any Liverpool player that

Bob Paisley ever made. It was a case, in Bob Paisley's eyes, of Liverpool's Way meeting Kennedy's Way and producing something hugely productive for the club and its supporters. But as Alan Hansen also says, by any sensible measure, though he may not have had the technical and creative gifts of others – he was no Dalglish or Souness or even a Ray Kennedy – Alan Kennedy was actually a 'great' professional footballer for Liverpool: he held his place on merit in a number of great Liverpool sides; he won virtually every honour in the game; he played in the greatest-ever Football League defence; and he even scored crucial goals in major matches. What other measures of capability and achievement in football make any real sense? It is a reasonable point.

After the official club dinner at the Meridian hotel, the Liverpool players took taxis and the European Cup to the Paris Lido, securing the best tables in the place. And this small fact is a suitable little descriptor for the influence and importance of the *players* at Liverpool Football Club. Because none of the club staff, and certainly not any of the directors nor the board at Liverpool, had either the will, or the power, to insist that the most valuable football club trophy in the world club game should stay with the official party this night, to be caressed by directors' wives or be ogled by the club's sponsors. This cup – indeed, this football club – belonged to the players and to the fans of Liverpool, who had swamped Paris that night by train, ferry and plane. Together they had earned this triumph and the players of Liverpool would now celebrate it in their own way, the European Cup standing proud among them, whilst eyeing up the dancers at the Paris Lido. Could life really get much better than this?

When the players and staff finally returned to Liverpool, half-a-million people turned out for the players' motorcade. It proceeded under a huge 'Thanks, Barney' flag, Kennedy's new nickname in the city. His picture was in every national paper, usually with the European Cup in one hand and a mug of beer in his still-bandaged other. Back in the St Helens area Alan, local hero, world football star, began sorting through the offers from sponsors and grifters that began pouring through his front door. He soon met Jane Garrett, whom he later married, indirectly through some of this work, and although it was mostly small-scale, local stuff, this was actually fine by him. Alan Kennedy didn't want much razzmatazz: he just wanted a place in the Anfield dressing-room, to steer clear of injuries and keep his Liverpool career on track. It was a sobering thought that, amidst all the hype, his first notion on scoring against West Ham at Wembley in the League

Cup final in 1981 was simply: 'Will this mean another season for me at Liverpool?' After scoring in Paris he was entitled to think that, with his injuries behind him, he might be allowed to settle back into the left-back slot and to see out his time at Anfield. Too easy: as it turned out, initially at least, nothing could be further from the truth.

Chapter 7

BROTHERS IN FOOTBALL

A FAMILY IN FOOTBALL

Almost 50 years ago now, a new modern English football myth was about to start writing itself in the soccer-daft streets of the North-east of England. Growing up in the tiny village of Shiney Row and then in Penshaw in the 1960s, two football-obsessed young brothers, one a Newcastle United follower and a delinquent grammar school boy, the other a Sunderland fan and an 11-plus failure, both set their minds, independently, on becoming professional football players. What type of family madness was this? It looked a very long shot indeed that even one of them might actually make it in the hard business of professional football. After all, they had no strong family ties in the game, nor knew any local families that had produced professional players. Their own parents had no more than a passing interest in football and they were also determined that their sons' sporting obsession did not interrupt the school studies that were likely to offer both boys much better long-term prospects than the endless hours they spent together scrapping and kicking a battered football.

The Kennedy boys were bright enough but they spent little time pressing for knowledge at school. Even with their 'play all hours' approach to football – like many lads in the area – it was still very hard to imagine that even these eager and competitive lads, good physical types, might one day mix it with the hardened professionals who made up top football clubs at the time. And that one of them, the fast whippy one who played too much with his head down, might then go on to score the winning goal in two European Cup finals. A visit to Mars might have been more believable. Brothers in professional football are unusual, of course, but not unheard of. The Charlton brothers, Bobby and Jack, are probably the most famous examples in the English game, if not the world, and they are lauded World Cup winners to boot. Bill and brother Bob Shankly were both football professionals and an amazing four Clarke brothers played for pay, including Allan and Wayne at the very top level. Even Alan's former Newcastle teammate Terry Hibbitt shared the football plaudits in the '70s with his Wolves-based brother, Kenny. More recently the Neville brothers, Gary and Phil, have both played for Manchester United and for England, glittering football careers not yet spent. There are also a few cases – as is the story of the Kennedy brothers – in which one brother plays at the very top level of the game while another toils honourably, mainly in the lower reaches of the profession: battling Scouser Peter Reid, for example, won England caps, League championships and European honours at high-flying Everton in the '80s, while his brother Shaun played most of his own professional career, relatively unheralded, at modest Rochdale. Light and shade in the same family and in the same sporting occupation.

What makes the story of the Kennedy brothers unique, however, is the fact that, early on in his career, Keith Kennedy was in direct competition in the early '70s with younger brother Alan for the same left-back position at the same top English club, Newcastle United. Indeed, for a while it seemed that these two 'manufactured' left-footed defenders, Keith, a converted centre-back, and Alan, a younger one-time flying left-winger, would challenge each other in pursuit of Frank Clark's old full-back berth at St. James' Park. By this time, Keith was already in the reserves at Newcastle, and pressing for first-team opportunities, while Alan was coming up fast through the club's junior teams and was predicted by the club's coaches and manager Joe Harvey for a glowing career in the game. They were very different boys, Alan and Keith, with more than two years between them, but it was already clear that something had to give – and fast – if they were not to end up clawing, at the same time, at the very same Newcastle United first-team shirt.

Keith, a strapping youngster, had been physically well advanced in his football development at school and at junior levels and was actually acknowledged by most people to be a better player than Alan: more composed, more comfortable on the ball and a better passer. But Keith had stopped growing at a below average 5 ft 7 in., and was regarded by the coaches at Newcastle as much too small for his favoured stopper role in the biff-bash English game. He also lacked some of the pace and guile that was now being demanded at the very top levels of English football, even from previously hod-carrying full-backs. Alan was less of a thinker about the sport and less naturally talented than Keith, but he had some useful tricks and also a forward's attacking verve: he could do more out of the wide defensive position, including score goals, and he had that priceless attribute in the modern game, real speed. For a short time, the Kennedy boys played balancing right and left full-backs in Newcastle's reserves, and it was soon clear that Alan, especially, was very focused on taking his chances at Newcastle, brother or no brother to overtake. So it was for Keith to decide exactly how far brotherly love might be allowed to give way to something beyond routine sibling rivalry: how far, in short, he wanted to see his competitiveness with his younger brother develop into hard-nosed, cut-throat professional rivalry.

As things turned out, the Kennedy family was to develop a lasting link with a friendly, small North-West football club, Bury. Keith was offered a loan spell at Bury and, briefly, he buddied up with an effervescent young Scouser at the club, Terry McDermott. Terry Mac was a man whose career in the game was later famously to follow similar lines, via Newcastle and Liverpool, to that of Alan Kennedy. But back in the early '70s McDermott's hard-running game at Bury was attracting the attention of First Division scouts, while Keith Kennedy was growing increasingly frustrated at the lack of first-team opportunities at Newcastle United and was worried by what he saw as a growing queue of quality left-sided players coming through at the club, including his own better-equipped kid brother, Alan. The first-team buzz at Bury was a whole new world for the Newcastle man: Keith liked the crowds and the attention which followed a bright, young First Division prospect down to the lower divisions. He settled in well in good landlady digs – so well, in fact, that he soon decided to make the move to the North-West permanent. Bury paid a £5,000 fee and Keith left Newcastle, reasoning that he might be better spotted by a larger club playing in first-team football in the lower divisions than rotting away in Newcastle United's reserves – or worse. He also left to save the Kennedy family from the potential friction of brothers possibly destroying each other's ambitions and dreams. Another twist followed: Keith's bedroom at the Kennedy home in Durham would soon be put to good use by another professional player whose arrival at Newcastle offered none of the familial football tensions recently experienced in the household: one Terry McDermott moved in to replace brother Keith, signed by Newcastle United, from Bury.

The truth that lay behind Keith Kennedy's move to Bury was that he had sussed that he might be squeezed out altogether at Newcastle, which would mean he could be forced to start his putative career again at non-League level. It was not an inviting prospect. Both Keith and Alan knew lots of decent players in the North-east – better football men than themselves – who were playing in the lower leagues because they lacked the application, had missed the breaks, or had not found the right doors into the professional game. Luck played a major role here, and once you had plummeted out of the professional ranks, there was just no guarantee of an easy passport back. So Keith's move into the lower divisions was a brave strategy, as well as being an admission, of sorts, that he might never make it in the game at the very highest levels. But it was also smart thinking: after all, top English clubs were still recruiting from the lower levels, with Liverpool, themselves, picking up Neal, Keegan and Clemence from the bargain basement – all later European Cup winners. Keith would bide his time in the first team at Bury, watch his brother's likely progress at Newcastle – and wait for something good to happen.

During their very different professional trajectories in football the Kennedy brothers met regularly, usually in Bury, to discuss issues in the game and in their own careers. There were few airs and graces when the footballing Kennedy brothers met: this was still even-handed brother-to-brother talk, professional footballer to professional footballer. It was also still hugely competitive: both brothers longed for the occasion when little Bury and mighty Liverpool might be drawn together, David and Goliath-style, in one of the game's cup competitions. It only happened once, in the FA Cup at Anfield in 1980, but for a short spell at least both Keith and Alan were famous together as the press and television excavated their family connections once more for stories of the 'Kennedy Brothers at War'. With both playing left full-back at Anfield, the two men never directly opposed each other in a tackle in the entire 90 minutes. They did not lament the lost opportunity. The match itself ended with a predictable Liverpool win, but with all the glory and the necessary cash going to a resilient Bury. The press pundits agreed that there had been only one decent left full-back on show that afternoon at Anfield – and it was not Liverpool's international, Alan Kennedy.

As it turned out, Keith's football career was never to make it beyond the lower divisions, despite his many rousing leadership performances for Bury and the considerable interest shown in him from larger clubs. Perhaps his height always counted against him. He later finished his impressive lower division career at Mansfield Town after a move there in 1982. Instead, it was Alan's star that continued to rise, culminating in his heart-stopping penalty heroics in Rome in 1984, which was watched with a mixture of excitement and horror on TV at home in Bury by his professional footballer brother, Keith. It was not easy viewing, even for a man who knows how it feels being exposed on a football field. Notwithstanding the obvious glamour of the job, this was a period when top football players in England earned 'good money', but hardly the riches many ordinary professionals earn today. This means that although we can say that, in some ways, they played the game in different football universes in the '70s and '80s, financially Alan and Keith Kennedy were never really massive poles apart. Indeed, it was Keith who had the necessary plans and skills to adapt, better than Alan, to life after football, and it was he who worried about Alan's prospects after his brother left Anfield in 1985 and, eventually, the professional game itself.

Today, the Kennedy brothers live broadly similar, comfortable, but not affluent, lives in the North-West of England, one still strongly attached to the town of Bury, the other by now wedded immutably to the Merseyside area. They meet regularly and their families also spend holiday time together. They both have growing young families and Keith's own middle son, Tom, has just broken through into the first-team squad at Bury: another left-footed left-back. Justifiably, Keith oozes pride about this latest Kennedy family football success and he thinks his lad might have what it takes to play in the game at a higher level. You sense he might not be too disappointed, though, if his son goes on to become another longstanding local football servant at Bury. As Keith remarks below in this recently recorded conversation with his more famous brother Alan, if the two brothers are out together today in Bury, there is still much more pub talk among the men who stop them to chat about Keith's driving performances for the Gigg Lane club 20 years ago than there is about Alan's massive contributions for all-conquering Liverpool. You see, Keith Kennedy is a true local football hero – and one who is immensely proud of his younger kid brother, Alan, a man who also, as it happens, once played a decent game of professional football himself.

* * *

GROWING UP FOOTBALLERS

Keith: At Shiney Row school I was one of the big lads and that helped me get on in football there. Alan was two and a half years younger than most of us when he got into the team at outside-left, and that was unique in itself. I also played for the Hetton and District representative side. At the time I went to Washington Grammar School they always asked you, at about 12 or 13 years of age in a questionnaire, what you wanted to do in your life. I put down I wanted to be a professional footballer, but it was only at about 14 years of age that I actually started playing in the Washington school team – it wasn't a very football-orientated school. At 15 I went on to Chester-le-Street Boys, the district side, and then one or two people started looking at me and I got taken on by Newcastle United.

Alan: Keith and I weren't the best footballers, even at Shiney Row: but he was the biggest kid there and I was probably one of the quickest. He was a centre-back and I was an outside-left. Both being left-footed was a big help, because not many kids could kick with the left. Keith was the dominant one – he always thought he was right – but he also thought he had to look after me when I got into scrapes, usually because of things that had happened during football.

Keith: We did a bit of fighting as kids, I have to be honest with you. I always had to win at things and Alan would get frustrated. Alan was also the worst timekeeper in the world and if my dad said to him, when Alan was a nine year old: 'You're coming in at eight o'clock,' there would be no sign of Alan at that time. So my dad used to send me to find him and bring him back. I used to get it in the neck a bit because of Alan's lateness, but then he'd get grounded, or a belt, when he got home. I used to keep a watch on him to make sure he was where he was supposed to be. When we used to play over at Sandy Banks there wasn't even a football field, just a piece of wasteland. Alan, being that little bit younger, just had to learn to deal with problems. He was skilful and quick and the bigger lads, of course, would catch him with late tackles, and we had some right dos over that. But by the time he was 12 or 13 he had learned to look after himself. After the 11-plus, Alan went to a different school to me and he started to really show up as a player. I started to flunk my exams, because, at 15, I began playing with Newcastle United. I had to hide my school reports from my dad for the whole summer, because I slumped from a 'B' level to about an 'E' level. A PE teacher, Neville Norton, really encouraged me to play football at school, even though cricket and athletics were the main sports there.

Alan: We both got warnings from my dad that if our results at school didn't improve we were going to be stopped from playing football. Our results both improved somehow. At 14 or 15 you had no idea what you wanted to do. My dad didn't point us in any real direction. I used to tell my mother I wanted to be a footballer, but she still said we had to do well at school in case we didn't make it. Everybody laughed at us because we put down 'professional footballer' when we had to write what we wanted to do. The teachers laughed, because the usual jobs for kids like us were working in a factory or some kind of manual work.

Keith: A lot of kids do believe they can make it in football but, either by luck or skill, we both managed to get a job in the game. I had no idea what I would have done otherwise. Alan and I were extremely competitive at home in any sport. In the winter nights, when we couldn't go out, we used to rig up some fireguards in the kitchen and we'd play hockey, using cricket bats or stumps and a little ball. My mum and dad used to go mad, but we always wanted to be playing something. In the street, we would play 'kerbs': you hit the ball off the kerb and you had to hit it again before it reached the kerb on the other side of the road. That was difficult, a good skills game. Between about 11 to 15 years old we always played games with each other; we didn't have many other close friends.

Alan: I always wanted to be with the older lads, but of course Keith wanted his own mates and I wanted to be with them, too. There was a game of football for us every day for at least two or three hours and our parents knew where we were. I liked the speedier players then in football because defenders were just stoppers. At this time, I was closer to my mum, who was a Sunderland fan, and Keith was closer to my dad, a Newcastle fan. Sunderland support far outweighed Newcastle in the Washington area, so that caused some trouble for Keith too. But he stuck with Newcastle.

Keith: I knew only one lad who had any contact with a club, a guy called Colin Suggett at our school who was a couple of years older than me, and who had started to play a bit at Sunderland. He eventually became a professional and in my last year at school we started talking a bit to each other. I was approached to go to Preston North End when I was 15, but I thought it was too far to go. When a Newcastle United scout came in for me to go training on

Tuesdays and Thursdays it was a dream. They put me in the 'Ns', which was the fourth team. I used to train with the district side on a Tuesday night, from about four o'clock until half five, and I'd get a bus from there straight through to Newcastle and train from seven o'clock until nine o'clock, getting home at about half ten or eleven: and this was as a 15 year old! I was very determined to make it. I was playing as a left-winger first, and then a sweeper: I was 19 before I played my first game as a left-back. I had a couple of decent games in the reserves and even made one appearance for the Newcastle first team.

Alan: Until we played with Newcastle United we had no experience even of playing on a flat pitch. Where we lived, everything was, basically, on a hill: everywhere was sloping. Playing on the Hetton Lyons school pitch, we used to call it 'Ocean Waves' because it was so up and down. So, once we got on a decent surface with a reasonable football the game seemed a bit easier to us. We knew, deep down, that we were going to be professional players but at what level, that wasn't in our hands. I was really happy for Keith when Newcastle picked him up, because a lot of people were leaving school at 15 with no jobs. But I was envious, too, because Keith would come back home now with stories about seeing Bobby Moncur or Frank Clark. I just had these footballers' cards to collect. Keith was now mixing with real footballers, the players I had on my cards! It sounded fantastic, and Newcastle United were a good First Division team at that time. They asked Keith if he knew anyone else who could play, and he recommended me.

Keith: By then I was signing as an apprentice, so Alan and I didn't get to see a lot of each other. I bought my first car at 17 and then I used to go and watch Alan playing in his school games that started at about four o'clock. He had just recovered from Osgood Slatters disease, a bone growth problem in his knees, which meant that he'd had two operations and hadn't been playing for about nine months. I remember thinking how much his thighs had developed and how powerful he had become, bombing down the wing. I hadn't seen him play at all for almost a couple of years. I knew what he could do, but I'd also seen a change in his body shape. He had always looked frail, but all of a sudden he'd filled out and had become a powerful runner. I have my mother's build – shorter and stockier – whereas Alan took after my father. When Temple Lisle, the scout at Newcastle, asked me about players, I asked him whether the club had looked at my younger brother. 'He's just had an illness,' I said, 'but he has developed really well since then.' He said to bring Alan down and they'd have a look. They got Alan for nothing – and cashed in on him later!

Alan: Yeah, notice they told Keith to *bring* me down to training. Newcastle wouldn't even send someone to watch me play! They only had so many scouts in those days, and they were, basically, old fellahs wearing a little flat cap. I remember when we first started playing together at Newcastle in the reserves because I would play right-back and Keith would be on the left. I was 17 and he was 19 and we were trying to get into the same team then.

Keith: I think it was the other way around, because I used to play a lot on the right-hand side. I was a full-time pro then, at 19, and that's when the real competition between us started to develop. Personally, I felt threatened by this. There were other good players there at Newcastle who were also damn good full-backs. That's why I asked for a transfer. Alan and I didn't talk about it, but I was a little naive and went for some advice from some of the older pros at the club: for example, I talked to Malcolm Macdonald about it. He said that if I went to a lower division club I could always come back up again. I knew I didn't want to compete with Alan because I knew I'd lose out: I couldn't win against him. I thought that if I stayed at Newcastle I'd end up going non-League somewhere in the North-east and then I might be outside the pro game for good. An opportunity to move came up so I said to Joe Harvey: 'Look, my brother's coming through. You don't want me blocking his way and I can't go back playing in the "A" team, I'm too old. It would be better if I moved on.' I thought I had worked it all out, because at the time Newcastle seemed top-heavy with full-backs. It was a massive, massive step for me: leaving the North-east, leaving my mum. I came on a month's loan to Bury and we did well under the manager, Alan Brown. We played Chelsea in the FA Cup: there were 16,000 there and I loved the atmosphere. I was on £35 at Newcastle and Bury offered me £37.50 with £750 signing-on fee, which was a decent sum in those days. But when I signed I remember arriving at Bury and staying in some poxy hotel and crying my eyes out. I wondered what I'd done, especially when we had to go to places like Crewe and Hartlepool. I played in the Bury reserves at Blackpool and I couldn't wait to get back to Newcastle at the weekend. It took me a long while to settle in Bury, but at least I soon started playing in front of crowds of 5,000 or 6,000 people.

Alan: I always said that Keith was a far better footballer than me. He could use the ball better than me, but pace got me everywhere. Keith could play football the way it should be played: I just had a trick or two. He was an out-and-out defender, whereas I was a forward who was coming back to play in defence. That was the difference between us: I could run at players. Technically he was a better player than me, he had everything. I thought he could have played at a higher level, but he had made the decision to leave. I thought he would get spotted at Bury eventually.

Keith: Terry Mac was at Bury when I first came down. I was brought back up to Newcastle with Terry when they signed him for £25,000 – which was a steal for the quality of player he was. But he was a little immature and a little raw and we decided he should take my bed in our house. I used to come back for the weekend for nights out and I used to sleep on the couch and Terry would keep my bed! He was a great lad and we had some great times.

Alan: Terry Mac was only supposed to be living with us for two months. It ended up being two years! But we didn't mind, he was a good lad. Once Keith left, Frank Clark was still a big obstacle to me getting into the first team at Newcastle. But now there was nobody else to put me under pressure. Frank knew his days were numbered and for about 18 months or so he moved around the Newcastle defence, at centre-back and right-back, and I started coming in at left-back. I respected Frank as a good pro, but I wanted to get into the first team. Whatever they told me to do at the club, I would have done it if it meant getting a chance to play.

'HE WAS THE HERO AT BURY'

Keith: To be honest, I was surprised at how quickly Alan made it into the first team at Newcastle. All of a sudden there had been a clearout at St. James' and it did pave the way for Alan to step into the first team and he made phenomenal strides once he got there. He had a couple of dodgy games and he dropped a backpass short in the FA Cup run in 1974, but I went to watch him in the 1974 Cup final. A pity Newcastle didn't turn up. I did think at Wembley: 'I could have been playing here.' I was pleased and proud for him, but I thought it could have been me. Even now I can't be sure I made the right decision to leave Newcastle. It doesn't haunt me, but who knows what would have happened if I'd hung on that season. I still believe that Alan would have finished off where I was playing, and in the first team. I ended up playing 16 years professionally and I might have had none of that had I stayed at Newcastle. Mind you, it was a complete shock to the system, coming to Bury. The ground was falling down, but Gigg Lane was a great playing surface, better than at Newcastle. The training facilities were grim. There was a smaller squad at Bury, so things were much more intimate. I became a big fish in a little pond, though I thought I was good enough to move on. I had two really good seasons and the first year I was there we got promoted. I knew clubs were watching me, but there was something about my make-up they obviously didn't like. Maybe it was lack of height, but I don't remember ever getting beaten much in the air. I know clubs made inquiries – Derby County and Man City – and I was playing as well as ever at Bury. I was enjoying myself in the town, and I was a bit of a jack-the-lad, really. And when Alan moved to Liverpool it was handy to get there from here and I met up with all the Liverpool lads after matches at Anfield.

Alan: But look at Kenny Sansom and even a player like Gary Neville today or Roberto Carlos: they are not tall players. I think clubs were worried then about taking a chance with a player from the lower divisions. And that was stupid because Liverpool had recruited some great players from the lower divisions. If only we had had agents in those days, because they would have touted Keith about and found him a club. People would have seen him on video. He was a great leader as well as being a really good player.

Keith: When Alan went to Liverpool I was pleased for him. Coaches and managers noticed when he bombed forward and I suppose that it stuck in people's minds. This is what they were looking for in full-backs then, so he had that going for him. I was surprised it was Liverpool who came in for him and I didn't think Alan would move. I thought he was too settled at Newcastle. But once a club like Liverpool come in for you, you don't really have much choice, do you? You have to go. I know he struggled, staying in a hotel in Liverpool, for the first few months, so I went across to give him some moral support. When I was over in Liverpool I definitely became 'Alan Kennedy's brother'. I know when he first arrived he had some trouble with one or two Liverpool players who wanted to show him that they were the bosses. He used to tell me about these things and I just told him that, at some stage, you just had to answer them back. At all football clubs you always have arseholes and bullies and you either handle them or else you keep away from them. Hard players respect you more if you answer them back. I've been involved in lots of similar things in training situations. Players can't always be nicey-nicey with each other.

Alan: It really helped me that Keith came over for some of the night games at Anfield. When I came over to Bury to watch Keith play in the late '70s, when we went out Bury people still called me Keith's brother. He was the hero at Bury, no doubt about that. But after a few beers on a night out, we didn't really care who we were, to be honest! Keith was married then and I was still single, and although I tried to save money I couldn't do it. Keith always got his rounds in but I was buying the drinks for others because people simply thought that top footballers had the money to buy everything.

Keith: We were on pretty ordinary wages at Bury. I moved, after ten years, to Mansfield and right away I got another £50 a week. Bury were a club that was always in financial trouble, so I had to be far more careful with money than Alan. He would just fritter his money away. He was more generous than me – and a bit gullible. He also used to look after mum and dad a bit more, because he had the cash. We always did well in the FA Cup at Bury, so it was inevitable that one year we would get Liverpool, and I was over the moon when we did, in 1980. The hype was amazing, from the draw to when we played the game. All the Kennedy family was involved, of course, and it was important to me that I had at least one game against him in my career. I thought we played quite well and we even hit the bar in the first half. Then they just brought on David Fairclough and he put two goals away. That finished us off, but I was pleased and I thought I'd done well on the day.

Alan: A typical Liverpool performance. We had to go through, of course. Bob had told me to forget about families: that this is not about families, this is about Liverpool Football Club. He didn't like all the media attention on us, the football brothers, because he thought it would distract the team. But he made me captain for the day. Bury played well and we were rubbish. But if you don't take your chances against Liverpool you don't win the game. Bury were happy in the end because their bread and butter was the League. They also had a big payday and a lot of their fans came to Anfield and had a good time.

'I WASN'T CHEERING FOR LIVERPOOL'

Keith: I was in Paris for Alan's first European Cup final in 1981. I must say it doesn't really hit you at the time that it's your brother who is out there doing all of this. I was with our sister, Bev, but the game itself was so boring that when Alan scored that goal I ended up about three rows further down because of the celebration. As he burst through with the ball, I remember thinking: 'I can't believe this, he's in with a chance here.' He just hit it so true. Trying to put into perspective that *he* has just scored the winning goal in the European Cup final is not easy. It's the pinnacle of any player's career. Alan has always been a positive player: rightly or wrongly, he'll always try to do something. He decided to make that run, one of their players decided to bottle out of the tackle – when he should have cut Alan in two, basically – and because Alan's done something positive it has changed the whole game. It was a breath of fresh air in a poor game. It is hard now to relive those emotions. It's funny, because I was still a Newcastle fan, of course, so it was a personal thing, seeing Alan score that goal. I wasn't cheering for Liverpool: it was all for my brother, Alan Kennedy.

Alan: It was great for me scoring in Paris, and it changed a lot for me. But I must say I was still disappointed that Keith wasn't going any further in the game. He was a good talent, a good player and we had a lot of time for each other. I think he feels he could have done a lot better. Maybe he thought Bury was the only opportunity he was going to get. I often wondered why more people weren't in for him. He was experienced and reliable. I also think he really left Newcastle all those years ago because he wanted to give me a real chance of making it at the top. He knew in his heart that I was the more exciting player and that's what Newcastle wanted at that time; that was the kind of club it was. So I'm sure I owe him something for that goal I scored in Paris.

Keith: It produced a lot of attention for Alan, scoring the winning goal in 1981, but he took it all in his stride. His attitude never changed in any way. He still treated me the same, but I realised that he was now on the national stage, especially when he played for England later on. He had got to a level I never thought he could reach. But locally, here in Bury, it made no difference to me. Let me give you an example: myself and three friends go out in Bury these days, every Friday night, without fail. We did last night. And I must have spoken to half a dozen people who came across and said: 'I remember when you played for Bury in the 1970s. Those were great days.' They still remember me and know who I am, even after 25 years. In my own way I was quite a high-profile figure here. I lived in the town and did a lot of the local presentations to football clubs. People do the same with Alan in Liverpool now, of course. But if Alan left Liverpool and walked in the street somewhere else, not many people would know who he was. One of the people who stopped me last night said: 'Your name's Alan, isn't it?' I said: 'No, Alan's my brother, I'm Keith.' And his mate said: 'There, I told you that it wasn't him.' It was funny. We then had a bit of banter a chat, no problem.

Alan: He is more of a hero here in Bury than I am in Liverpool! It was good coming over here as a Liverpool player on a Thursday night in those days. Nobody bothered you, and me and Keith could have a few beers, well out of Bob Paisley's way.

Keith: Alan brought the Liverpool team for my testimonial at Bury. It was 1982, when Scotland were in the World Cup finals and the day after my event here the Scottish players from Liverpool were going off to join up with the World Cup squad! Kenny kicked the match off and all the other Liverpool first-team players played, apart from Souness. It was a great atmosphere. At first it was really serious and we just couldn't get the ball off Liverpool. Then, after half-time, we messed the teams up a bit. I swapped shirts with Alan and played in Liverpool's team and Brucie Grobbelaar played out, with Sammy Lee going in goal. I was so impressed that their players all turned up, with all the Liverpool backroom staff too.

Alan: Keith had a testimonial year and because it was the end of the season we decided to put a team together. I just approached Bob Paisley and asked if there was any chance of getting a team out. I don't think Bob was exactly happy about it, but he was accommodating and he said it was up to the players. We didn't do it on a professional basis, let's put it that way. It was a great turn-out by the Liverpool players and the football was good, considering the lads had been on the bevy beforehand. We had a few beers before the game and everyone went home happy. Terry Mac, Alan Hansen and Kenny all knew Keith and they were very happy to do it.

Keith: I watched the 1984 Rome final here, in this room, on the TV. My wife, Karen, was doing things around the house and putting our son, Richard, to bed. I was watching the match, and I'd had a can or two. When the match was coming to the end at 1–1, I began to think about penalties, but not in my wildest dreams did I think that *Alan* was going to take one. It was nothing to do with him striking the ball or his temperament: I just thought that Liverpool had enough midfield and forward players who were good enough to take one before him. But as it went through the sequence, it only struck me as the last Liverpool penalty came up after Roma had missed, that our Alan actually had a chance of taking this deciding penalty. And I'm not joking, the hairs on the back of my neck just stood up.

And all of a sudden Alan's even got the ball in his hands and now

I'm thinking: 'Oh, my God, he *is* taking it.' So then I'm shouting: 'Karen, Karen, Alan's going to take a penalty here.' Now I'm thinking that, as far as I knew, Alan has never taken a penalty in his life before. I felt that I was taking the penalty with him because I could actually feel the whole thing: the crowd against him; this overwhelming sense that the crowd wanted him to miss. My heart was beating so fast: I felt I was really there alongside him. As he ran up I had everything crossed and as he stuck it away looking like the calmest man in the ground I suddenly thought: 'Flaming hell: I could *not* do that, I could not do what he's just done for Liverpool.' Alan had stayed so calm in front of that crowd and millions watching on telly. He was so brave to do that. I can take a penalty, but in those circumstances it was *so* difficult. Everything was against him. When he put it away, with all that emotion and happiness, the phone here never stopped ringing for the next half hour. We had to go to the pub to celebrate with all my mates. And I was still shaking when we got to the pub. To score one European Cup final winner was amazing – but *two*! His life could have changed completely in that moment. You also think later that, if he had missed that kick, football clubs are mercenary and he was getting towards the end of his time at Liverpool anyway. It would have been an ideal opportunity to let him go. But I tend to think that Alan is a lucky lad in his life. If something either will, or won't, happen in his favour it will usually happen positively for him. I don't mean that in a bad way: I just think that he was always destined to do all right, especially in his football career. I just don't think you can do better than what he's done. It won't be beaten, certainly not by a full-back. His contribution to Liverpool's success just can't be measured.

Alan: I thought about all of my family when I was walking up to take that penalty kick in 1984. I can tell you now I was feeling much worse than Keith! We often talk about it now in the pub. Keith knows what that feeling is like, facing a situation like that. Okay, he's not played in a European Cup final, but he has played a lot of professional football, and having someone who is as close as we are, but who is also a player, was very important in sharing those sorts of moments.

Keith: I was very worried for Alan when he finished at Liverpool. I was adapting myself to running a business and for several years, really, Alan was in the doldrums. Once you left Liverpool you could only go downwards, which is what he did. He did okay at some lower clubs, but he was really just filling in time. Alan's love of football kept him going and I was the same: I had six or seven good years of top non-League football when I stopped playing professionally. He didn't really make a lot of money when he was playing, and he was certainly never the best paid player at Liverpool. They undervalued him, really, that's my view. He could have done with an adviser to help him with his money. But after a while Alan picked up on the sportsmen's dinners – which I never thought he would be successful at. Now he's one of the top five in the business. I went to see one of his first nights and it was horrific! He is happy now with his media work and he is good at it, he talks quite well. It is just so difficult when you finish at the very highest level in football. I just had to step off a little step when I finished playing, but he stepped off a massive step because of what he had achieved. I'm very proud of him – but I know that he would say the same about me. We are just the Kennedy football brothers: Bury and Liverpool.

Chapter 8

NEVER STOP: BUILDING
A NEW LIVERPOOL

BARNEY, BARNEY

Paris, thought Alan Kennedy, had proved to Bob Paisley that, given a run free from injury, he was the man for left-back in the Liverpool first team. Alan also felt that he was making some welcome headway with his doubters among the Liverpool fans and, of course, that scoring the winning goal in a European Cup final could do no harm at all to local relations. All right, he still had his critics, especially among the football boffins and moaners in the Kemlyn Road Lower. And Ronnie Moran was still cursing him from the home team bench. But he felt that, rather than focusing all the time on his obvious weaknesses, the wider Anfield crowd had now decided that he was something of a working-class football hero: a player who wore his heart on his sleeve and was a full-on Kop trier. He was also now a proven goalscorer in major finals. All football crowds like a talisman and a willing enthusiast and so the Anfield regulars had even created a new identity for him: they had looked to a TV character, one that seemed rather a good fit for Kennedy's increasingly craggy features, his occasional gaffes, and his honest, no frills, conscript approach to the job of being a top professional footballer. Rise up, Barney Rubble: 'I think the Liverpool crowd thought that Alan Kennedy was just an ordinary man and that's why they identified with me, especially on the Kop. I was one of the fans – I always was. I knew they would all like to be in my position. I came from the North-east, from a city similar to Liverpool, and Bob and the supporters always knew they would get 100 per cent from me. The nickname Barney Rubble definitely came from the fans. I heard them singing it and pointing to me. I hadn't a clue it was me! So I had some press pictures taken with the caveman outfit.

'These fans used to associate with Emlyn Hughes and Joey Jones, I suppose, the big fist shakers. They loved the fact that I was competitive. I always felt under pressure: that I needed to work harder than anyone else, and I think I won people over because of that. Some Liverpool fans expected perfection, so they weren't best pleased with me if I gave a bad ball. I think they saw me as a limited player, but one who would always give 100 per cent. I was also a bit of a cavalier: I would maraud forward, bashing people out of the way. But I was a sidekick, more than the main man. Graeme Souness or Dalglish were Fred Flintstone. I was just Barney.'

Visualising Kenny Dalglish as Fred Flintstone is not an easy connection, but you can see the point. Alan was also beginning to enjoy, a little more, the attention he was now receiving from sponsors and the press. He had no agent, of course, hardly any player did. And, like most players, Alan was doing very little planning for his years outside the game beyond listening, distractedly, to the basic financial advice offered by the club's own advisers. He had no major business interests, no fancy investments. He had not even bought a house and never checked his earnings. He used to pick up Terry Mac, who lived with his parents in Kirkby, in his club-sponsored car, an unfashionable Lada. Kenny Dalglish refused to ride in this heap. When Kennedy told him it was actually a Lada EX, Kenny was still unimpressed: 'The EX doesn't stand for expensive, does it?' This was far from the high life.

The city of Liverpool itself was in turmoil at this time, with its street revolts and highly publicised 'far left' City Council opposition to Thatcherite policies. Few of the players bothered with any of this politics stuff. Graeme Souness appeared in the *Boys from the Blackstuff* anti-Thatcher TV drama series about Liverpool, although his own politics differed markedly from those of the author, Alan Bleasdale, or series star Bernard Hill. Howard Gayle brought in some radical news and views from the Liverpool streets and Steve Heighway had some informed liberal/left leanings. Players like Alan Kennedy, from broadly working-class backgrounds, had a residual Labour-voting tradition, inherited from their parents. But once the Tories got in and reduced tax rates for higher earners, most of the players soon followed them. Bob Paisley once made a little speech to the Liverpool players about how they should forget all the city's problems, not lose their focus, and concentrate on the football. Bob thought that the football, and Liverpool's successes in this area, could also help compensate people locally for the 'bad' image of the city he argued that the street riots and the left-wing council had brought.

By now Alan was making around £500 a week basic, supplemented by bonuses. For winning the European Cup, each Liverpool player in the final received £6,000. This was a fair sum but, in fact, Alan spent his money very quickly: he was young and liked to be liked, and he had cash to spend. Why not spend it? Alan probably needed better guidance and more financial discipline, but life was sweet. Even after scoring the goal that made him famous in Paris, he still lived in digs in Rainford and he still felt awkward outside the group of Liverpool players and the football club, and the sorts of working people he still knew best back in Durham and on Merseyside. There is a lot of time to fill for reasonably wealthy footballers, even quite stable ones who were still – like Alan certainly was – a little immature and lacking in confidence. Finding something to fill in the lengthy gaps between the extraordinarily intense highs of playing big football matches was not always easy. Drink was an obvious and comforting outlet: 'I spent money like it was going out of fashion. I wasn't bothered if I had anything in the bank as long as I had a good time. It was hard to earn a living in those days and a lot of working-class people found it hard, whereas they've got a bit of money now. In those days I used to buy a lot of people drinks, I suppose just to get them on my side and make them feel comfortable. I wanted to make them want to like me. I would always be in the areas where there were working-class people, people from that kind of environment. I felt comfortable there: local pubs, shops, whatever. I felt I didn't really want to be in town and I didn't really want to be in areas like Southport and Formby where people seemed to have a lot more money than I was used to. I liked two things: drinking and going to the racing. I liked the racing mainly because of the drinking. I wasn't a gambler – I didn't even like gambling.

'Booze was a way of dealing with the time you weren't at training. I think the club were happier I was drinking than risking getting injured doing something else. As long as we came in the next day, Bob was happy. We were being treated as men at Liverpool whereas at other clubs we heard that players were treated like kids. How we became so successful, the amount we drank, I just don't know.'

Of course, drinking together and the camaraderie it produced was *part* of the reason why Liverpool FC was so successful. Alan Hansen, among others, says today that he misses the *playing* side of football hardly at all, but he does miss the Liverpool dressing-room and the players' nights out. Alan Kennedy's other 'public appearances' before Paris were largely down to a few invitations to push over piles of charity pennies in Liverpool pubs and, for a few quid, to opening new shops in Rainford and the St Helens area where he lived. Top Liverpool players, like Dalglish and Souness, were much more canny and made plenty of personal appearance money. Alan was too shy to ask, or to do much more work, and Bob would not have wanted much more than this outside the drills at Melwood. Even when Alan had become a national hero after scoring the winning goal in Paris, he ended up travelling miles to obscure venues in Britain for personal appearances for a pittance in pay. He was just too nice – and too gullible – to make much hay out of his new stardom. The wiseacres in the Liverpool dressing-room sure let him know about it. Football boot manufacturers were also now in touch with Alan – at least a couple of new pairs a season when he signed up with Dunlop. Phil Neal once managed to agree to two boot deals simultaneously, so wore one boot from each manufacturer for coverage in TV matches. Today he would probably be sued. Alan was also now in reasonably regular demand from the press and media, both local and national. This new public exposure brought its own challenges and disciplines.

The picture Kennedy now paints of player/media relations at Liverpool at this time is difficult to comprehend from the perspective of today's frenzied media outpourings about modern footballers and their private lives. After all, although they were welcomed in most places in the city for the glitz and the public attention they brought with them, some Liverpool footballers were also banned from a few local bars at the time – Thompson, Kennedy, Hansen and McDermott, for example, were outlawed from the Hen and Chickens pub near Kirkby for a time because of their heavy drinking and rowdy antics. The single players had lots of spare time to fill and no one wanted to go back home to family digs in the middle of the afternoon. 'We had drinking games, swearing games, anything we could do,' says Alan. 'Sometimes it can get a bit boring when you're in a pub for five or six hours and sometimes longer. What else could we do, apart from drink?' Someone would then inevitably end up driving the group to another venue, trying hard to avoid the drink police, of course.

Terry Mac once fell foul and was banned from driving. It was pretty minor stuff, but none of this tomfoolery ever really made the press or local media outlets in Liverpool, as it would instantly today. The public better protected their local sport heroes, and sports journalists had much less space to fill with their stories then. They also had professional and personal relationships to maintain with their local clubs and especially with the players. They feared club officials, as Alan Kennedy knew well: 'There were no clear guidelines for players, with the press. You had your little rulebook that Liverpool gave you, from the PFA, about bringing the game into disrepute, but this was very general stuff. No one at the club said: "This is what you can and can't say." The local reporters were very good to the players, but we didn't get much cash from the *Echo* or the local correspondents of the national papers. They needed us. And the press could approach players directly about a match and Bob would have no problems. Maybe it was John Smith saying to them: "Look, you can have all the stories you want but if you cut us up we will make sure you're out of here." The club was bigger than the press boys because if they did something bad they would be in trouble. They would be hauled before the chairman and dressed down.'

News reporters spent very little time on the football beat. There were lots of rumours flying around the city about Liverpool and Everton footballers, of course, some of them true. The Liverpool players had a well-worn drinking beat, so they weren't too hard to track down. But even the news guys seemed to want at least *some* hard evidence about incidents rather than rely on the, 'It was alleged . . .' kiss and tell approach of today. The players looked for bars where they would be left alone to play some snooker and do some drinking. Despite their fame, this was usually possible.

The sports reporters also enjoyed the lively drinking sessions they sometimes had with famous footballers. With Liverpool, they even got fully paid-up trips abroad with the star names, who were earning big, but not enormous, salaries. As Roy Evans observed: 'We could tell more stories about the media than the media could tell about us. They got away with murder!' The public envy and moral outrage that is routinely aimed at top footballers today, and is part of the heightened circulation wars between the tabloid newspapers, was simply just not a feature of the culture in the same way 25 years ago. Once the police became involved, of course, it was impossible to keep a good football story out of the papers: the news guys then stepped in. Otherwise, why would any sensible sports writer, even from a tabloid paper, want to risk losing this kind of access and enjoyment with glamorous, affluent young athletes like these? Players, in any case, were easily accessible and usually made themselves available as part of their job at the club. This was not hard work for the media men.

Players could also use journalists – as they do now – to get stories out about their unhappiness or their unjust treatment by a manager or official. This was more dangerous ground, of course, and it needed careful handling. Bob warned his players about getting too close to journalists and about saying something stupid to the press that might rile the staff or future opponents, such as Liverpool are going to 'hammer' some poor, unsuspecting victims. He also liked the Liverpool players always to be positive in the media about all things at the club: he told Alan Kennedy late in the 1979–80 season to remember to tell the press that he'd really meant to curl in a shot at Leeds, when it was obvious to all the players and staff that the goal he'd scored there was actually a mis-hit cross. This was, partly, a little joke on the journalists, but why not also make opponents fear a Liverpool goal directly from out wide? It was one of Bob's little tricks.

In fact, as Alan Kennedy now recalls, rather than exploit and distort players' comments, sometimes the press guys themselves were happy even to tone down the sorts of things that were said by players in the heat of the moment, in order to make sure that their informants – and the journalists themselves – stayed in the good books of the manager and so were available for a good quote on another slow news day. This tack also prevented players from revealing things inadvertently or making statements that might make them a laughing stock among 'the lads', a much more important consideration in the Liverpool hothouse of dressing-room stick. This is a generalisation, but the whole approach of football journalists then suggests a very different sporting and media world: 'They could have reported a lot more than what they did, because they were with us a lot of the time. In those days a lot was kept under wraps by the reporters. We were a little frightened of talking to them at first, but the journalists would even sometimes warn you and say "I don't think we should put it like that", because they knew what would work best at the club. They were very good. They had some great European journeys with us. We also used to go drinking with them at the Press Club in Liverpool. The journalists could help you get a story out that you weren't happy. Generally, they were pretty good to the players. I wouldn't say players trusted them, but we had socialising nights with them. Bob made the point: "Don't trust them as far as you can throw them. If you give them a little they might take too much."'

Bob himself didn't enjoy talking to the press or TV and he did as little of it as possible. He was uncomfortable with the media attention and, later on, he had difficulty coping with the endless (and pointless) media questions about his personal contribution to Liverpool, and the team's success. After all, for Bob, a successful team was all about a solid work ethic, good players and sensible habits, plain and simple. He could have a laugh with favoured reporters, but if he said something to them off the record they could never repeat it, or they were gone. Most of them didn't step over the line. Joe and Ronnie seldom ever spoke to the media when Bob was in charge at Liverpool, even as their profiles grew. After a defeat at Ipswich Town, Bob once talked a little carelessly to the media about players he called playboys or 'fly-by-nights': those who came to clubs for the money and who behaved unprofessionally. Phil Neal and the senior players were hurt and Bob's comments were the talk of Melwood the following day. The players wanted to know exactly *whom* the Liverpool manager could possibly be referring to. Nobody was brave – or foolhardy – enough to ask.

MARKING TIME

'I found it hard to take,' says Alan today. 'Bob never even came up to me to talk about it.' Three months after scoring the winning goal in Paris, a fit and fresh Alan Kennedy watched from the stands as Liverpool lost the opening day's fixture in the 1981–82 League campaign, away to Wolves. He had been left out by Paisley. It was a shattering blow. That new players would be brought into Anfield, even after a European Cup win, was no shock at all to Liverpool players or fans. Bob had started to rebuild his new Liverpool on the tried and trusted basis of always adding new players from a position of apparent strength. The problems in the League the previous season also told the Boot Room that new recruits were urgently needed to boost and strengthen the squad. Conveniently, Paris had provided the necessary cash, so why not spend it? Suddenly last year's new flavours, Richard Money, Gayle, Irwin and Cohen, were all effectively out of the Anfield picture, deemed below Liverpool's testing standards despite their contributions in Germany and elsewhere. Jimmy Case was also sold to Brighton: his Liverpool 'twin', Ray Kennedy, would soon follow him out of Anfield.

But a real shock was that Shankly's keeper, Ray Clemence, left for Tottenham, apparently feeling the pressure behind from new recruit, Zimbabwe guerrilla fighter and general exhibitionist, Bruce Grobbelaar, and claiming he needed a new challenge away from

Liverpool – and a payday. Bruce was a popular, brash new dressing-room influence at Anfield, a man who could easily be wound up by the Liverpool wags, but who also had plenty to say for himself about his mad adventures in Africa. Bruce was a skilled all-round footballer with a great physique and was super-confident: he wanted to reorganise the Liverpool defence, and even suggested new training approaches. He also had all the required physical attributes to be a top goalkeeper. He loved his jungle combat stories and swore by the restorative powers of South African salt beef: 'It's good for you, man' – though the rest of the players hated it. In, too, came Craig Johnston from Middlesbrough, a non-stop £575,000 Aussie pest on the Liverpool right and an obvious alternative to Case and the declining powers of Terry McDermott. Bob lectured Johnston, endlessly, about the need to pass the ball sooner, to get his head up quicker: to do the obvious, not always the difficult. But Johnston, for all his wasteful faults, added plenty of zest and persistence on the Liverpool right-hand side.

Ian Rush was still snarling at Bob, but at least he was scoring goals and now he actually wanted to play for Liverpool again, pushing the veteran David Johnson all the way. Rush still looked too thin and awkward and he had taken time to settle. Alan Hansen, for one, was convinced that Rush had no chance of ever becoming a top footballer. But the Welshman had big pace and an eye for goal and Kenny had started to enjoy playing with him. It seemed he might make a Liverpool player after all. Ronnie Whelan was graduating, meanwhile, with excellent reports from the Liverpool reserve side and he was groomed to step in, eventually, for a disillusioned Ray Kennedy. Ronnie was a good socialiser, a very positive dressing-room presence, with a silky smooth touch on the field on both sides. Ronnie could also stick his foot in when he needed to and scored goals: he was perfect Liverpool midfield material, in fact. Finally, the man who became, for a while, the source of Alan Kennedy's new fears, Mark Lawrenson, was recruited for £900,000 from Brighton. Preston-born Lawrenson was also courted by Manchester United and Arsenal and was, arguably, the most sought after and talented defensive player in Britain at the time, a man who could play on either flank, anywhere across the back and also anywhere in midfield. Mark was actually recruited by Bob mainly because he was available, and because his sale elsewhere would strengthen Liverpool's opponents. He was also comfortably better than any of Liverpool's defensive cover. In fact, Mark Lawrenson could play just about anywhere, and it was clear that he had not been bought to fester in the club's reserves or to sit on the bench. He could well hold his own, too, in the tough Liverpool dressing-room, matching the word games and jokes of the Jocks and Terry Mac. In short, he was all round quality.

This was turning into a season of huge change at Anfield and in the game at large, with three points for a win on the League slate for the first time. The early aim at Melwood, then, was to convert more draws into wins, and to find a system that would best suit the club's new acquisitions. Unusually, Liverpool had experimented in pre-season with a three at the back formation of Hansen, Thompson and new man Lawrenson, with Alan Kennedy and Phil Neal pushed forward into a five in midfield. Neal and Kennedy seemed perfect candidates for the wing-back slots, but somehow it didn't work, producing holes at the back and cramping both Dalglish and Souness for space. As the first League game loomed, Bob was faced with a real problem: where was new man Mark going to play? Alan Hansen argues that Paisley just had to get Lawrenson into the first team *somewhere*: that the sheer quality of the player simply cried out for his inclusion. The Liverpool centre-backs were solid and still playing well as a partnership and Phil Neal was showing no signs of slowing up on the right. Ray Kennedy still just about merited his own spot and, in any case, Bob would stir up a right hornets' nest if Ray was omitted. Which left Alan Kennedy.

Kennedy was a better left-back than Mark, but Lawrenson was a much better player. Bob's unlikely saviour in Paris, the great Liverpool enthusiast, began to be seen in the Boot Room as the easiest 'established' player to bump for their new man. The message started to come through. In the traditional pre-season match between the Liverpool first team and the club's straining and talented reserves, Alan, ominously, was selected for the stiffs, while Mark Lawrenson played up against a Howard Gayle who was still trying to prove things to Bob and Joe. Predictably, Howard murdered the new man with his pace, the reserves eventually running out easy 5–1 winners over the first team. A crestfallen Bob drew the slaughter to a close, saying: 'All right, forget it, let's get in.' 'This new team,' thought a watching Joe Fagan, 'would actually take some thinking through.' Alan Kennedy afforded himself the thinnest of smiles, but he was still being left out in the cold.

Alan had played in the pre-season fixtures, but he was left out of the first three League matches of the new campaign. He then, briefly, replaced the injured Lawrenson, before being left out again for a further run of seven matches. By Boxing Day 1981 he had started only seven League matches in total. This meant that all his comforting rhythms were abandoned: a decent performance and a win at Liverpool usually guaranteed you a place in the side the following week. This is how he had paced his time at the club, week by week. Now, when Liverpool's form was poor, as it had been at the start of this new season, he couldn't even show what he could do. Maybe his time here was already up? Not that the team without him was flying. A pressing problem for Paisley was that his new goalkeeper Grobbelaar was causing huge uncertainty at the back. Bruce had too many distracting business interests off the field for Bob's liking, and was an athletic, if erratic, shot-stopper, a man who even liked to have a chat, during matches, with the crowd. Bob often bawled Brucie out to focus more, to stop showboating and to improve his concentration. But Bruce remained a poor talker and organiser and he was inconsistent in coming for, and taking, the high ball. Joe Fagan told his defenders, 'Get round Bruce if he comes for it – he'll drop a few.' This meant that the Liverpool centre-backs had to come deeper to cover for the keeper's many early mistakes, and Phil Thompson's game, especially, was beginning to suffer. All of this disturbed Liverpool's essential defensive equilibrium.

Added to these adjustments and instabilities at the back, Ray Kennedy was contributing inconsistently on the Liverpool left, so putting extra strain on new man Lawrenson, and David Johnson's spark was also fading up front, his coveted and deserved European Cup medal having now finally been secured. For all his ability, Mark Lawrenson was just not getting forward effectively on the left, and the shape of the side looked wrong. It certainly lacked energy and pace. The low point came with a 1–3 Boxing Day home defeat against Manchester City, Alan coming on as a substitute and City pouring through the Liverpool left side for the third and clinching goal – scored in his own net by a frustrated and under-performing Phil Thompson. Bob claimed, a little implausibly, that Liverpool were still suffering from the effects of the trip for a 0–3 hammering by the Brazilians, Flamenco, in Tokyo in the World Club Championship some two weeks before. In fact, Liverpool had looked a mid-table shambles for some time. They were down to 12th in the League table. Bob talked to Joe Fagan, who said as much in the Liverpool dressing-room afterwards. It was certainly a lively exchange, but one dominated by Joe: 'Pull yourselves together,' he barked, simply but firmly. 'Get it sorted out among yourselves.'

But Bob and Joe also realised that *they* needed to do something to get the side back to Liverpool basics. They needed to shore up the leaking Liverpool left side, for one thing, while promoting a bit more 'oomph' in the dressing-room and on the field. Phil Thompson was struggling, so Graeme Souness was made captain to add some much needed urgency and direction to the cause. Thompson hated the change but Souness offered more leadership on the field, though he also liked to sort out the problems of others and frequently warned off opposing defenders who had started, for example, to target the elusive Dalglish. This kind of tribal response caused some frustration for Bob Paisley, who told the combustible midfielder to let his teammates 'fight their own battles'. Souness would not come to everybody's rescue, of course, and he accepted that not all players would, necessarily, get on in the same successful football squad. When he was given the Liverpool captaincy by Paisley, he took the dressing-room unease well in his stride. 'It ended any pretence of friendship between Phil Thompson and me,' he said. 'He took it as a personal affront and it was a long, long time before he would even say hello to me.' The two remained respectfully frosty for the rest of their time together at Liverpool – and resumed their open enmity much later in Liverpool managerial and coaching positions.

On 2 January 1982 a 'new' Liverpool visited high-flying Swansea City in the third round of the FA Cup. Alan Kennedy was recalled at left-back, Rush and Ronnie Whelan both started, for Ray Kennedy and David Johnson respectively, adding pace and youthful drive to the side. Bruce was finally settling in goal and Mark Lawrenson was pushed up into midfield to add a little class and strength to that department and scored in a 4–0 rout, Ian Rush also scoring twice. The old Liverpool fight, determination and confidence as a team seemed to have returned, fired by an injection of hungry new men and a stabilising dash of some of the old stalwarts. This was also a much faster, a more forward-thinking Liverpool unit than the one that had played in 1980–81. Alan Kennedy was now more determined than ever that he would become Liverpool's left-back for the rest of his time at the club. Remarkably, he remained a constant there for more than three years, until he was injured in March 1985 against Manchester United and was finally replaced in the Liverpool side by Irishman Jim Beglin. Bob Paisley's new Anfield Empire was, finally, beginning to strike back.

From 5 January 1982 until the season's end, this reconstituted Liverpool won 20 out of 25 League matches, including a winning streak of 11 games, losing only two and drawing three, one of which was the 'dead' final match at Middlesbrough. The stats show 63 points taken by Liverpool from the last 25 League matches compared to only 24 from the first 17. It was an astonishing turnaround in anybody's book and was enough to produce yet another League title for Paisley and Anfield. During this amazing unbeaten run in the League, on 10 April 1982, in front of the *Match of the Day* cameras, Manchester City were demolished 5–0 by Liverpool at Maine Road. Alan Kennedy even got on the score sheet again, an outrageously mis-hit right-foot cross that totally fooled Joe Corrigan. Kenny Dalglish visibly roared with laughter in the players' celebrations that followed. Liverpool, missing the injured Souness, fielded six players in this match who were still to win a championship medal, the core of another new Paisley side. The comedian, Eddie Large, sat on the City bench: it looked as if he had organised the home defence. Memorably, the City manager, the usually ebullient John Bond, was interviewed again on TV after this humiliation, looking like a man whose entire family had been taken by an Act of God. How had this new Liverpool compared to his City team? Bond growled: 'They were so superior to us in every way: in their determination; in their will to win; their skill; their habits and their methods; the way they knocked the ball around. I would have been ashamed, really, to have been a Manchester City footballer today, to have succumbed as easily as that. It looks, in many ways – and people in football will know what I mean – as if Liverpool do what they want to do, when they want to do it. And when you're not able to change it around too much you have to live with it. It's sickening really.'

Bond looked like he needed rehab – or Prozac. New boys Rush, Johnston and Sammy Lee had all scored for Liverpool, with Phil Neal also finishing from the spot, a penalty won by Rush. At 3–0 the Maine Road crowd began chanting: 'What the fuck is going on?' They might have guessed it: Liverpool were back. 'How could we doubt Liverpool earlier in the season?' twinkled an obviously contrite TV presenter, Jimmy Hill. The Higson's pale ale that the Liverpool players were always given by Ronnie Moran on the bus back from away games tasted especially sweet that night as they swept west along the M62. The Reds now led the table by five points from Ipswich Town, with 11 games remaining: they were to remain unbeaten in the League until the end of the season.

The record 13th Anfield League title was finally secured, at home, on a dank day and on a wet pitch, against Tottenham, with Liverpool playing in what looked suspiciously like red shirts and *pink* trim: had the Anfield laundry ladies got their wash settings correct? Spurs, without an Anfield win since 1912, even took the lead, Glenn Hoddle scoring from long range. But the match was turned by two interventions by Mark Lawrenson soon after half-time, as Liverpool attacked the Kop. The first was a towering header over the returning Ray Clemence, from a Sammy Lee corner; the second was a half clearance by Spurs that Lawrenson hooked back into the danger area for an unmarked Dalglish to slot home from near the penalty spot. Ronnie Whelan's volleyed late goal from a Grobbelaar punt just served to signal the influence this young Irishman would continue to have on this new Paisley side. He had already contributed ten League goals in 31 games, with Ian Rush notching 17 in 32 starts and 30 goals in all major competitions. Rush had found his feet and was even beginning to warm to the Liverpool dressing-room. Bob, as usual, had been right all along. These new boys were already a key part of a changed Liverpool. At the final whistle, Chairman John Smith presented the championship trophy to his own club – though 'presenting' is a little grand for what occurred: he actually handed it, in a centre circle mêlée, to Graeme Souness. The Liverpool captain was more expansive, chucking the old silver pot irreverently between his players. The Kop simply purred its appreciation. Liverpool had ridden the storm – and emerged stronger.

CUP TALES

In Europe, the picture had been less positive for Liverpool. After Oulu (again) and Dutchmen AZ '67 Alkmaar had been seen off in the early rounds, the holders met CSKA again, in March at Anfield. The Bulgarians had clearly learned to press higher up the pitch and even Liverpool's fine domestic form was found wanting here, the Anfield club managing only a 1–0 win in the first leg, thanks to a Ronnie Whelan goal in front of a meagre 27,000 crowd. In Sofia, in a poorly refereed physical contest, Liverpool missed chances galore and had dreadful luck, but still looked comfortable. That is, until a bored Brucie had one of those inexplicable rushes of blood, a kamikaze moment, coming for a cross and then retreating. His hesitant two-step allowed Mladenov to nod the ball easily into an empty net on 78 minutes. It was a dagger through Liverpool's heart. Mladenov scored again in extra time, this time via a deflection, while Liverpool twice struck the post. Mark Lawrenson struck something else late on: he was sent off, for retaliation, to complete an entirely miserable night for Paisley's men. Bob blamed the Austrian referee, claiming that Liverpool had had too little protection from the officials. It was a shock and an undeserved exit, certainly, and one that left the way open for Aston Villa to continue the amazing run of six straight European Cup wins for English clubs.

In the FA Cup, the turnaround Liverpool destruction of Swansea City had promised real progress – until, that is, Chelsea sank any serious Liverpool weekend-in-London plans in May, at unloved Stamford Bridge with a 0–2 defeat in the fifth round. In the following League game, Liverpool also lost 0–2 to Swansea, producing from Bob his first vocalised thoughts that he just might jack it in altogether if things didn't pick up. As ever, the League Cup offered more possibilities of Liverpool success, and a gentle first-round meeting with Exeter City provided Ian Rush with an early chance to get some goals – he scored 4 out of Liverpool's 11 over the 2 legs. Defeating Arsenal took both a replay and extra time, as did beating more modest Barnsley in the quarter-finals. The semi-finals brought Liverpool up against League championship rivals, Ipswich Town, Rush and McDermott seeing off the Suffolk men at Anfield. Liverpool were always comfortable in the 2–2 return draw at Portman Road, having pulled away to 4–0 on aggregate just after half-time, with strikes from Rush and Dalglish. Wembley beckoned once again.

Tottenham proved a tougher nut to crack in the 1982 League Cup final, which was played with that daft, wobbly, coloured Football League ball again on an afternoon of sun and showers. With Ardiles, Hoddle, Perryman and Archibald all in their side, Spurs were on a 16-match unbeaten run and had yet to concede a goal in their League Cup journey. Spurs had also never been beaten at Wembley and were on a remarkable 25-match unbeaten spell in all cup-ties. They expected to win. Alan Hansen missed out through injury for Liverpool, Phil Thompson returning, but it was a mistake by Hansen's replacement at the back, Mark Lawrenson, that allowed Archibald to put the Londoners ahead after 11 frenetic minutes. Liverpool piled it on before half-time and in the second half, in search of an equaliser, with Alan Kennedy playing exceptionally well. But Archibald should really have closed it up for Spurs, with Grobbelaar beaten, only for Souness to clear the Scot's shot off the line. It was the turning point. David Johnson soon replaced Terry McDermott in the second half, in his big match swansong for Liverpool, and it was Johnson's low cross from the right that was swept in, first time, past Clemence by Ronnie Whelan. Tottenham had led for 76 long minutes. 'I thought we'd lost it,' admitted Alan Kennedy. 'But once Ronnie scored we knew we'd win.' It was that close. Bob bluffed it for TV afterwards: 'The rule says you play for 90 minutes, yer know.' But he also knew that this was a late, late saving Liverpool show: almost too late.

At full time, Joe and Bob were quickly off the Liverpool bench, with Joe, especially, visibly relieved and telling all the players to get on their feet: that Spurs were drooping, finished. Rush and Kenny Dalglish, who had been brilliant throughout, finally got through down Tottenham's right flank with nine minutes left, but Kenny still took an age to decide to feed a pass back to Ronnie Whelan – who else? – for the youngster to lash his right-foot shot over Clemence from the edge of the six-yard box. Rush's late goal, following a bad miss by Johnson, was a welcome, if unnecessary, piece of Reds' insurance. Weirdly – perhaps uniquely – Liverpool collected *two* cups up the Wembley steps: the old League Cup, from ex-Red, Sir Matt Busby, and the new Milk Cup from some Dairy Council face. Thompson and Souness, old and new Liverpool captains, fittingly each came down the famous old staircase carrying their own silverware with handles. It was fitting too that Alan Kennedy was voted man of the match for a relentless performance on Liverpool's left flank, compensation for the award he never got in Paris in 1981.

In the newfangled and risky dressing-room TV interviews later, a choirboy-faced Ronnie Whelan was filleted on screen by the rest of the Liverpool squad as he was asked by some inane TV interviewer to: 'Tell us how you felt, Ronnie, as the second goal went in.' Poor Ronnie tried to play it cool in front of the lads, nervously toying with the TV format and providing some pointedly football-speak answers. But he was betrayed by the videotape: it showed him – to loud dressing-room cheers, behind – ecstatically vaulting advertising hoardings to get to the Liverpool fans. Later, Bob even tried to make his own little joke for TV: 'I almost went sour on the Milk Cup,' he suggested. Time, it was universally agreed, for a visit to the pub.

ONE FOR THE ROAD?

Unusually, there was also time for ale *before* Liverpool's last League game of the 1981–82 season, a meaningless midweek affair at Middlesbrough. The Reds had just won the title, of course, after a poor start and much media criticism. This trip to the North-east was the fag-end of the season as the World Cup finals loomed. Liverpool captain Graeme Souness obviously wanted to mark his first title as skipper with a unique gesture. Earlier in the season, Souness had fallen out with Bob over the Scotsman's plans to return from injury away to one of his old clubs, Tottenham. Convinced the manager was leaving him out, Souness had angrily hit the afternoon gin and tonics in London as he waited to confront Paisley. Bob actually put his captain on the bench and Souey came on at half-time, apparently none the worse, to help turn a two-goal deficit into a vital point for Liverpool. Maybe the Scot thought he was immune to the effects of drink? He now suggested that the Liverpool squad celebrate their achievements on the afternoon before the evening kick-off in Middlesbrough. It seems like an incredible development today, but there was more than a hint of Liverpool demob rebellion in the Teesside air. The players probably also wanted to prove that the mighty Liverpool could beat most First Division fodder, even with a pissed-up team. Some of the Liverpool players were also annoyed that there had been no formal celebrations organised by the club to celebrate the championship win. Why not have one now? They also knew that this would be the last time all the Liverpool players would be together before the World Cup finals took hold in the summer.

Whatever the reason, a few welcome lunchtime pints of lager were downed by the Liverpool squad. It was as if some of the greatest football players in Europe were preparing for nothing more than a Sunday League afternoon hack-around. Roy Evans and Ronnie Moran knew nothing about this illicit outing, as all the Liverpool players were back in their hotel rooms, sleeping it off, in time for the early evening checks. But the Liverpool coaches must have smelt the booze later: certainly, some of the Middlesbrough players did, as the two teams fought out a less than competitive 0–0 draw in front of 17,000 fans. It was, to say the least, an unusual way to end what had already been a strange Liverpool campaign.

GOODBYE MR PAISLEY

Bob Paisley had already decided, after the ups and downs of the season, that 44 years' service at Anfield would be quite enough, thank you. He announced at a football writers' dinner in Durham that he was stepping down at the end of the following season. Liverpool made it clear that 62-year-old Joe Fagan would take over from Bob, much to the Liverpool dressing-room's relief and delight. No one wanted an 'outsider', possibly a disciplinarian manager, to take charge. Why spoil all this? The players all knew and trusted Joe, who would be happy to let things operate just like before. For Bob's last throw, with Ray Kennedy already gone to Swansea City and David Johnson and Terry McDermott both departing from Liverpool with thanks on £100,000 transfers, Middlesbrough's David Hodgson came in for a hefty £450,000 as a replacement. The striker was Paisley's last major signing – if not his best. Steve Nicol had also joined Liverpool from Ayr United back in October 1981 and had been learning his trade in the Central League side. But he was now ready to fill in when needed, another talented player – and something of an entertaining dressing-room space cadet – who could cover a number of defensive and midfield positions. David Fairclough was also back from injury, though he had few illusions about convincing Bob now that he was worth his place.

Alan Hansen missed the first seven League matches of the 1982–83 season with injury, so Hodgson began up front, partnering Rush, with Kenny Dalglish moving back into midfield and Lawrenson playing at the back. Dalglish's vision and Rush's pace and finishing were now starting to impress everyone at Liverpool. Alan Hansen rates the 1978–79 Liverpool team as the best he ever played in at Anfield, but add Ian Rush to it, he argues, and it becomes unbeatable. Things started well for Liverpool, seven games unbeaten in the League and the dangerous Ipswich Town already dumped out of the League Cup. It was looking good for Bob's last stand. Alan Kennedy also felt much more secure now. The experiment of playing Lawrenson at full-back seemed to have passed. If anything, Phil Thompson's position appeared most at risk, though Bob was also happy to use Lawrenson to strengthen the Liverpool midfield whenever he felt it was needed. Also, the promise of having Joe Fagan in charge was a big plus for the future: Joe rated Alan's game, which meant that the new boss – not the same as the old boss – was unlikely to be looking to bring in a new left-back: 'It wasn't obvious that Bob was thinking about leaving but I remember we wanted to give him a good send-off. We felt that nothing was going to change when Bob left. We knew that Bob was the main man but we also thought that Joe could do the job. Joe was always in the middle between the players and the manager, so he was the obvious choice. I was pleased it was Joe, because he understood my game. Joe's only problem seemed to be speaking to the press, but no one in the club enjoyed that side of it, because it was seen as an infringement on the football side of things. By the time Bob was finishing the team was really running itself anyway. Later, I suppose David Hodgson didn't feel he was part of things and Joe had to talk to him to get him to go out for a drink with some of the lads. He started to fit in a little more after that.'

Four Liverpool players, including Alan, started every major

Liverpool match in 1982–83, 59 games in all. Dalglish, Neal and Grobbelaar were the others. Alan felt his injury problems were over, he felt strong and more confident in his game, and his new left-side partnership with Ronnie Whelan was also working out well. Bob had also opted, occasionally, for a new midfield chemistry, with Kenny Dalglish playing a more withdrawn role to accommodate new signing Hodgson. This gave Liverpool a little more flexibility in the middle of the park. Hodgson could sometimes play deeper too – and Dalglish continued to score goals, even when played in this deeper position – 18 goals in 42 League games. The big problem was Hodgson, who would go on to score only four goals in 20 League starts. He was a willing worker, certainly, but he still looked cumbersome and was finding it difficult to fit in at Anfield. Was he the right stuff for Liverpool?

In Europe, Irish champions Dundalk were despatched before, against tiny HJK Helsinki, Liverpool lost a near comic away leg 0–1. Normal service was resumed at Anfield, however, with the Finlanders hammered 5–0, Alan Kennedy getting two goals in the match, a strike from distance after a forceful run and a crisp penalty area volley. The draw for the quarter-finals in March offered Liverpool another daunting Eastern European challenge, this time from little known Widzew Lodz from Poland. To the untutored eye of the Merseyside visitors, life in Poland still looked unremittingly grim, the mustachioed locals in Lodz huddling together in uniform grey against the snow and the mining slagheaps, causing Kennedy to reflect on just how privileged the lifestyle of English footballers was by comparison. Alan and his teammates had other reasons to feel thankful: the flight to Poland on British Airways had been forced to land in bad weather and had ended up overshooting the runway, necessitating a second approach. By this time the Liverpool flight card school had been suspended until further notice – 'I'd had a really good hand, too,' moaned Alan – and nervous flyer Kennedy was trying hard to climb underneath his aircraft seat. The soothing words and apologies of the pilot were no consolation. It had been a close call – '50 feet from death,' Frank McGee wrote, dramatically, in the *Daily Mirror* the following day.

This testing experience might well have coloured a lifeless Liverpool display the following day. In fact, Bruce Grobbelaar was again at fault, dropping a deep cross from Surlit just after half-time for Tiokinski to tap home. 'Nice catch, Brucie,' mumbled a mordant Alan Hansen. 'Better luck next time.' A goal in football, especially a clown's concession such as this one, is sometimes worth much more than just a goal. Conceding in a place like Lodz suddenly makes you see much more clearly how hostile and difficult life is there. Now the home crowd roused itself and the pressure started to build on Liverpool, though Alan brought a great save out of Mlynarczyk with a 30-yard bomb and, for a time, the visitors even took charge. Joe and Bob knew, of course, that, in Europe, a 0–1 away result is acceptable, retrievable, but 0–2 is almost impossible to claw back against a decent side. So when Wraga scored for Lodz with a spectacular diving header with just ten minutes left, and Liverpool were unable to reply, it already seemed like curtains. 'We knew we were struggling,' admitted Alan. 'You always say to the press after the game: "Of course we can get those goals back at Anfield," but 2–0 means that if you concede at home, effectively you're gone. We weren't confident. Bob was down but, to be honest, we were just glad to get home.'

A stomach bug for Kenny Dalglish meant a chance for David Hodgson in the second leg and an early Liverpool penalty, scored by Phil Neal, even got the home crowd thinking that this might still be possible. But Graeme Souness, of all people, dithered on the ball on the edge of his own box just after the half hour and was robbed by Smolarek, who was then brought down by a panicky Grobbelaar. Tiokinski scored, leaving Liverpool faced with the prospects of scoring four goals, without reply, to qualify. No chance. In fact, after the excellent Smolarek had put Lodz ahead in the second half, only late goals from Rush and Hodgson rescued the match for Liverpool – but not the tie. It was a bitter blow: Bob's last season and out, once again, at the quarter-final stage to Eastern Europeans, with no English team left to continue the run of successive European Cup victories that Liverpool had begun in 1977. Europe had, suddenly, felt much harder to win over.

In fact, this was the second cup competition in a month from which Liverpool had departed early. By the '90s, Sunday play was just another part of the satellite TV football revolution, but when Liverpool met unfancied Brighton at Anfield on 20 February 1983 in the fifth round of the FA Cup, it was the first time in the Merseyside's club's entire history that they had played on a Sunday. It proved a disastrous debut, manager Jimmy Melia and returning player Jimmy Case masterminding a shock 1–2 televised victory for the visitors. Phil Neal even missed a penalty for Liverpool. Bob Paisley would now never win the FA Cup for the club as either a player or a manager, and gone was Liverpool's 63-game unbeaten run at home in all cup competitions that stretched back over eight years. A bad day at the office, but Bob simply shrugged it off: after all, everybody knew the League Cup was really his favourite domestic cup competition.

BOB'S BIG DAY OUT

Liverpool's path to Wembley for the third successive season in the League Cup was smoothed by a series of home draws after the tricky two-legged opener with Ipswich Town. Burnley were eventually overcome in a difficult semi-final, which meant a meeting with Ron Atkinson's Manchester United at Wembley, and a chance for revenge for the FA Cup defeat by United in 1977, Bob's only Wembley reverse as a manager. Phil Thompson missed out in the final, Paisley fielding his new Liverpool 'A' team, with Craig Johnston preferred to Hodgson. Again Liverpool fell behind in the first half but rallied later, grinding United down. Alan had been prominent against Steve Coppell on the Liverpool left and with 12 minutes remaining he moved forward, once again, to pick up a pass from Sammy Lee. As United retreated Alan struck a low shot through a group of players and across Gary Bailey into his bottom left-hand corner. Another vital full-back's goal at Wembley for Liverpool. In extra time, Liverpool poured forward, Dalglish having a shot blocked on the edge of the United area. The ball broke to Ronnie Whelan, with Alan, still full of running, steaming up in support. Ronnie's first attempt at a left-footed pass to Alan was blocked by Stapleton. His second, a right-footed shot, curved beyond the United man and the unsighted Bailey into the United net. There was no way back; Liverpool were simply too strong and too sure of themselves in another Wembley final. At the whistle, Bob Paisley tried to sneak off in his flat cap to the changing-rooms for interviews and a celebratory drink with his staff. But Souness and the senior Liverpool players had decided that Bob himself should go up first to receive the cup. How else could one properly mark the passing of a man who had offered 44 years' service and won, as a manager, three European Cups, six League titles and three League Cups in just nine years for Liverpool? With a paltry OBE? Where was Bob Paisley's knighthood? It was an easy question to answer, of course. Bob was, simply, in the wrong sport, from the wrong city, and working in football at the wrong time.

Bob refused the gesture at first – 'Football is all about players' – but he could see that his squad were set on this special goodbye. They were not to be turned down. So, almost 33 years after Bob Paisley had been denied his chance at the 39 Wembley steps as a Liverpool player, the greatest-ever English manager strode up to receive the Milk Cup for Liverpool Football Club on his final Wembley occasion. A fan threw a Liverpool scarf at the grey-suited Paisley as he climbed to the Royal Box, and the scarf draped over one shoulder, like a jaunty Highlander's cape. Bob looked as if he was in a daze. Followed closely by his captain, and with his hair scraped up into little peaks, the man from little Hetton claimed the cup for his players, his staff and for Liverpool supporters everywhere. It was an unforgettable moment and the last time Liverpool managed to get the better of United in a major final until Michael Owen and Steven Gerrard sank Ferguson's men in the same League Cup final, some 20 years later, in Cardiff. It was too long a wait.

In the League in 1982–83, the opposition to Liverpool had been weak all season, with little Watford, under Graham Taylor, trying hard to hang on to Liverpool's coat tails. It was a hopeless task. The highlights were clear and occasionally historic. At Goodison Park in November, following the sending off of Everton debutant Glen Keeley under the League's new disciplinary code, Liverpool ran riot, Ian Rush becoming the first player to score four goals in a Derby game in a 5–0 drubbing. The exposed Keeley never played for Everton again. Southampton, Manchester City, Notts County and Stoke City were all hit for five in the League by Liverpool: poor, benighted Manchester City conceded nine goals in their two Liverpool fixtures. The title 'race' was over effectively by the middle of April, with Rush and Dalglish ending up with 42 League goals between them and Alan Kennedy claiming three goals, all away from home, and all in Liverpool victories. His goals signalled that this was, above all, an attacking Liverpool side and one that might, playing at full throttle to the end, even have threatened the magical 100 goals League scoring target. Except that, astonishingly, some weeks before the season's end Liverpool's players just downed tools. Maybe it was tiredness or a simple loss of competitive edge. Maybe winning titles and setting new standards was becoming a little dull to Hansen and Neal, Souness, Kennedy and Thompson. This seems unlikely. 'We just couldn't get up for matches,' says Alan Kennedy. But, just as they had done at Middlesbrough the previous season, the Liverpool players gave up on the job of going all out to win football matches once the title was secured. The last seven Liverpool League fixtures read: W0 L5 D2 F4 A11. Only two other League matches had been lost by Liverpool all season. This was relegation form and the sequence was compared later to Gérard Houllier's disastrous winless run with Liverpool in season

2002–03. Except, of course, that Houllier's Liverpool had not already sewn up the League title and were not struggling to stay awake or to keep the rest of the League opposition in sight.

In some ways, this winless run was a slightly sad end to Paisley's managerial career at Anfield, but it was also testament to just how dominant his Liverpool side had become. Bob was leaving the club in fine fettle, a slew of new young talented players recently recruited to supplement an experienced core of the highest quality. With the unlucky David Fairclough finally moving on, only David Hodgson seemed out of place and unhappy at Anfield. Joe Fagan would need to find some forward and midfield cover, but the necessary surgery was slight. The club had qualified, once more, for the European Cup, the Holy Grail, and Joe's team would certainly be competitive in that competition right from the start – if they could only avoid an early banana-skin way out east. Liverpool would also be clear favourites to win the League title again, though neighbours Everton would soon prove themselves, under Howard Kendall, to be dangerously on the rise once more. Moreover, another Liverpool championship would match Arsenal's record of three consecutive League titles that had stood since the 1930s. It was just another target, but something that Ronnie Moran and Joe could at least flag up to the Liverpool players when pre-season came around once more. They need have no fears: Liverpool under Joe Fagan would display no obvious lack of appetite for winning football matches – or football trophies.

Chapter 9

JOE FAGAN'S WAY

AND HERE'S TO YOU, MICHAEL ROBINSON

Joe Fagan had seen, from the inside, Bob Paisley prosper as Liverpool manager even following the mercurial Bill Shankly, so the top job at Anfield now held few fears for him, especially with key senior players still in place at Liverpool and with Moran and Roy Evans still solid in the Liverpool backroom. The Liverpool board wanted Joe for the job for reasons of continuity and to stabilise the Liverpool players. Why shake up, any more than was absolutely necessary, something that seemed to be working and could be expected to do so for the foreseeable future? In retrospect it was a short-sighted policy, but Joe was almost certainly told by the Liverpool board that his services as manager would be needed only in the short term. Phil Neal, Souness and Kenny Dalglish were all potential Liverpool managers or player–managers for the future who understood the Liverpool Way, so Joe was trusted to direct the Anfield ship through any immediate choppy waters created in the wake of Bob's departure.

Crucially, the influential Liverpool captain, Graeme Souness, was right behind Fagan and immediately called the senior players together to point out that he was determined to try to win the very top prizes – another title and the European Cup – for Joe. Souness, of course, was already secretly anticipating his own likely departure from Liverpool for a spell in Italy at the end of the season. He wanted to leave the club on a personal high and with his own and Joe Fagan's reputations both intact and enhanced. He liked and respected Joe, and like many people inside the club thought that Fagan's role was undervalued by the wider football community.

Kenny Dalglish also thought that Joe was the perfect choice to pick up the reins from Bob: 'He has a lovely way about him and is a very charming man. In football matters he is shrewd but his strongest asset is the way he can handle people. He rarely loses his head and can make a point usually without raising his voice. He and Bob had been so close for so many years that we hardly noticed the difference. We were using the same hotels, the same training methods and things ticked along very much the same. Joe's approach is similar and, if anything, he made the game even simpler than Bob.'

As Kenny pointed out, with Joe Fagan in charge no one at Liverpool expected anything to change: set up for the season, League title, the bread and butter; get the early European Cup games sorted and then wait until March when the serious European competition kicked in; pick up the League Cup, four on the trot; try to beat the Paisley FA Cup jinx. What could be simpler? However, Joe wanted his own stamp on the Liverpool squad and to continue the Anfield tradition of buying quality players from a position of strength. He may also have wanted a slightly more attacking policy than the more cautious Bob Paisley, because when Ronnie Whelan developed hernia trouble before the 1983–84 season started, Joe decided to shop in the store marked 'forwards' rather than search around right away for a replacement midfielder. Ironically, Liverpool had only recently sold probably the most talented left-sided midfielder in the country to Everton, of all clubs. 'We all thought Kevin Sheedy had a back problem,' says Alan Kennedy. 'He couldn't play 20 games a season.' Sheedy would remind Liverpool of their misjudgement. Not that the club were short of midfield talent: Steve Nicol, the kind of play-anywhere man of the sort championed by Bob, was ready to burst into the Liverpool first team at any time now. Joe was covered.

Joe was searching for a new forward, partly, of course, because David Hodgson was still under-performing. The Liverpool players first heard about the signing of Michael Robinson from Brighton while on a pre-season tour of Holland. Robinson had been championed by Malcolm Allison early on in his career, but he looked like a stock workhorse. Alan Kennedy remembers that not all the Liverpool players fancied the new man: a powerful forward, and one who had played well against Liverpool in the past, but he was not out of the very top bracket. The club's centre-backs, top assessors, rated him only average. Joe Fagan's big football test, of course, was not whether he could handle the Anfield players: everyone knew the answer to that question. It was more whether he could judge his major signings as astutely as Bob Paisley had generally done. Here was his first big test. With Phil Thompson now out of the first-team picture, Joe's plan was to move Lawrenson to centre-back and place Dalglish behind a front two of Robinson and Rush, with Craig Johnston – or Steve Nicol – on the left of midfield and Sammy Lee on the right. This brought the two main Liverpool strategists, Souness and Dalglish, closer together in the centre of the action, where they could plot the downfall of opposing defences. This was the theory. But the ultimate success of this plan probably hinged on Robinson getting his full quota of goals and/or Kenny keeping his own scoring record intact from the previous season. In fact, neither of these things happened. In an injury-hit campaign, Kenny scored only 7 League goals (from 33 starts) and Robinson weighed in with only 6 (from 23). Joe's first big dip into the transfer market seemed to register only a 'must try harder' rating.

Rather than Robinson's arrival or Dalglish's goals, there were two other defining stories from this first Joe Fagan season in charge: the first was about the Liverpool defence. Having one top defender as a reliable ever-present in the biff-bang that was the English First Division is a good effort, a reward for any manager. But in 1983–84 the Liverpool back four and goalkeeper missed only one League match *between* all five players. This meant amazingly consistent form and that the vulnerable, like Hansen and Alan Kennedy, were injury-free for once, hamstrings and knees in fully working order. It also meant that this Liverpool defence generally operated on automatic pilot, like a slick unit – despite a few notable lapses. It could not match the 1978–79 Paisley defence, of course, mainly because Joe Fagan's defensive midfield shield in front was more porous and his goalkeeper much less secure. But no Liverpool side since the Second World War – and quite possibly no modern First Division club ever – could match this collective consistency and this appearance record: 210 possible shows and 209 actual starts. It is an astonishing achievement in modern sport, one built on a refusal by the Liverpool players and the staff to bow to minor injuries and on an approach to defending that was about intervention and reading the play rather than full-on, last-ditch tackling. So who was the missing man, the horrible single absence that spoilt this otherwise perfect defensive record? This is going to kill you, because the never-absent Phil Neal got injured at Manchester United at the end of September and was missing his first

League game in nine seasons, at home against Sunderland, as a result. Who could blame the rest of Fagan's ever-present defence that season for cruelly labelling the indestructible Neal – 'crock'?

The second defining story from Joe's first season in charge was the incredible scoring feats of Ian Rush: 32 goals in 41 League games and 48 goals for Liverpool in all major competitions. Rush even scored 14 *headed* goals, a supposed weakness in his make-up. Rush was now entirely comfortable in the Liverpool set-up, his coltish early anxieties well behind him and he liked Joe and wanted to do well for him. Rush also certainly benefited from Dalglish's more withdrawn role, the Scot's pinpoint longer passing and the Welshman's speed and clinical finishing on both sides taking him beyond and through defences and into the Liverpool scoring records. His shots on target ratio must have been astonishing, in an era before daft records like these were ever kept or even imagined. Once Rush was beyond the final defender, with ball at feet, the Liverpool players felt the game was up for the opposition. No one expected him to miss: he was icy in front of goal. Having this sort of assurance up front was a huge lift to any team – and a massive blow to the opposition. Routinely, under Bob, Liverpool had had many of the League's best defenders and midfielders and, in Kenny Dalglish, certainly the best all-round British forward. Joe Fagan's reward for all his back-of-the-house duties at Anfield was now to be blessed, as Liverpool manager, with the fruits of Bob Paisley's work in recruiting the man who was the League's best striker. Ian Rush seemed unstoppable.

With new man Robinson in the side, Liverpool began the new season steadily, with four wins and two draws in the first six games. But Liverpool's first loss of the season, at rejuvenated Manchester United, seemed potentially crucial. Alan was culpable, caught out of position on the halfway line on the Liverpool left, a mistake which allowed Arthur Graham to escape Alan Hansen and drift wide before the Scottish winger cut back a low cross for Frank Stapleton to drive home. With Phil Neal missing, replaced by Steve Nicol, a shock 0–1 Liverpool defeat followed, at home to Sunderland. Joe's new plans, seemingly, were going off the rails, as Liverpool faced a tough visit to top of the table West Ham on 15 October. Craig Johnston's sending off did little to slow Robinson – or Liverpool – down, the new man claiming a hat-trick. Maybe this was an inspired new Fagan signing after all? When Bruce Grobbelaar allowed in a Devonshire consolation late on, Alan Kennedy gave the keeper a fierce verbal hammering. He was a frustrating man, Brucie, mixing up incredible stops with these sorts of stupid, stupid mistakes.

NICOL AND RUSH

October and November 1983 was all about Rush and Steve Nicol, who had replaced the injured Craig Johnston and now played in front of Alan Kennedy on Liverpool's left flank. Nicol, signed from Ayr United, actually began life in Scotland as a centre-back. He was a delight, a man who had 'sunny, small-town Scot' written all over him, much to the Liverpool Jocks' obvious dismay. He, naturally, became the butt of Liverpool dressing-room banter, a bit of a relief for Alan Kennedy and others. But on the field he was a revelation, showing pace and real invention in scoring a late winner for Liverpool at Queens Park Rangers in October. Ian Rush then took over, netting five against a hapless Luton Town at Anfield, 30 years on from when John Evans had last done the same for Liverpool against Bristol Rovers in the Second Division. In the derby game at Anfield in November the youngster Nicol starred, laying on a goal for Rush, who did the same for Michael Robinson, before Nicol scored himself with a late header from a Mark Lawrenson cross for a 3–0 Reds' rout. A centre-back, playing right winger in the dying minutes of a derby game that was already won? Fagan's team was certainly not dull. Not with Dalglish around: the Scot scored his 100th Liverpool goal, with an outrageous left-footed shot at Ipswich Town in a 1–1 draw.

In Europe it was a struggle, though Danish side BK Odense offered lightweight resistance only in the opening encounter, Kenny Dalglish scoring three times in the 6–1 aggregate Liverpool win to pass Denis Law's British scoring record of 14 goals in the European Cup. A pitiful crowd of 15,000 attended the second leg at Anfield: 'The ground was dead,' says Alan. 'Half the crowd were from our families on free tickets.' Liverpool seldom seemed to draw Italian or Spanish clubs in the early stages in Europe, partly because of seeding, but here was a new name, Athletic Bilbao, and a welcome break from the usual slog to Eastern Europe. Not that this was a plum tie: Bilbao's anglophile coach, Javier Clemente, had studied the English game and had set his team out to frustrate Liverpool, led by Andoni Goicoechea, the colourfully named 'Butcher of Bilbao'. Rush and Robinson were shackled in a 0–0 deadlock. 'They were a good team,' remembers Kennedy. 'They played good football, and as soon as we got off the pitch Joe said right away: "I'm happy with that. Well done." He knew we'd played a decent side, and conceding no goals at home was vital.' The second leg saw Liverpool at their defensive best in Europe, solid at the back and with Souness in imperious form in midfield. As Alan Kennedy remembers: 'Souness really intimidated their midfielders. It was cat and mouse early on – but we were definitely the cat.' With time running out, Alan Kennedy, himself, managed to get free down the left only to pull the ball back onto his right foot for a cross: 'Ian Rush, the cheeky bastard, told me later that he thought there was no chance of me crossing it with my right foot.' Rush headed home Kennedy's teasing centre – and Liverpool were through a difficult test.

Liverpool also seemed to be back on track and cruising to another halfway lead in the title race: cruising, that is, until Bruce Grobbelaar struck once more. Grobbelaar certainly entertained TV commentators and away football crowds – if not always the Liverpool defence – with his quirky dribbles and unpredictable headers outside the box and his acrobatic antics inside. Coventry City's Highfield Road had hardly been a favourite hunting ground for Liverpool under Paisley, but under Fagan and Brucie things suddenly got much, much worse. Alan knew a bad day was in store: he wore red leather trousers to the game, a wild affront to the Liverpool dressing-room fashion police. It took exactly 40 seconds for the Liverpool goalkeeper to shovel the ball out for Nicky Platnauer to score for City. With a new left-back, Stuart Pearce, growling at Rush, and the elusive Dave Bennett totally messing up Hansen and Kennedy on Liverpool's left, little Terry Gibson soon scored – and then scored again – as Grobbelaar fumbled away the visitors' chances. Being 0–3 down at half-time, Liverpool returned to the dressing-room to find Joe in uncharacteristic crockery-smashing mood, to Alan Kennedy's surprise: 'He went absolutely berserk at half-time, at everybody. We just couldn't get near Gibson and when Joe started to throw the cups around, I started chucking them too! Then Souey and Ronnie Moran started barking in and Roy Evans had to come in from outside to calm it all down. It got out of hand quite badly. Joe was blaming everybody. And we didn't even win the second half. It hurt us badly – it was shocking.'

Three-nil down became four, as Gibson grabbed his hat-trick after the interval – 0–4 at Coventry City: it was chaos, sheer chaos at the back for Liverpool. Poor Notts County didn't want to be the next visitors to Anfield: they knew what was coming, a 5–0 redemptive thrashing. Not that this convinced too many Liverpool supporters: only just over 22,400 fans turned up to see the rout. It felt like returning to football in the Second Division in the late 1950s. By the time Liverpool next lost in the League, a surprise 0–1 defeat at

Wolves, they had played 23 League matches and were top, just ahead of Manchester United and West Ham. But by this stage, too, Kenny Dalglish had been seriously injured, a nasty depressed cheekbone fracture picked up against Manchester United. There would still be some toil to do before Joe Fagan could claim his first title as a manager – and before Liverpool could match Herbert Chapman's Arsenal record from the 1930s of three League championships in a row.

MAINE MEN

The League Cup, Liverpool's exclusive property it seemed in recent years under Bob Paisley, was proving harder work for Fagan. After an 8–1 aggregate hammering of Brentford, it took three games and two portions of extra time for Liverpool to dispense with Second Division Fulham, Graeme Souness finally closing the tie at Craven Cottage by the narrowest of margins. Away draws at both Birmingham City and Sheffield Wednesday were then followed, in turn, by resounding 3–0 Liverpool victories in the home replays, Ian Rush liberally on the score sheets in both encounters. Little Third Division Walsall in the semi-final looked a Liverpool banker, but only two goals from the returned Ronnie Whelan saved the home blushes in the first leg at Anfield, where a lazy Liverpool were outplayed in a 2–2 draw. Alan Kennedy had a nightmare at left-back up against a rapid, if uncomplicated, winger called Mark Rees: 'This guy was really fast and he ran the backside out of me. I was so bad, he put the ball 30 yards past me and by the time I'd turned to get after it he was ten yards clear. I could just see his backside and I thought: "Oh, God, please don't cross it." Fortunately it went behind, or it would have been a certain goal for them.' Rush and Whelan, again, finally restored some order at the dilapidated Fellows Park, where a collapsed wall halted the match as injured fans were decamped onto the pitch. A revived Everton awaited Liverpool in the final, a delicious Merseyside prospect. Sadly, though, Joe Fagan had no better luck in the FA Cup than Bob Paisley had before him. Second Division leaders Newcastle United, including Keegan, Beardsley, Waddle and Terry McDermott, were dumped 4–0 at Anfield in the third round, but the previous season's bogey team and finalists, relegated Brighton, did for Liverpool again on a poor pitch and a windy afternoon at the Goldstone Ground in the fourth round, a conclusive 0–2 defeat. Maybe Liverpool's League Cup successes were rendering the FA Cup somehow less important at Anfield? Whatever the reason, it was back to the domestic knockout drawing board for Joe and the Liverpool staff.

The historic League Cup final against Everton, the first Merseyside Wembley final, was a major social event for the city – and a vital one to win for both clubs. It flagged up both Everton's rapidly rising potential under Howard Kendall and Liverpool's gritty resilience and spirit, even when struggling for their best form. Many of the players from the two clubs knew each other, of course, from international matches, social events and the fact that Everton's Alan Harper and Kevin Sheedy had both recently been in the Liverpool camp. Not that this eased the competitive edge between the clubs at all: it simply added to it. Kendall, after coming very close to getting the sack, was now suddenly developing an effective and talented side at Goodison, one with both width and plenty of bite. The likely Wembley match-ups were intriguing: Alan Kennedy up against Trevor Steven; Phil Neal against Harper; Heath and Sharpe up front against Hansen and Lawrenson; Souness against Peter Reid; Ian Rush against his Wales captain Kevin Ratcliffe. The Liverpool players and staff knew they faced a dogfight against a quality Everton team desperate to unseat their local rivals. It promised to be a typical 100-mile-an-hour derby blast, with lots of 'dig', in front of a passionate Merseyside crowd. Winner takes all.

In fact, the Wembley setting defused much of the tribal temptation to mix it, in a timid, disappointing match played out in a raucous atmosphere. Evertonians left London convinced that Alan Hansen had handled in the penalty area, so robbing the Blue half of Merseyside. Liverpudlians argued that Alan Kennedy had scored a late goal, wrongly disallowed for offside. It was honour dissatisfied, and if no one exactly came home from Brent contented, then no one left with their dreams dashed either.

The replay, at Manchester City's Maine Road, was much more the red-raw northern encounter for local bragging rights that many supporters – and players – had expected. A Souness goal won a fierce encounter for Liverpool, but it was a very close call, as Alan Kennedy remembers: 'The replay was really tough, played on a dismal night at Maine Road. It was made for their style and they made much better chances than us. Sharpey had one at the far post, over my head, but he headed it wide. Andy Gray had a couple, as well, and he was obviously told to really get at Alan Hansen: whack him; he doesn't like it in the air; flying elbows, the lot. We coped with it and, surprisingly, we took the lead, a great turn and shot by Graeme Souness: it lit the match up. That seemed to knock the stuffing out of them for a while. At half-time you could feel that Kendall must have said to them: "Listen, don't let these bastards have a go at you. C'mon, get out there and really start battling." It was alehouse stuff after that, from our point of view. We didn't play any football whatsoever and Rushie, who was up front on his own, got absolutely no service. Kenny was pushed right back and we were under the cosh. Bruce was outstanding. Even in the final minute they had a great chance to equalise, and you could see that they were really gutted that they'd got beat. We probably didn't deserve to win it, really, because we all said later: "Bloody hell, we were lucky there." We were happy with the result, but not the performance and we came back to Liverpool for a meal in a restaurant afterwards and a few beers. You could go out later if you wanted to, but we knew we'd get trouble if we went into town. Great if you met the Reds, like, but not so good if you ran into Blues.'

This clash illustrates well the great conundrum facing top English clubs at this time. Joe Fagan and his backroom staff needed to build a Liverpool side capable of manning the trenches for the most intense physical battles the English game had to offer, but at the same time produce players with the technique, decision-making capabilities and finesse needed for the sort of cerebral football which was likely to be required at the highest levels of the European game. In this one month, March 1984, Liverpool faced: three important meetings with a very physical but clever Everton team, including one away League match in which Alan Harper equalised for Everton, while suspiciously unmarked on Alan Kennedy's watch; two meetings with a subtle Benfica side, Portugal's champions, in the European Cup; two high-tempo League matches against Tottenham at home and Watford away; and a League trip to Southampton, where the home side bombed Liverpool with high balls for a 0–2 result. Eight games in twenty-nine days, only two played at home, and many different styles to face: four won, three drawn and only one lost. This was a 'normal' Liverpool programme at the time. One-dimensional, faint-hearted footballers need not apply.

Benfica were a good test in the European Cup quarter-finals and provided another opportunity for Alan Kennedy to lay on a headed goal for Rush, a terrific cross that bemused the international goalkeeper, Bento. Liverpool took only a 1–0 lead to Portugal, a stick or twist scenario, and one that was common in the season. Alan Hansen remarks that Liverpool 'had it all to do away from home' throughout the 1984 European Cup run. But when Ronnie Whelan scored after only nine minutes in Lisbon, the goal severely damaged Benfica and paved the way for an outstanding Liverpool performance. Craig Johnston scored the second after half an hour.

Benfica had simply not worked Liverpool out: 'They didn't press us at all and they couldn't seem to work out how we were playing. Nobody could pick Kenny up and Ronnie Whelan kept getting forward into the box every time Rushie took his defenders wide. Everything we tried came off: they just couldn't work it out. It was so easy in the end, an absolute doddle. They were so open we couldn't believe it. They did get a consolation goal in the second half, from Nene, when he looped one over Grobbelaar, but they were never going to get any more than that. Rushie and Ronnie Whelan got a couple of late goals for us for 4–1, but the tie was well over by then. A fantastic performance.'

Dinamo Bucharest now lay ahead and eventually Roma in Rome. Alan Kennedy had had a real influence throughout the Liverpool European run, probably his best sequence in Europe, but little did he know what still lay ahead. With Bucharest dismissed by Liverpool over two stormy legs, there were now two weeks to burn, after League matches were completed, before the European Cup final.

A Liverpool 'friend' in Israel, the infamous agent Pini Zahavi, set up a 'relaxing' club visit to Tel Aviv. The Anfield staff allowed the players to mix light training with some R&R and a bit of boozing before working back up to full fitness for the final. The players arranged to meet the British press on the beach for a morning conference carrying a large bin, full to the brim with iced orange juice, Coke and water. When the press left, the soft drinks also disappeared, revealing cans of ale at the bottom of the bin. After a skinful, a few of the Liverpool players, including Alan, went to the main square, which was now full of tourists, Liverpool fans and military personnel. The players began playing Buzz, a drinking game, but David Hodgson was too far gone by this stage, and ended up pissing under the table over other players' legs. In the confusion that followed Alan stepped in to try to prevent a fight between Hodgson, Rush and reserve centre-back John McGregor – and caught a haymaker from McGregor flush in the eye. Returning to the hotel, and with Alan by now feeling groggy, the players bumped into venerable Liverpool director Sid Moss, who had been told that there was fighting in the square: 'Lock them up, lock them up!' shouted Moss, believing it was fans who were involved. 'But it's the players, Mr Moss,' came the reply. Joe Fagan called the 'guilty' men in the next morning. His European Cup warriors looked a dishevelled bunch. 'Just keep it quiet,' said Joe. 'Have a drink out of town, away from the media.' The players found a Scottish bar out of the main area, a perfect haunt – nobody remembers paying for drinks.

In the League, meanwhile, Joe Fagan had chosen to steady the Liverpool ship by bringing in John Wark, a classy Terry McDermott-style midfield passer and scorer from Ipswich Town, who immediately replaced Craig Johnston. Wark could play no role in Europe this season, and with him in the League team Liverpool rather limped home to the title. Two wins and five draws in the last seven League games, including the vital point at Notts County in a 0–0 draw on a blustery day and on a dry pitch, clinched Joe Fagan his first League title. Joe beamed in the TV interviews that followed, two trophies already in hand and the European Cup final still to play. 'What about Liverpool's first Treble, Joe?' asked an agreeable John Motson. 'No comment,' answered Joe playfully, flashing a warm grin. It had been an outstanding season for Fagan and his players and an extraordinary one for Alan Kennedy. But they would need all of these good memories – and more – to face the trials that lay ahead for the Liverpool club in Europe.

Chapter 10

HEYSEL AND OUT

ALAN AND JANE

After all the excitement and public attention connected with Rome 1984 had died down a little, Alan Kennedy began to look at his football and personal life rather more critically. He was approaching 30 years of age, the age of reason for most professional players of his generation. At 29 an outfield footballer is seen to be mature and at his peak, but at 30 he is rapidly supposed to be moving into the veteran class, looking for another life. At least that is how it can feel, and players' contracts can suggest the same thing. Kennedy had lived through one generation of Liverpool FC winners and drinkers and was now part of another younger school at the club, made up of Ian Rush, Ronnie Whelan, Bruce Grobbelaar and other players in the new Fagan team. At the same time he was becoming, along with Phil Neal and Dalglish, one of the elder statesmen at the club, and he had finally gained his two England caps in the spring of 1984 in the home internationals against Northern Ireland and Wales. It had been quite a year, and it was time to take stock and to try to think a little harder about what the future might hold.

Two major things had changed in his life. First, after his heroics in Rome, the Liverpool board offered him a new three-year deal as a reward for his service and recent performances for the club. He had been injury-free and ever present at Liverpool since January 1982, fighting off challenges to his position from home and abroad. He had delivered in the League and had more than showed up in the finals: he deserved a decent new deal. This sort of security at a club like Liverpool, making him contracted until he was over 32 years of age, seemed like an excellent opportunity, so he signed at £750 per week basic. He could rest easy for a while on the playing side – or so he thought. But he would need to start to think more about what to do when he stopped playing professionally. Injury or loss of form could move things on quickly at this stage of a player's career.

His personal life was also changing. He had first met Jane Garrett in January 1982 on something of a blind date after initially asking out Jane's older sister, Bobbie, whose house Alan was now using for digs. The occasion was a restaurant opening, in Warrington, the sort of event players and wives or girlfriends were often asked to help out with. Bobbie suggested her sister for the date. Alan had often seen Jane – and liked what he saw – in his minor celebrity round of knocking over piles of pennies for local pubs and especially on nights out in the Bottle and Glass pub in Rainford. Alan was shy and disorganised and typically left the telephone call to Jane until the last minute. He then asked Jane if she could drive them both over to the venue: his own new snazzy E-Type Jaguar was in bits. Jane agreed, but discovered when they arrived in Warrington that Alan knew neither the name nor the address of the restaurant. She would learn to live with this kind of chaos. They eventually found the place, and Alan lived to tell the tale.

The meal went well and after some playful messing around with the apple pie and cream desserts – Alan somehow found his face pushed into his dish – Jane drove Alan home and he made a very quick getaway: shyness again. The next morning he telephoned and the relationship began in earnest. Jane was no real football fan, and she certainly had no plans to become a footballer's wife: 'I thought you had to be blonde and glamorous. In that era everyone wore fur coats.' But she soon enjoyed the social side of Anfield life, meeting the players and their wives and girlfriends and travelling to the major matches. As Alan puts it: 'She soon got to know the way of Liverpool – out drinking every night of the week!' Jane worked as a nursery nurse in a local special school and Alan began to visit the kids at the school to talk football, as well as arranging for other Liverpool players to visit. When he won his £3,000 prize for being voted man of the match at the League Cup final in 1982 he donated the £1,000 charity segment of the award to the school.

Jane lived with her mother and stepfather in Eccleston near St Helens, so Alan next decided to buy a bungalow a few hundred yards from her home and eventually, late in 1983, Jane moved in. Alan finally had a real base in Liverpool, a retreat from the bookies and the snooker clubs: a home. About 18 months later, in February 1985 the local vicar, a regular visitor to the new Kennedy/Garrett home, airily suggested that the couple should now think seriously about getting married. As a joke, he suggested three possible dates: the couple chose one of them, 6 July 1985. Naturally, Keith Kennedy was Alan's best man. Naturally, he got very drunk for the occasion – and made a great speech.

EVERTON'S REVENGE

So as the new football season began, Alan was already settled in a stable relationship in a new shared home, with a lengthy and improved contract from Liverpool, and his full England debut behind him. He was now Liverpool's undisputed first-choice left full-back, with a long run of consecutive appearances, a man who had been through the European penalties fire – and had come out the other side as something of a national celebrity. Life was good and he was slowly taking ownership of his new responsibilities. Liverpool had recruited new young players, of course, including defenders Gary Gillespie and the young Irishman Jim Beglin, midfielder Jan Molby from Ajax and striker Paul Walsh, one of the few southern footballers signed by Liverpool during the entire Paisley/Fagan era. Molby, a brilliant passer of a football, though lacking the mobility of much inferior players, was bought by Joe to replace Graeme Souness, while Walsh had some of the attributes, at least, of an ageing Kenny Dalglish. But the inevitable decline of Dalglish and also Souness's departure to Sampdoria would effectively signal the beginning of the end of an era of Liverpool dominance that had brought five League titles, three European Cups and four League Cups to Anfield in just seven seasons – a run of success that was largely built around these two magnificent Scottish footballers. Whisper it: the new challenge to Liverpool in domestic football in England looked like it would come strongest from neighbours Everton.

Without Souness and with Rush injured, and now trying a much less abrasive and less mobile midfield quartet of Whelan, Lee, Molby and Wark, Liverpool made a slow start in the League. Goal scoring was a problem again, and from 8 September until 20 October, when Liverpool lost 0–1 at Anfield to title rivals Everton, Fagan's new side, now captained by Phil Neal, was winless in the League, losing four matches, drawing three and scoring only two goals. Joe's experiment of playing both Dalglish and Walsh was plainly not working. Once

Rush returned in late October Liverpool's form picked up, with nine matches producing only one League loss, away to bogey club Chelsea. But scoring away from home remained a problem all season – only 23 goals in 21 matches – while at home Liverpool mixed occasional ruthless efficiency against weaker opposition with a vulnerability to defeat on more difficult home days. John Wark scored more than his fair share – 18 goals in 40 League games – but Jan Molby could be quite brilliant one match and overrun the next. Five losses at home was the worst Liverpool record in this department for more than twenty years and Liverpool home attendances continued to show it, albeit in a period of national decline in football crowds. On 18 December 1984 only 27,237 watched Liverpool beat Coventry City, barely 60 per cent of stadium capacity. Fagan bought left-side Leicester City trundler Kevin MacDonald to try to lift Liverpool's season – if not their crowds – but eventual champions Everton went on to do the Double over Liverpool for the first time for two decades, which all added weight to the sense that another convulsive period of change was now likely at Anfield after the relative stability of the Shankly/Paisley/Fagan dynasty. But it also felt like English football itself, with its deep-seated problems of poor facilities and hooliganism, might now be in irretrievable decline.

A signifier of the game's problems in this respect was the visibly worsening relationship between the supporters of Liverpool and Manchester United. Liverpool fans felt United were fawned on by the press for not much achievement, whereas Liverpool's successes were underplayed in the media and regarded as functional, dull even. United fans had little in the way of sustained success to show since the late '60s and the domination of Liverpool, for the past decade, was particularly difficult for Manchester regulars to swallow. Add in some local tribal rivalry and problems of high unemployment and crime, and these meetings were becoming increasingly poisonous affairs: eventually Liverpool supporters even attacked a United team coach on the way to Anfield for a League match. Much worse, however, was now going on between the rival fans. By the time these clubs met in the FA Cup semi-finals in 1985 at Goodison Park and later in a replay at Maine Road, the atmosphere at these games was positively seething with hatred. Liverpool scraped an undeserved draw in the first match, a late Paul Walsh extra-time equaliser, but lost the replay. Fan disorder was now a major blight on the English game. The League Cup was not going to rescue Joe Fagan this time, a 0–1 away defeat to Tottenham Hotspur in the third round meaning that Liverpool would not now play in a major final at Wembley for the first time since 1981. Briefly, in fact, it was *Everton* that threatened a football Treble, deservedly winning the League title for the first time in 25 years, winning the club's first European trophy, the European Cup-winners' Cup against Rapid Vienna, and just missing out to Manchester United in the FA Cup final. Perhaps the balance of football power was finally shifting on Merseyside.

In Europe, if the Champion's Cup had produced a testing list of opponents for Liverpool in 1983–84, in 1984–85 the gods looked down more kindly on Fagan's spluttering team. In September and October the inexperienced Poles, Lech Poznan, were easily seen off, 5–0 on aggregate, John Wark scoring four. Next up Benfica tried again, in the pouring rain, at Anfield, but an Ian Rush hat-trick in a 3–1 win meant the 0–1 reply by the Portuguese in a difficult second leg, with Grobbelaar giving away a stupid early penalty and Kenny Dalglish being sent off, was simply not enough. Liverpool would play in Europe in March once more. There they met Austria Vienna, frankly poor European Cup quarter-finalists, who were overrun in the first hour in the return at Anfield for a 5–2 aggregate score after a comfortable 1–1 draw in Austria. This smooth Euro passage meant that Alan Kennedy was starting to dream of another European Cup winner's medal, especially when the semi-final draw paired Liverpool, not with the favourites Juventus, but with European outsiders, the Greek champions Panathinaikos. It was counting chickens. After three and a half years without serious injury, at Anfield in late March the bruising Manchester United forward Mark Hughes bundled into Alan, who fell awkwardly on his left leg. The immediate, extreme pain in the calf area told him right away that this was more than just a routine knock. It was, in fact, a stress fracture, five or six weeks out – and no European Cup semi-final. His absence gave Jim Beglin an opportunity to stake his claim for the Liverpool left-back slot, and the young Irishman started to do worryingly well.

Beglin played confidently against the Greeks at Anfield, who resisted bravely for 35 minutes, before conceding 3 goals in the next 15, 2 of them to Ian Rush. Beglin himself scored the fourth, with a header, showing Joe Fagan that he could also contribute with goals, an obvious Alan Kennedy strength. The return in Athens was a formality, Mark Lawrenson scoring the only goal on the hour. Jim Beglin was a strong tackler, good in the air and a man with an educated left foot: but he had no fierce pace and his passing could also weaken under pressure. Nevertheless, unless Alan could get fit quickly, the improving Beglin was now in pole position for a European Cup final place in Brussels on 29 May. Alan worked diligently at getting his leg right, and Joe desperately wanted him to be ready for the final. Perhaps they both tried too hard, or simply expected too much. Alan returned against Aston Villa at Anfield on 11 May. It was way too early for him: in the second half he couldn't even strike a stationary ball with his left foot, as the injured leg broke down once more. He had to face the truth: after two extraordinary personal tales of European Cup glory he would probably now have to sit out the 1985 final. He wished Beglin luck, without yet knowing, of course, that this game, Europe's blue riband football occasion, would turn out to be one that no player or fan would ever want to remember.

BRUSSELS

Alan actually made the Liverpool squad of 18 for Brussels but Joe knew that he was still carrying an injury. Alan hoped that Joe might think back to last year, or even to 1981, and pick him for his experience and for his record of coming up with big plays for Liverpool in major finals. Surely he was worth a place on the bench, even if he was only half fit? When Joe named the Liverpool substitutes on the evening of the match, European Cup final hero Alan Kennedy knew the worst: he was reduced to one of those players who was faced for the next few hours with hanging around the dressing-room and tunnel area in a suit, struggling with security men and toying with the pain of watching – or just waiting. He says now that the Liverpool players hated the Heysel Stadium from the moment they trained there the evening before the match. It looked antiquated and flimsy. 'The stadium looked horrible, tatty. The changing-rooms were terrible. The whole place felt like a very poor venue for a European Cup final, even though the pitch was half decent.' The Liverpool camp certainly rated Juventus, led by Boniek and Platini, more highly than the venue: Liverpool had played the Italian club in January 1985 in the Super Cup and had lost 0–2 on a frost-bound surface in Turin. These Italian boys, with their foreign stars, could play.

Alan understood Joe's decision to leave him out, but he still wandered morosely around the pitch before the match, he and substitute Craig Johnston kicking a football around with Liverpool fans, who were booting it from the terraces onto the pitch. He noticed then how poorly segregated the rival supporters were at the 'Liverpool' end of the ground. This didn't look right. Jim Beglin had other concerns: he was in another football world entirely, a young man who was confident, happy, looking forward to his first big final. Kennedy and the left-out Kevin MacDonald were soon back with Beglin in the Liverpool dressing-room, looking for something useful to do or say as the players began to get changed, when things started going horribly wrong outside. The players heard the terrible rumble of the collapsing wall outside but were unsure what it was. Alan Kennedy became the 'runner' between them and their wives and girlfriends upstairs. He was sent out to do some research, to check on the official party at regular intervals and to convey messages to the wives that the Liverpool players were safe and to the players that their partners were not being attacked in the stand. He also saw, first-hand, the panic unfold outside, because he was soon right next to the wall that had collapsed. He saw the injured and the already blue bodies of the dead being carried away from the area. These were laid out at the back of the stand, where some of the Liverpool wives claimed that they even saw fans going through the pockets of dead spectators. 'It was a horrible, horrible atmosphere,' said Alan. 'I had a feeling I was in danger, that I was going to get knifed, because everybody in this area was so angry against Liverpool.' This football match was turning into a war zone.

Eventually a UEFA official came down to tell the Liverpool officials and players that there would be a delay to the kick-off because of 'crowd trouble'. The players knew from the reaction of those, like Alan, who had been outside that something very serious had happened, some wanted to know the full extent of the problems, others wanted to try to stay focused on the game they thought they would still have to play. Alan took out some playing cards to distract some of the players and he batted off players' questions as best he could, struggling with images of what he had seen, until Phil Neal and Joe Fagan went out to try to calm the Liverpool fans. 'It shouldn't have been played, but with 50,000 fans there it probably had to be,' says Alan today. 'But the game was irrelevant to Liverpool. A lot of the players – Bruce was one of them – asked why we were even playing the game. They didn't want it to go ahead.' UEFA officials decided to play the match to avoid a riot.

Kennedy watched the match from the Liverpool bench but he could think of nothing else but the bodies he had seen being dragged out of the wreckage and lifelessly lined up at the rear of the stadium. He is sure now that the game, if not exactly rigged for Juventus, was played and refereed to make sure the Italian club won. No other result was safe or acceptable, a dubious Platini penalty dividing the teams in a haunting atmosphere. Plenty of English, and especially Italian, fans had long since left the stadium. No Liverpool player talked in the dressing-room afterwards, and back at the hotel after the match the Liverpool squad sat around silently and numb and were advised not to leave the building for their own safety. The next day the Liverpool players' bus was attacked by enraged Italian fans. 'It was a sad time, a terrible time,' recalls Alan. 'I remember Joe Fagan coming back on the plane and saying: "That's enough now, I've had enough of football" – which you can understand.' Kennedy and Fagan had together experienced the ecstatic highs of two European finals: these were the unimaginable depths.

Back in Liverpool, Kenny Dalglish was announced as the new Liverpool player–manager in a city stunned by the previous evening's events. Phil Neal thought that *he* had been promised the Liverpool job, injecting more anger and unhappiness into an already murky business. Although some players – including Alan Kennedy himself – questioned whether carrying on playing football professionally made any sense any more, this feeling of revulsion soon turned to anger as the case against UEFA and the Belgian authorities began to mount up. With a month off, the players now drifted away, but even when pre-season training resumed it was still doom and gloom at the Liverpool base. What was there to look forward to? There was no football in Europe and Liverpool's reputation was utterly tarnished, disgraced – and wrongly, as the club's players felt. Everton fans and officials were also outraged, of course: the blanket ban from UEFA on English clubs meant that the Goodison club would not play in the European Cup after all. With Gary Lineker recently signed and with the best midfield in Britain, if not in Europe, Everton would have been heavy favourites to win a trophy eventually claimed, on penalties, by the unimpressive Steaua Bucharest. But Alan Kennedy had other things on his mind. Maybe the time was approaching when he would have to start thinking about where his career was heading. Events were about to spur his thinking.

MOVING ON

Like all Liverpool players, Alan started the next League season under a cloud. New manager Dalglish relied on Bob Paisley to help him ease his way into the new job and his first-team meeting at Melwood was impressive enough, the Scot pointing out forcefully that the Liverpool Way still meant something to him, despite recent events. Surprisingly, both Beglin and Kennedy started the new campaign in the first team, with Beglin beginning in midfield. But Alan felt that his game was already suffering from the pressure of having the youngster involved and pressing. He thought that it was only a matter of time before the Irishman forced him out of the Liverpool side. In fact, both the full-back spots were now uncertain at Anfield because Phil Neal was also looking for a way out because of his recent rejection for the manager's job. Leaving Liverpool also suddenly seemed like an easier option for these experienced players, with the club in the doldrums and Europe no longer offering that very special incentive for being there. Not that this had an adverse effect on early results: after eight League matches Liverpool had lost only one game under Kenny, to struggling Newcastle United.

Alan Kennedy's last match for Liverpool was Steve McMahon's first, on 14 September 1985 at the Manor Ground, Oxford, a tough 2–2 draw. 'A poky little ground with terrible floodlights. They had this centre-forward called Aldridge, who wasn't bad.' Oxford went in front, before Ronnie Whelan was in a head clash and was stretchered off. Rush and Craig Johnston then put Liverpool 2–1 ahead until another defining moment in Alan Kennedy's life occurred. In the dying minutes, Alan was shepherding a crossed ball back towards his own goal and he stuck out a boot to direct it back to Grobbelaar. Sadly, Bruce had already strayed, assuming the ball had passed Alan. Own goal – and with virtually his last kick in a Liverpool shirt. It looked like this really was the end: 'Kenny went crazy in the dressing-room afterwards. He totally blamed me – he had a right go. All right, I wasn't brilliant, but I hadn't had a bad game. He picked me up on a few things I wasn't doing right, even though I thought that the problem was that Paul Walsh kept giving the ball away. All the lads afterwards said the own goal was Bruce's fault anyway. Whether Kenny alerted the papers about me I don't know, but by the weekend it was all over the Sunday newspapers: that Newcastle had made a bid of £100,000 for me. I thought that wasn't a bad price, so I was given permission to talk to them.'

Alan went to see Kenny, who confirmed that a bid was in from his old club. The manager, basically, said that the decision was up to Alan, but that if he stayed at Anfield he had a fight on his hands for his place. Although Alan still had 18 months left on his contract, after which he was in touching distance of a Liverpool testimonial, the manager's words didn't take too much decoding. 'When a manager says that it's up to you, he really means that you're not in his plans any more.' He had some security at Liverpool and he could stay to fight for his place.

Peter Robinson reassured him that he could stay if he wanted to. He could even wait and put some feelers out to other clubs. But Alan made arrangements, instead, to see his old friend, Newcastle United manager Willie McFaul. Although a move to the North-east was attractive, Alan still had a nagging doubt about going back to his old club. Would people there still expect to see the young flying Alan Kennedy of old? Right away, Newcastle offered him a healthy £35,000 a year and pre-contract forms were signed to enable him to play pre-season. Alan passed his medical and had photos taken with his new manager. Everything seemed to be moving at breakneck speed: seven amazing years as a winning Liverpool player were suddenly disappearing in an instant. He now began to doubt the move, though he felt that things were out of his control: he wanted to undo what he had already agreed.

Lawrie McMenemy, the new Sunderland manager and TV pundit, then rang asking Alan for a meeting, which took place in a hotel car park in Washington. McMenemy, a smooth and plausible operator, went to work. He completely sold Second Division Sunderland to Kennedy as a club reborn, a mix of established older professionals and talented new blood that was really going places. Newcastle looked like First Division relegation candidates, said Lawrie, whereas ambitious Sunderland was bound for promotion back to the top flight. McMenemy even seemed to imply he had contacts that could help get Alan back into the England set-up. Alan had no idea Sunderland had already lost their first five League matches, but he was impressed. Who wouldn't be? But he decided, first, to discuss matters with his father and sister Bev, promising McMenemy he would have his answer in the morning.

Bold Lawrie had other ideas: the next day the North-east press was splashed with 'Kennedy signs for Sunderland' stories. An angry Willie McFaul called Alan, who explained that nothing was decided but that, yes, the Sunderland offer was attractive. McFaul made his own mind up: 'Kennedy snubs Newcastle' were the next day's headlines, with McFaul publicly badmouthing Alan for letting down Newcastle, having agreed to join and even signing forms. 'I'm no villain,' Alan told *The Sun* the next day. No Newcastle United fan was likely to believe him now. Kennedy had trusted McMenemy, who had made him look unreliable and devious by going to the press. This was an old football ploy, of course, making up a player's mind by salting a press story, but it was a sign about Lawrie that Alan later regretted he had ignored.

At 31, after playing over 350 times in League and Cup for Liverpool, scoring 21 goals over just over seven seasons and winning 5 League titles, 2 European Cups and 4 League Cups, Alan Kennedy signed a new 3-year contract at Sunderland. 'It is frightening the power a football club has over a family's life and the speed at which everything changes,' says Jane Kennedy. 'One minute you have a home on Merseyside, the next you're in a hotel room in Washington in County Durham.' Alan knew, almost immediately, that the move was a mistake. As at his first club, Newcastle United, favoured senior players at Roker Park were too influential in decision-making at Sunderland. McMenemy's assistant, Lew Chatterley, perhaps also contributed to unrest in the Roker camp by feeding back to Lawrie stories about the players' lifestyles and about their private comments in the dressing-room. Training seemed to be reduced to a series of exhausting practice matches or distance running and no one at Sunderland appeared to be interested in organising a decent training session. Team meetings degenerated into players slagging off each other. Lawrie himself, a man with many commitments, seemed to spend relatively little time actually managing Sunderland Football Club. There was also growing boardroom unrest at the club as the Roker men began sliding towards the Third Division. This kind of thing never happened at Anfield. In short, Sunderland was not a happy camp and was showing few signs of recovery later. McMenemy had released 14 Sunderland players and in an attempt to rescue the situation brought in Frank Gray, Bob Bolder, George Burley, David Swindlehurst, Eric Gates and Alan himself, all solid top-level professionals on high-cost contracts. None of it worked. The new team didn't seem to gel and it was difficult for the experienced, older men to adjust to playing with much poorer younger players in a frantic division. It was short-cut football management, with Sunderland's debts booming. Kennedy was number 1 choice for left-back at the start at Sunderland, but when things failed to take off there McMenemy seemed loath to justify his big wage by switching things around or motivating his players. Suddenly, 18 months in the Liverpool reserves or a season under Willie McFaul at Newcastle United was starting to look very attractive indeed to Alan Kennedy. He still has a copy of that redundant Newcastle United contract.

Sunderland struggled on the brink of relegation to the Third Division for most of the latter part of the season. Alan said all the right things to the press about the players letting the manager down, but, privately, he despaired of McMenemy. He also began to be left out of the side, in favour of Frank Gray, as his form inevitably suffered because of the stress and his regrets at leaving Anfield. He was angry with himself for ending up in this mess. When Sunderland eventually survived, things still failed to improve. In September 1986 an old Liverpool teammate, Howard Gayle, who was also at Roker, slammed McMenemy as 'a joke' in the Sunday tabloids for his bullying management style and his coaching ineptitude at Sunderland.

In November, in a strange twist, Phil Neal, now manager at Bolton Wanderers, made press noises about trying to sign Alan from Sunderland. Wages were probably the stumbling block, so the two full-backs remained close friends but no longer clubmates. Mercifully, Lawrie McMenemy left Sunderland towards the end of the 1986–87 season and, now managed by Bob Stokoe, Sunderland battled against relegation again – but this time to no avail. With the Roker club looking urgently to slash its wage bill, Alan now needed to set himself up with another club at much lower wages and then take the money Sunderland were contractually obliged to give him for the final year of his contract followed by a free transfer. Instead, he just took the cash. He had no job and no club.

STAYING ALIVE

In December 1987 Alan sold a bitter story to *The Sun*, blasting Lawrie McMenemy for 'ruining' his football career. It was a way to make some money, get rid of some of his frustrations and also to advertise the fact that he was still available and fit for work in the game at 33 years of age. But it read like a fall from grace. Here was a man pictured holding the European Cup aloft just three and a half years ago, who was now signing on the dole in Durham to support his wife and new baby son, Michael. Alan also said how much he regretted leaving Liverpool, though he was probably correct to think that his first-team opportunities there had been diminishing fast. Since leaving Sunderland, Alan had spent a few enjoyable months with Swedish Third Division side Husqvarna FF, had a short spell at Fourth Division Hartlepool United, a pretty disastrous week with the Beerschot club in Belgium, a flirtation with Northwich Victoria and had even joined Grantham under old Forest adversary Martin O'Neill in the Beazer Homes League. He was getting desperate and was tentatively applying for work outside football, but the game was all he really knew. The *Sun* story seemed to have the desired effect, though, because Ray Mathias at Third Division promotion chasers Wigan Athletic came in at Christmas and offered him a month's trial and then a deal, sponsored for 24 weeks by a local company, Port Petroleum. Alan snapped it up. It was difficult to work out the details: Alan trained at Hartlepool for the first three days of the week before staying with Jane's parents in Eccleston from Thursday. Wigan missed out on promotion, but his return to the North-west area generated plenty of warm media coverage, and playing in a positive environment at Springfield Park also felt like Alan had a bit of self-respect back and that life had started up again. But now, in May 1988, he was on another 'free'. The pressure of short-term contracts increases tensions at home and offers no security for the future. How would the Kennedys survive?

Brother Keith came up with Alan's next move. Keith had played for ambitious big-spending HFS Loans non-League side Colne Dynamos at the end of 1987 and he put in a word for Alan with Colne's manager and funder, Graham White. White snapped up Kennedy for high-rolling Colne, and this attractive new contract and a club move back to Lancashire provided the opportunity for Kennedy to relocate his family home back in the Merseyside area. Alan enjoyed the new challenge, but the entire Colne dream was precarious and when in March 1990 Brian Flynn came in to invite Alan back into League football at struggling Fourth Division Wrexham, he jumped at the chance. The move enabled him to complete his 500th League game. There was more. In October 1990, 12 years after they had first battled over the left full-back spot for Liverpool, Joey Jones and Alan Kennedy actually played together for Wrexham against Manchester United in the European Cup-winners' Cup. It was a marvellous story for the man who had scored winning goals in two European finals – and who had hit the depths just over three years later. In January 1991, at the end of Alan's stay in Wales, the managing director at Wrexham, D.L. Rhodes, wrote a letter of thanks to Alan. In some ways it sums up his whole approach to the game at all the levels at which he had played: 'Thanks for all your help and assistance during your short stay with us. You arrived in our darkest hour, and with your professionalism and good humour were able to see us through to a happier ending. It was also an honour for the club to have you here at Wrexham for your 500th League appearance, considering the many famous grounds you have graced.'

After Wrexham, Alan's stint in non-League football continued via spells as a player at Morecambe and Radcliffe Borough and as a player–manager at Netherfield. By this time he was also raising some cash by running soccer schools and doing part-time radio work. Jane was the driving force here, encouraging and organising, doing the marketing and the admin and keeping his spirits up. The organisation was not always waterproof: the Kennedy team used players and ex-players to make presentations for their soccer schools. Alan once rang Alan Hansen to see if he would get involved: 'Can you do a presentation?' asked Kennedy. 'Sure, when is it?' asked Hansen. 'Actually, now – we're sitting in your drive.' It was still very hard work making ends meet, but this was a little more like it. At 40 years of age, in 1995, Kennedy was starting to earn reasonably again – he now had two children to support. But he was still turning out for Barrow in the Northern Premier League (average gate 900, £60 a match) and making the 190-mile round trip from the family home for this purpose. It was his 15th football club and his presence in the centre of midfield on muddied fields was a thrill for any player he faced and anyone he spoke to in the bar afterwards. 'If anyone dismisses me during matches as a has-been,' he told the press, 'I just say: "Listen, mate, it's better to be a has-been than a never-been."' It was a nice put-down. But, then, Alan Kennedy, double European Cup winner, has never been a has-been.

Chapter 11

CLOSING TIME

TALL TALES

Like a lot of old sporting warriors, Alan Kennedy was reluctant to accept that his best football days were now over. In January 1987 Jim Beglin broke his leg playing for Liverpool against Everton, and Alan, in the depths of despair at Sunderland, sent a note to Kenny Dalglish, saying that he was still available if Liverpool needed a stand-in. Kenny replied with a photo of himself and a message: 'Don't phone me, I'll call you.' Alan was 33 and still dreaming. Ten years later, he could no more easily face hanging up his football boots. The truth is he was probably afraid to face up to a life without football and while his body held out, why not continue to enjoy the security and comradeship of the football dressing-room and try to block out bigger, more important questions? Like what, exactly, was he going to do with the rest of his life? Instead, regardless of any needs at home, he insisted on travelling hundreds of miles, at any opportunity, to play non-League football, charity games and especially to meet up with some of his old Liverpool mates and try to hold on to memories of old times. Who could blame him? Even 20 years after their greatest triumphs, Liverpool teams from the '80s are still being invited all over the globe to meet with fans and to play against scratch local sides. Their achievements only seem to grow over time and their values increase in importance when compared to an era in which cash and celebrity seem much more important than any sporting credo.

As his contracts with League clubs began to become a thing of the past, Jane Kennedy was beginning to get frustrated and afraid about Alan's future and that of his family. Alan had spent most of what he had earned in the game and his pension could barely cover the essentials. He seldom talked about his anxieties and after decades of being cosseted by football clubs Alan had precious few transferable skills outside the sport: he seemed incapable even of making telephone calls to follow up job opportunities. He tried selling perimeter advertising in stadiums for a while, but hated it, and in the midst of one of his depressions Jane even rang up Gordon Taylor at the PFA to ask what, exactly, ex-players did at the end of their playing careers and what sort of support the players' union offered. There was nothing. And then Alan Kennedy had a break.

Alan had become friendly with ex-Everton player Duncan McKenzie, a natural comic and one of the very first football after-dinner speakers. Duncan suggested that Kennedy put together a few stories about the Paisley years at Liverpool and with the help of a local comedian, Willie Miller, maybe they could get 15 minutes of usable material that could be fitted into a McKenzie speaking engagement. Now, Alan could play football in front of 50,000, but he could barely talk to the postman, never mind a room of drink-softened golf club members or football anoraks. Nevertheless, he practised his short set for three weeks in front of mirrors and with Jane and the kids as an audience. He was hopeless. He called McKenzie to cancel. No chance: they were now expecting 200 punters at a pub in Parbold, many of them drawn by the promise of a few Liverpool tales. At the event, Alan ate nothing and couldn't even look at the sea of expectant faces in the audience: he was numbed with nerves. A strippergram offered a brief if welcome distraction, but then the evil clown McKenzie messed up all his cue cards. Kennedy eventually stood up on the sort of wobbly legs that Grobbelaar would be proud of – and was predictably crap. But he did manage to squeeze out nine excruciating minutes and even the occasional audience giggle. He told McKenzie 'no more', but a week later the ex-Everton man was back with another booking – and a £50 fee. Alan swallowed hard – and said he'd do it.

THE NEW LIVERPOOL

At first, his old mates at Liverpool scoffed at the idea of making a new life out of telling hack Anfield stories: why was he making such a fool of himself, and selling so cheaply the Anfield brand? But as the market for this sort of service grew, Alan's list of clients expanded and, with experience, he even became a half-decent performer. His fee also rose, up to £1,000 sometimes in recent years – and all this for a bit of driving, a few hours of nostalgic story telling, and some pressing the flesh with his public: for *being* Alan Kennedy. Soon, other Liverpool players swallowed their pride and asked him how to make a start, and he began to put these new Liverpool stand-up merchants in touch with clients. Today, a local cottage industry has grown around Liverpool's glorious past. Alan has a list of ex-Anfield men, who mostly live in the Merseyside area, who can all do good shows and no one is laughing any more – except occasionally, perhaps, a few lucky people in the audience. It is just one way that the club's fantastic heritage is kept alive. Alan Kennedy, the shy ex-footballer who thought he had no skills outside of his feet, now spends most of his non-football playing life on the telephone, negotiating, organising gigs, doing radio phone-ins, setting up Liverpool tours and holding the attention of large audiences. Mind you, he still finds it hard to resist throwing everything off course in order to accept an invitation to play football: a large group of ex-Liverpool players travel, at the drop of a hat, around the globe to take on all-comers. The Liverpool legend from the '70s and '80s dies hard.

This is one of the reasons, of course, why the managers and teams that followed the great Paisley and Fagan sides at Liverpool found it so tough to make things work. Kenny Dalglish, briefly, built a great Liverpool team in the late '80s, but the terrible pressures of Hillsborough and some poor signings eventually dimmed Kenny's resolve and he suddenly left the club in 1991. Alan and a number of the older players were also involved in the aftermath of the Hillsborough disaster, attending the funerals of fans, playing in charity games, saying words at family gatherings. It was a way to reconnect with the club and its followers in tragic times. There were plenty of Liverpool greats left to pick up the Anfield managerial mantle after Kenny. His old mate Graeme Souness arrived on a moderniser's ticket and performed some necessary surgery, with Ronnie Moran, Sammy Lee and Roy Evans still on board, making changes to the old Melwood training regime and bringing in his own recruits. Perhaps it was too much too soon, because Souness's Liverpool were plagued with injuries and, despite an FA Cup win in 1992, the tough old master found it difficult to keep some of his senior players on board. Some of Souness's signings also reflected more his hard-man ethos than his own brilliant playing skills. Alan Kennedy was especially bemused by the Souness recruitment of Julian Dicks for his prized Liverpool number 3 shirt. Dicks seemed to be an alehouse signing, a man who also valued little of the Anfield traditions when, unforgivably, he ended up slagging off Ronnie Moran and the club staff in the Liverpool dressing-room.

Roy Evans followed Souness into the hot seat as Liverpool sought some in-house stability once more and Roy tried, honourably, to continue the Anfield traditions but in very different times. Player power, massive wages and the new media-driven celebrity culture for players all contributed to scuppering the Evans ship, which actually produced some marvellous football. During Alan's time at Liverpool, the club's players lived hard but also operated under the strong guidelines laid down by the staff and the senior players, including Roy himself. Under Evans as manager, the senior Liverpool players – Ruddock, Wright and even the magnificent John Barnes – were less ideal role models for the exciting younger stars who were now helping to shape the new Liverpool. The famous cream suits at Wembley in 1996 and especially Ruddock's later stories that the Liverpool players sometimes passed a pound coin between each other during matches as part of a betting game were signs that the priorities among the new generation of players were very different to those which applied under Bob and Joe.

The Frenchman Gérard Houllier then arrived at Liverpool, initially to share the job with Roy, in order to bring in the new scientific approaches to player conditioning and coaching that were popular on the Continent. The old Liverpool Way of minimum coaching, an intuitive response to injuries and recruiting and keeping the best players had been overtaken by the new global market for footballers and the chasing of the football dollar. The Houllier years at Anfield began very promisingly, and in 2001, with Phil Thompson as his assistant, there were even trophies to show for his efforts, including the first European silver at Anfield, the UEFA Cup, since Alan's penalty triumph in Rome in 1984. In 2002, the Frenchman got the club back in serious European Cup contention until a bad night in Leverkusen (a 2–4 quarter-final loss) ended Kopite dreams. But Houllier's approach was very different to the one championed by Paisley and the Liverpool Boot Room. The flexibility and invention on the field promoted under Paisley and Fagan seemed much more difficult to achieve under Houllier, and the club's players sometimes seemed to be performing in a defensive straitjacket, fashioned by the manager.

Poor Liverpool signings in the summer of 2002 meant Houllier had to grind out results while using statistics to try to create a fog of misrepresentation. As results failed to improve, the Frenchman's popularity on the Red half of Merseyside fell. A small number of Houllier's foreign recruits – Sami Hyypiä and Dietmar Hamann, for example – proved lasting successes at Anfield, but too many others struggled.

Indeed, of the players at Liverpool over the last decade, it was actually the local talent – Steve McManaman, Steven Gerrard, Robbie Fowler and Michael Owen – who would have had the best chance of getting into some of the great Liverpool sides of the late '70s and early '80s. But even these players would have needed to be at the very top of their games to be serious contenders.

With a troubled Houllier now frantically trying to recapture the club's old glories, Alan Kennedy still watched football matches at Anfield, and he also enjoyed working the Liverpool sponsors' lounges, making cracks and discussing the club and its players with the punters. He was desperately hoping, like all the older Anfield players, that a new Liverpool could rise to the very top once more. He was certainly not living in the past: like every fan, he just wanted today's Liverpool to respect what had gone on before – and better it. And every time Alan Kennedy watched some penalty shoot-out football drama on TV, he didn't have to try to imagine the highs and lows of the test; he only had to remember Rome 1984 and the time that Liverpool FC were, indisputably, the greatest football club in Europe. Little did he know that, under another new Continental manager in 2005, Liverpool Football Club was destined to revisit the penalty shoot-out white-knuckle ride in the world's greatest football club competition. Alan Kennedy, a Liverpool penalty hero from 21 years before and a non-playing veteran of Heysel, was there in Istanbul to witness what some informed commentators would claim was the most dramatic ever European Cup final.

EPILOGUE

AU REVOIR, GÉRARD

The summer of 2004 and the 2004–05 season that followed were something of a watershed for many of the ex-Liverpool players, such as Alan Kennedy, who still lived in and around the city and who continued, through one means or another, to make a living by commenting on their own Liverpool FC past or on the new regimes at the club. Alan continued to do his after-dinner presentations, his occasional match-hosting at Anfield and he had his nightly phone-in *Legends* football show to manage on Century Radio. He also offered news commentary on football in Liverpool for Sky Sports and other TV channels, so in many respects his was a pivotal media position in this area. The early part of 2004 was a difficult time for anyone who cared for Liverpool Football Club, especially those who were routinely asked for their professional opinions on the state of health of the club and about its likely future under manager Gérard Houllier. The nightly radio phone-in shows for Reds fans had become pretty much fixated by now on Houllier's alleged failings and the associated shortcomings of his team. Despite the potentially exciting signing of Harry Kewell from Leeds United in 2003 and the claims now made by Houllier that his Liverpool would begin to show more attacking intent, the team had continued to struggle and was already way off the Premiership-title pace early in the new season. The Frenchman, in the fifth year of a five-year plan for Liverpool success, was in trouble.

This near-uniform kind of panning of the staff of a local football club is hard to manage well on a local media outlet. Alan, himself, was placed in an especially difficult position here. He was deeply concerned about the direction of the Houllier project and he had real disquiet about recent developments. But these views had to be set against his deep loyalty to the club and his need to maintain good contacts inside Liverpool FC. He also knew well that Houllier monitored keenly all local press and media commentary on his management of the club. The ex-left-back had already had some experience of Houllier's increasingly paranoid tendencies in this department: his experience with the Liverpool manager in 2003 was a signal of how things were to spiral rapidly out of control later at Anfield.

At this time, Alan was acting as a match-day host at Anfield for club sponsors Carlsberg. But this role was threatened when he was accused by Phil Thompson and the manager of 'disloyalty' to the Liverpool club. His alleged 'crime'? Showing a story that was critical of Liverpool Football Club in the *Liverpool Echo* to Blackburn Rovers boss Graeme Souness before a match. The article's subject was how far Houllier's Liverpool had fallen behind Manchester United. Alan was further accused of not supporting the club when he differed from them in his views about a bad tackle on Jamie Carragher and when he appeared not to talk up Liverpool's chances on the Sky Sports *Soccer AM* Saturday-morning show. When asked to forecast the result of a Liverpool match, Alan held out his palms and shrugged as if unable to predict a positive outcome for the club – who were then on a terrible run. Carlsberg were contacted by Houllier's office and told that if Kennedy worked in the sponsor's lounge the following match day, no Liverpool players would visit the lounge after the game. Alan had to withdraw temporarily from his Carlsberg work – though he needed the cash – and for seven weeks he tried to get a meeting with Houllier to resolve the issue. There was only silence.

Eventually, Alan was summonsed, by Gérard Houllier, to a meeting at the club training ground. He takes up the story now: 'I was called in to see Houllier at 5.30 p.m. on a Tuesday evening at Melwood; it was supposed to be a 15-minute meeting. He knew I had my radio show to do, but he finally saw me at five to six. I'm feeling like a little kid now, going to see the headmaster to be told off. I sat there with him for forty minutes, three times watching a tape of myself on the *Soccer AM* show. I couldn't see the point of it, but Houllier kept saying to me, "But Alan, look again, look again." There was nothing there! But he accused me of disrespecting Liverpool Football Club and the players. I spoke to some of the players later, who thought nothing of it. Lots of ex-players had voiced their opinion by now. We could all see what was going wrong, but he couldn't. And I was often defending him on the radio show for some of the things he had said! I don't think anyone at the club was happy with him at the end. I think he was probably, eventually, trying to run the whole club, control everything that was done or said. It became a bit sad, really.'

The Liverpool FC Annual General Meeting on 5 January 2004 – usually a limp rubber-stamping for the manager's good works – proved a pretty stormy affair for once. Angry Liverpool shareholders openly criticised the team's performances and the manager's own showing, with one claiming that even loyal Liverpool fans were now 'running out of patience with the team' and that 'money has been spent on foreign players, many of whom have been of questionable quality'. Few could argue with that point in relation to Houllier's more recent signings. Local millionaire builder and potential Liverpool investor Steve Morgan had confronted the club chairman David Moores, who was visibly shaken by the very dark mood of the meeting. Some frustrated Liverpool fans were even beginning to think that a change at the top table might be worth having – with a rather more forceful and interventionist chairman.

Ian St John was one of the ex-Liverpool players who had spectacularly attacked on this front by publicly and unequivocally condemning the Houllier approach; the Scot had argued that Liverpool fans were being turned into 'zombies', who were now being asked to watch 'pre-programmed', boring football of some of the poorest quality seen at Anfield in living memory. This idea – that the current manager was a negative, controlling influence on the Liverpool players – seemed widely shared locally at this point, and it was anathema to those players looking on who had grown up in earlier coaching regimes at the club. In these earlier eras, Liverpool managers and coaches had always given the Liverpool players both the freedom and the responsibility to perform. When Bob Paisley and Joe Fagan were asked by the media to explain Liverpool's 'secret', this wily pair had always replied, without blinking or hesitation, 'good players'. For them, it was almost that simple. To some ex-players, it seemed that the current Liverpool manager believed, unlike Bob and Joe, that his role was as important – or even more important – than that of the players. This seemed deeply at odds with the Liverpool Way, and it seemed to be damaging the long-term prospects of the club. Something, clearly, had to give.

Alan remembers this period, early in 2004, as one of great

uncertainty – and some unhappiness – around the Liverpool club. Sometimes, when the managerial regime is in trouble at a football club, this lack of positive direction, and the sense of suspicion and fear it can generate, permeates tangibly throughout the club. Liverpool FC did not feel like a happy ship at this moment: instead it felt like one that was rudderless and heading for decidedly choppy waters.

But the club was still in contention for the crucial fourth Champions League qualifying place (which it eventually secured) and Gérard Houllier was even being allowed by the Liverpool board to set up a £14 million summer transfer for the French striker Djibril Cissé while preparing to offload an earlier £11 million signing, Emile Heskey. These were hardly the actions of a board planning to sack its manager. 'I thought Houllier was going to be around for another year,' admits Alan, 'though the talk, at that time, was that he wasn't really wanted at the club any more. Liverpool had really stuttered. They'd not played good, attractive football at all. They hadn't entertained. They were going backwards rather than forwards. The board, and the chairman, was under pressure to sacrifice someone and, in the end, it was a brave decision to sack the manager. But I was surprised by it.'

What, finally, went wrong for Houllier? Alan, like many people in Liverpool, thought that the manager's illness in 2001 was a factor. During a routine home League draw with Leeds United on 13 October 2001, the Frenchman had complained of chest pains and at half-time was rushed to Broadgreen Hospital in Liverpool, where he received 11 hours of emergency heart surgery on a damaged aorta. Exhaustion, more than stress, was the cause of his problems, and Houllier, being a football man, had seemingly pushed this beyond breaking point by denying his own vulnerability. He spent much of that season recovering from his near-death experience. Maybe this changed his outlook, made him even more sensitive to criticism: a desperate problem in a job as publicly exposed as that of a Premiership manager at a top club like Liverpool.

'After his illness, I felt there was something missing – maybe a spark was missing,' says Alan. 'He started to look even more at what the papers and the players were saying about him. The football became stereotyped: "If we go one–nil up, we'll protect that lead." We had [Didi] Hamann, who was a good defensive midfielder, but he only did that one job. Players were given instructions from the manager to go out and play the way he [the manager] wanted them to play. They became robots. A lot of the fans felt, like me, that it wasn't the right way to be going. But it took us two years to realise that.'

This alleged 'robotic' approach to play and preparation at Liverpool was quite at odds, of course, with Alan's own experiences at Anfield and Melwood over 20 years earlier. The relationship between manager and players was also very different then. Liverpool's coaching staff in the 1970s and early '80s had no problems recruiting 'big' personalities to Anfield, bringing in leaders, mature men who had their own views on the game – Dalglish, Souness and Lawrenson are all good examples here. They added value to the Liverpool squad and helped to shape how the team played and prepared for matches. They were certainly 'in charge' in the dressing-room and, once the Liverpool team stepped onto the field of play, they also, pretty much, dictated how the team played. If changes were needed, they were often made by the players on the pitch. Neither Paisley nor Fagan seemed worried about having these powerful voices in the Liverpool dressing-room and on the pitch; they thought, instead, that they added conviction and strength to the Anfield stock and improved performance.

Under Gérard Houllier, however, things seemed very different. The Frenchman seemed to favour younger players he could control and shape for his team. 'We always thought Bob Paisley had more knowledge of football than us, so we had a mutual respect there,' says Alan. 'The players Houllier brought in were players who, first of all, looked up to him, the manager. So whatever he said, they would do. But that's not how you should respond on the pitch. You need to have a bit of flexibility, to be able to express yourself. The manager has the overall say, but Bob [Paisley] never gave you instructions so that you couldn't adapt to situations on the pitch and show what you were capable of. You were your own man on the pitch. The Liverpool coaches, in my day, couldn't dictate the play once you had crossed the white line. Then it was up to you. If a manager is telling you how to play all the time, you can never be comfortable on the park. That's what happened here.'

Perhaps this lack of flexibility, or even his unwillingness to trust his own players in a way that had seemed second nature to Bob Paisley and his staff, counted against Houllier and also meant that he failed to recruit enough powerful leaders on the field. This is certainly suggested by the problems Liverpool had under Houllier: for example, in the team's failure to come from behind to win matches. Once Liverpool conceded a lead to an opponent, there seemed no useful 'plan B', nor the necessary strength of character on the park to haul them back into the contest. Mentally and tactically, Houllier's Liverpool seemed weak, and a very different group of men from those who Paisley and Fagan had gathered – including a raw Alan Kennedy – to bring trophies to Liverpool two decades before.

'A lot of fans were very suspicious after the manager brought in [El-Hadji] Diouf, [Salif] Diao and [Bruno] Cheyrou in 2002 and one or two others,' says Alan. 'We had to question the players he brought in at that time. None of them was good enough in my view. When Bob Paisley brought in someone, he also looked at the character of the person: what was he like, was he single, did he like to go out and have a drink? Gérard Houllier went down the French angle, but he didn't seem to know enough about what he was getting.' All three of the players mentioned above by Alan Kennedy had both technical and character defects for playing in the English game. Bob Paisley, like all managers, might have made occasional errors of judgement in this department: but three simultaneously? I don't think so.

In the end, too, the Liverpool manager had become embattled in 2004 and relied far too much on his own thoughts and opinions. Although Paisley and Fagan could be ruthless when it was needed and neither shied away from making difficult decisions, the Liverpool Way was also very much about having a more democratic input from players and coaches on the style of play the club should be trying to achieve. Bob and Joe were always keen on their senior players 'chipping in' at Melwood with constructive suggestions and comments on training and on how the team was playing, and they would also confer with the other coaching staff. By the end of Gérard Houllier's reign, however, it was clear that the manager's way was, increasingly, the only way.

'Houllier was fine when he started off, and he got Liverpool back on track,' is Alan's view. 'But you needed a different balance. Houllier, in the end, relied too much on himself; he stopped asking people's opinions and he made every decision his own. We were critical about the way the club was being run: one man needs other people to help him. In our day, we had Joe Fagan and Ronnie Moran and Tom Saunders who we could ask for advice – and the manager could ask for advice from them. Whether the manager wanted to take it or not was another matter. But by this time Gérard wasn't listening to anybody.'

The Liverpool manager, in short, had become unsustainably isolated and had lost the support and belief of his players and staff. He looked, increasingly, like a man under siege. On 24 May 2004, Gérard Houllier left Anfield, his departure announced with amiable words about him leaving the club as a 'friend' and, above all, 'on good terms'.

But, however you dress it up, he had been sacked. This was much to the delight of many of Alan Kennedy's Century Radio callers, though it should also be said that many callers to the show also wanted on record the enormous recent contribution Gérard Houllier had made to the Liverpool club, especially in the amazing 'treble' year of 2001.

OLA, RAFA!

So where next for Liverpool? There was no doubt that there was a local backlash now against the possible appointment of another foreign coach at Anfield. This message was coming through loud and clear on Century Radio and at Alan Kennedy's public-speaking events. After all, following a promising start this most recent Continental Liverpool manager had seemed to become obsessed with statistics and video analysis and, by the end, he had brought in, in many people's eyes, far too many foreign players with just the wrong sort of attributes for survival in the tough English Premiership. Maybe it was time to get back to basics and to appoint a solid British manager once more? There were even some around – and possibly available – who might be argued to have some of the attributes of the old Liverpool Boot Room. Alan was in Barbados at the same time as Rick Parry was there – June 2004 – ruminating over the next Liverpool appointment. Parry was giving little away, even as the usual rumours were flying around about who had been approached and who had bought real estate recently in the north-west.

Alan Kennedy was one of those who thought a return to a British manager might now be in the club's best interests. Bolton's Sam Allardyce and Charlton's Alan Curbishley had both been mentioned. 'I always like the British manager,' Kennedy said. '[British managers] have the right mentality, know what they want. There was press talk of George Graham or Martin O'Neill [coming to Liverpool] and they were all supposed to have bought houses round the area.' Alan's choice was actually for a couple of old Forest adversaries from the late-1970s. This might have proved an intriguing take on the idea of a move back to the old Boot Room era at Liverpool: recruit the guys who had proved such obstacles to the club 25 years ago. 'Personally, I would have gone for Martin O'Neill. He is a personable guy,' said Alan. 'He had the credentials to take things on, him and his assistant, John Robertson. I used to see them when I did hospitality at Leicester City matches: they would take me in to have a beer after matches. They used to say, "We're giving the players a couple of days off because they need it." That was treating them as men – you're not looking after them 24 hours a day. This was how it used to be done at Liverpool. But when the players come in, they must work hard and train hard. O'Neill understood all this.'

O'Neill certainly had his supporters on Merseyside, that was for sure. He had the British motivational qualities that some fans thought Houllier lacked, and he was unlikely to stand for the sort of abject performances that the team had begun to produce away from home under the Frenchman. He would give Liverpool more passion and a stronger will to win. He also wore his heart on his sleeve: the Anfield faithful might enjoy some of O'Neill's strange touchline 'supporter' antics as a welcome contrast to Houllier's increasingly inert bench performances, especially now the animated Phil Thompson had also left Liverpool following his manager's departure. But wasn't O'Neill being lined up to succeed Alex Ferguson at Manchester United? And did the Irishman even *like* Liverpool FC after all those great tussles with the club as a player 25 years ago? Alan Kennedy certainly thought so: 'I think Martin always set his stall out [as a manager] to try and beat Liverpool. He thought that if he could win against Liverpool, then he'd felt as though he'd beaten the best team. I felt Martin's attitude was that this was the result he really wanted: he really admired Liverpool. But Martin's tactics were also a little bit of the "long ball" mentality, in some people's eyes. I don't think Liverpool wanted to go along those lines.'

There was a strong perception of O'Neill – not always supported by the facts – that he liked only large, powerful strikers and an uncomplicated approach to the game: one that would not fit well with the more cerebral demands of the Liverpool crowd. Deciding there were no suitable British candidates after all, Liverpool looked abroad for a manager once more. Few of the ex-Liverpool players working in the media in the area thought that Rafa Benítez might have been their target, as Alan recalls: 'The ex-players would never have gone for Benítez. We went through everybody, but we didn't think it would be Benítez.' The Spaniard seemed secure at Valencia and he was not that well known in England, even among ex-players. Alan Kennedy also had his doubts about a foreign boss. 'I was a little uncertain about another foreign manager. You couldn't blame Liverpool for taking this route: after all, we had played Valencia two and a half years earlier and we had been taken apart by them. But the older Liverpool lads were quite shocked, actually, by Liverpool going for another foreign manager.'

This continuation of the recent Continental-manager policy at

Anfield also carried with it a troubling new direction, especially for the ex-Liverpool players still working in the media business. With Phil Thompson gone and Sammy Lee also leaving his coaching post at Liverpool to work full-time for the FA, for the first time for half a century there would be no ex-Liverpool player on the club's coaching staff. It was truly the end of the Boot Room legacy – and a much more difficult prospect for those ex-players working in the game who relied on their friendly sources on the coaching staff for social chat and information on what, exactly, was happening inside the club. 'I was very disappointed that Sammy Lee didn't stay on,' said Alan Kennedy. 'Sammy, obviously, had his reasons [for going], but I wanted someone to remain there from the old days – so we could have a chat, go down to the Boot Room and have a discussion about the club, and not feel uncomfortable. Because, even when Gérard Houllier was there, we had Phil [Thompson] and Sammy we could talk to about what was happening in the club. There was still a link then. Now there was nobody.'

This move away from the last vestiges of the old Boot Room connections – Benítez brought with him a collection of Spanish coaches – might have been designed to shore up Anfield against some of messages coming out of the club under Houllier, but the new manager also seemed, personally, much more secure than the Frenchman, even when Liverpool began performing erratically away from home under his new leadership. Alan points out that 'A lot of the fans thought Houllier offered feeble excuses or strange claims.' This was not what Liverpool fans expected from their club's manager at all – and it was not what they got from Benítez, even when the going got tough. Kennedy goes on: 'What this club is about is not excuses, but honesty and integrity and hard work. That's what we lacked under Houllier. Benítez doesn't come up with excuses and he's a realist. He's more likely to say, "OK, we're doing all right, but I know we are still some way from being a good team." He knows that. We want hard work and to be going in the right direction.'

This was a welcome and novel level-headedness from the new manager, as was his approach to younger players at the club. Houllier seemed to have fallen out with his academy director, Steve Heighway, and too few young players had recently been making the transition from Kirkby to Melwood. Under Benítez, the League Cup – and less successfully the FA Cup – was being used as a schooling ground for younger Liverpool players again, as Alan notes approvingly: 'Benítez has given youth a chance. They may not all make it, but I think it's good that he's given them a go in various competitions. Benítez needs three or four more quality players and he knows that players at the club are not the finished articles. But at least the younger players now know that if they work hard they will get a start in the first team. That just wasn't happening under the last manager.'

Not that Rafa Benítez didn't have things still to learn: for example, exactly when, and where, to give his younger players a first-team start. He had had some early success in the League Cup fielding young squads, much to the approval of the club's fans and local commentators. Liverpool even went on to reach the final of the 2005 competition before falling to Chelsea. But the FA Cup has quite a different stature and meaning for Liverpool fans: it took the club until 1965 to even win the FA Cup for the first time and Liverpool fans – like all English fans, if not always their clubs – do prize the FA Cup competition. Drawn away to Burnley in the third round on a dank Lancashire night was, perhaps, too big a risk to take with a young and largely inexperienced Liverpool team. Liverpool lost to a horrendous Djimi Traoré own goal. It was the first real crisis for the new manager. As Alan Kennedy recalls, maybe he lacked some important local guidance: 'We all felt he [Benítez] was going to put out a weakened team at Burnley, but the performance was really sub-standard. Maybe the manager didn't understand the importance of the competition. That's where someone like Sammy Lee could have come in and said, "Listen, boss, this is the FA Cup, an important competition for everybody at this club. If we win this, every fan will be happy about it." Alex Miller [a Liverpool coach] knows about this competition – maybe his input wasn't quite there? I do think Benítez misunderstood the competition. In Spain, they're not bothered about their own cup; it means virtually nothing to them.'

A terrible Liverpool defeat, then – followed by others in the League – and one laid at the door of a young Liverpool defender, a man playing in Alan Kennedy's old position at Liverpool, of course. What did Kennedy think of Traoré's tragic efforts to clear his lines at Burnley? 'Djimi Traoré scored what we would class as a "hilarious" own goal. He made a very, very poor decision there,' says Kennedy. 'He should have cleared the ball with his right foot. Players of today are technically better than we were because we didn't practice what they do today. But Djimi got tangled up, didn't know what he was doing. But that's the type of game in which you need to put a reasonable team out in order to get a result.' It wasn't all poor Djimi's fault: other things also seemed to be missing from this 'new'

Liverpool. 'The [League] games at Birmingham City and Newcastle were the same [as Burnley], argued Alan. 'We needed a leader out there, somebody who was in the Graeme Souness or the Roy Keane mould. Graeme wouldn't have stood for that. Not for a second.'

So were these the very same sorts of problems that Liverpool had experienced under Houllier: a lack of leadership and resolve on the pitch, especially away from Anfield? Certainly the League record of Benítez away from home was no improvement on that of his predecessor. Liverpool would also finish an injury-hit season a massive 37 points behind the title winners, Chelsea. The new man needed to learn quickly some tough lessons about the English game. For Alan Kennedy some things were already obvious: 'We have players who have come from Spain, but this is a tough, quick league. Fernando Morientes, for example, is a quality player but he will need time to fit into the team and to get to the pace of the game in England. We seem to be asking more and more from the local players: the Scousers, Jamie Carragher and Steven Gerrard, have carried Liverpool pretty much for the past 12 months.' And who did Kennedy think were the early imported successes of the new Benítez era? There could be only one man here: '[Xabi] Alonso looks the best of the bunch: he can pass the ball and read the situation. As a passer, he is already possibly the best in the Premier League. He can hit it long or short, and he likes to be involved. He is as good as any we have seen in the last ten years. But he also needs players to win the ball for him.' Balance: football is always a question of balance.

CHELSEA: (ALMOST) KINGS OF DEFENCE

The 2004–05 season under Benítez was actually set to recall Alan Kennedy's old Liverpool days very strongly in a couple of quite astonishing ways. Firstly, Chelsea, in their first season under José Mourinho, were to threaten Liverpool's daunting 1978–79 League defensive record right up to the last game of the 2004–05 season. Chelsea ended up conceding just 15 goals in 38 games (.39 goals per game) compared to Liverpool's 16 goals in 42 games (.38 goals per game). The record was saved, but it was a very tight squeeze, with Liverpool's defenders from the old campaign watching every Chelsea match like hawks. 'We passed the ball more than this Chelsea team,' claims Alan today. 'We could pass teams to death.' But Alan Kennedy also, very fairly, points out that, because of injuries, Chelsea had no settled right-back or left-back for much of the season. Like Liverpool in 1978–79, though, they had an immensely strong defensive spine to the team, with Petr Cech in goal, John Terry at centre-back and the non-stop Frenchman Claude Makelele in the key central defensive midfield slot. Chelsea played a 4–3–3 system to Liverpool's 4–4–2, or 4–4–1–1, but they couldn't quite match the Merseyside club's 85 goals scored in 42 matches in the 1978–79 season (2.02 goals per game): Chelsea scored 72 goals in 38 games (1.89 per game). This, arguably, makes Liverpool's just the more complete team of the two: one that was more successful in balancing both defence and attack. The Reds could score from all parts of the pitch, but the new Chelsea had also brought real defensive strength and quality back to the international football agenda for the first time for quite some time. And Chelsea in 2004–05 lost only one match to Liverpool's three losses in 1978–79. The West London club had seriously challenged a Reds defensive League record in England that had looked nigh on impregnable.

Alan had also enjoyed the impact of the controversial new Chelsea manager: 'Mourinho is a breath of fresh air. He's knowledgeable and is passionate about his team,' he says. 'This arrogance he has, people either like it or loathe it. I think he's good for football. Manchester United and Arsenal have had it too good over the past ten years.' But Alan was less sure about the impact of the new finances being pumped into the London club by Russian billionaire Roman Abramovich: 'The money is good for them [Chelsea] – but not for football at large. Only a few clubs can compete now.' There would be no Nottingham Forest, for example, to challenge the top clubs in the north and in London in 2005, as there had been in 1979, when Bob Paisley's Liverpool was in its pomp. Would there ever be such a provincial challenger again to the larger clubs in England in the era of Sky Sports and the Champions League? Sadly, it seemed very doubtful.

LIVERPOOL, 2005: CHAMPIONS OF EUROPE!

For a while in 2004–05, it also looked as if Chelsea might even replicate the great 1984 Liverpool team's achievement of winning the League Cup (by defeating Liverpool in the final), the League Championship (by a country mile) and the European Cup. As we know now, it was Liverpool that protected their own 1984 record, by defeating Chelsea in the 2005 European Cup semi-final. But what Mourinho had achieved so quickly – even with all the resources he had had at his disposal – was still astonishing, as Alan Kennedy was all to quick too point out: 'It took the 1984 Liverpool team a few years to come together. We just built it up, built it up: trophies kept coming in all the time, as we grew up together. He [Mourinho] has done it in one year! It could go on to become even better – or it could all go pear-shaped at Chelsea. He could make some bad buys, but over the next five years Chelsea could go on and win what we did.' This last one is a troubling thought. But if Chelsea were to go on to dominate the English and European game in the next few years, they would have to overcome the new European Champions – who were from England. For the first time since Alan Kennedy himself had scored the winning penalty in Rome in 1984, the unconsidered Liverpool won the European Cup in 2005, on penalties, on a quite unforgettable night in Istanbul.

Alan Kennedy is convinced that Rafa Benítez specifically concentrated his efforts in his first season at Anfield on winning the European Cup for Liverpool: 'I think it was not just the manager, it was the players who were focused on the Champions League. This was the one competition that could bring Liverpool back to being one of the top four teams in the country. It is a horrible thing to say, but we are talking only about being one of the top four teams. In my day, we were the top team!' Alan was, appropriately, in Istanbul for the match, working for television, and he spent much of his match day with his son Michael around Tacsim Square in the centre of the capital doing interviews, signing autographs and being photographed with hundreds of Liverpool fans, many of whom were way too young to remember him play. He dealt with all this with incredible patience, making sure every fan had their chance. He is a little like today's Jamie Carragher – a man who refuses to see himself as somehow 'different' or 'apart' from the Liverpool fans. They still love him for it and many still affectionately call him Barney. It was hard to believe that 21 years had flown by since Alan scored that winning goal in Rome, and then did his 'stupid little jump' of celebration. But that 1984 team was a hardened, experienced Liverpool side, one well versed in high-level European combat. Could this raw Liverpool team, under their new Spanish manager, really repeat this feat against the might of AC Milan?

Typically, Alan travelled with Michael to the stadium in Istanbul on a bus with 'ordinary' Liverpool supporters: they were soon shaking his hand and hugging him, chanting his name. He sang along to the Liverpool tunes and experienced much of what a normal supporter would have experienced: 'I was just one of the fans again – and it was an eye-opener. It was a fantastic stadium with a great atmosphere, but the arrangements were terrible. The ground was miles from the city and we had fellas hanging out of the bus all the way. It was quite frightening, actually. There were no directions at the stadium, it was just confusion, and we had to circle the entire ground before we could get in.' At the match, Alan and Michael sat opposite the Main Stand, waving to well-wishers and accepting the back-slapping that all ex-Liverpool players get from fans everywhere they go. He met with ex-Reds players Avi Cohen and Michael Thomas before the game and also the family of the late Emlyn Hughes, a moving moment. By half-time in this contest, they would all be wishing they were somewhere else.

With Liverpool 0–3 down at the interval and apparently overawed and outclassed by Milan, Alan was besieged by distraught fans asking him what had gone wrong. He also had to do a live interview for ITV during the break. He tried to be upbeat – but also realistic. 'I said changes would have to be made at half-time and that Liverpool had been caught cold, had invited Milan onto them, giving opportunities away in the first 30 seconds. Now it seemed like it was improbable – but not impossible – to recover from three goals down. But if I'm honest, I was really thinking about damage limitation.' But Alan had also noticed something that he knew Paisley and Fagan would have used in the past to gee up their Liverpool sides. 'When Milan scored their third goal, just before half-time, all the substitutes came on for the celebrations: they thought they had won it. Bob would have used that in the dressing-room. He'd have given us a right rollicking and said, "They think this is over now – but you go out and show all those Liverpool fans what you can do this half." Maybe Rafa Benítez did the same thing?'

In the second half it was, fittingly, Liverpool's left-back Riise who started the amazing Liverpool comeback. Alan was calling it from the stands: 'He had one attempted cross blocked and I was shouting at Riise to get the cross in. It was one of those terrific 50–50 balls defenders hate, a ball to make up Steven Gerrard's mind to attack it. It was a great header, but it was the cross that made it. It was the kind of cross I might have put in!' The revival was now brewing; Alan could feel all the familiar signs: 'Riise was coming back along the stand galvanising the crowd, calling for more support. You could feel it was "game on" now. Liverpool were much more positive coming forward. Bringing on Hamann at half-time had allowed other players, such as Gerrard and Alonso, to get into the game.' Further Liverpool goals from Smicer and Alonso took proceedings into extra-time and then to penalties. Alan's stomach was beginning to churn. Was it to be Rome 1984 all over again?

As the Liverpool players lined up for the spot kicks, plenty of grim-faced Reds fans in the crowd asked Kennedy if he fancied taking one, because his old club needed him once more. He might have stepped up, too, if asked. He wondered what was going through the mind of the Liverpool manager now, as he decided on his penalty-takers. Alan offered: 'You need to look for character and confidence on the basis of the players' performances on that night. Garcia wanted a penalty, but you can't just let players take one because they want to, or because they think they have a duty to. Their mind has to be right.' What Alan didn't know was that, just as Joe Fagan had approached him to take the crucial final kick 21 years ago in Rome, so Rafa Benítez had done in Istanbul with his captain Steven Gerrard. The key difference, of course, was that Gerrard was spared his trial, mainly because of the way Jerzy Dudek successfully aped Bruce Grobbelaar from Rome: the keeper's wobbly legs and goal-line antics disturbed the Milan spot-kick-takers, winning the penalty shoot-out 3–2 for Liverpool before Gerrard's turn came round. So, against all odds, Liverpool were European Champions once more – but using lessons learned from 1984.

Gazing down on the players' celebrations afterwards and being enveloped by ecstatic Liverpool fans, Alan Kennedy could now reflect that his 1984 team was no longer the last to win the European Cup for Liverpool. This huge burden, this weight of Anfield history, had been lifted from today's Anfield players at last. As the lion-hearted Scouser Jamie Carragher rightly commented later, 'We respect the past Liverpool teams, but we have our own history, our own stories, now.' It was another glorious European night for Liverpool Football Club, one enjoyed by all the club's great ex-players wherever they were in the world on that May evening. And the next time any of them met up with Alan Kennedy, for a dinner, or five-a-side tournament, for a veterans' trip to Barbados or Singapore, or for a Liverpool supporters' do in Denmark or Sweden, there would be yet another new Liverpool chapter to recall. And Alan Kennedy's phone-in shows on Century Radio would also be a little lighter – for a while, at least. Joe and Bob would be smiling down at us again right now. But could Liverpool's new Spanish manager deliver what was second-nature to these men back in the 1970s and 1980s: routinely being realistic Championship contenders in season after season? Only time, as they say, will tell.

SOURCES

INTERVIEWS

Roy Evans, David Fairclough, Alan Hansen, David Johnson, Mark Lawrenson, Ronnie Moran, Phil Neal, Ronnie Whelan

BOOKS

Allt, Nicholas, *The Boys from the Mersey* (Milo Books, Bury, Lancs, 2004)

Anthony, Andrew, *On Penalties* (Yellow Jersey Press, London, 2001)

Barnes, John, *John Barnes: The Autobiography* (Headline, London, 1999)

Clough, Brian and Sadler, John, *Clough: The Autobiography* (Partridge Press, London, 1994)

Dalglish, Kenny, *Dalglish: My Autobiography* (Hodder & Stoughton, London, 1996)

Gibson, John, *The Newcastle United Story* (Arthur Barker, London, 1985)

Hale, Steve and Ponting, Ivan, *Liverpool in Europe* (Carlton Books, London, 2001)

Hansen, Alan and Gallagher, Ken, *Tall, Dark & Hansen* (Mainstream Publishing, Edinburgh, 1988)

Heighway, Steve, *Liverpool: My Team* (Souvenir Press, London, 1977)

Hey, Stan, *Liverpool's Dream Team* (Mainstream Publishing, Edinburgh, 1997)

Hodgson, Derek, *The Liverpool Story* (Arthur Barker, London, 1978)

Hughes, Emlyn, *Crazy Horse* (Arthur Barker, London, 1980)

Joannou, Paul, *A Complete Who's Who of Newcastle United* (Arthur Barker, London, 1983)

Johnston, Craig and Jameson, Neil, *Walk Alone* (Fleetfoot Books, UK, 1990)

Keegan, Kevin, *Kevin Keegan: My Autobiography* (Little Brown, London, 1997)

Keith, John, *Bob Paisley: Manager of the Millennium* (Robson Books, London, 1999)

Kelly, Stephen F., *The Boot Room Boys* (Collins Willow, London, 1999)

Lees, Dr Andrew, and Kennedy, Ray, *Ray of Hope: The Ray Kennedy Story* (Pelham Books, London, 1993)

Liversedge, Stan, *Paisley: A Liverpool Legend* (Redwood Books, Trowbridge, 1996)

Murphy, Patrick, *His Way: The Brian Clough Story* (Robson Books, London, 1993)

Neal, Phil, *Attack from the Back* (Arthur Barker, London, 1981)

Paisley, Bob, *Bob Paisley's Liverpool Scrapbook* (Souvenir Press, London, 1979)

Pead, Brian, *Liverpool: A Complete Record, 1892–1990* (Breedon Books, Derby, 1990)

Rush, Ian, *Rush: Ian Rush's Autobiography* (Grafton Books, London, 1985)

Shankly, Bill, *Shankly by Shankly* (Granada Media, London, 1977)

Souness, Graeme, *No Half Measures* (Grafton Books, London, 1987)

Taylor, Rogan and Ward, Andrew, *Three Sides of the Mersey* (Robson Books, London, 1994)

Williams, John, *The Liverpool Way* (Mainstream Publishing, Edinburgh, 2003)

Williams, John, Hopkins, Stephen and Long, Cathy, *Passing Rhythms* (Berg, Oxford, 2001)

INDEX